African Diasporic Women's Narratives

UNIVERSITY PRESS OF FLORIDA

Florida A&M University, Tallahassee
Florida Atlantic University, Boca Raton
Florida Gulf Coast University, Ft. Myers
Florida International University, Miami
Florida State University, Tallahassee
New College of Florida, Sarasota
University of Central Florida, Orlando
University of Florida, Gainesville
University of North Florida, Jacksonville
University of South Florida, Tampa
University of West Florida, Pensacola

UNIVERSITY PRESS OF FLORIDA

Gainesville · Tallahassee · Tampa · Boca Raton · Pensacola

Orlando · Miami · Jacksonville · Ft. Myers · Sarasota

AFRICAN DIASPORIC WOMEN'S NARRATIVES

Politics of Resistance, Survival, and Citizenship

Simone A. James Alexander

Copyright 2014 by Simone A. James Alexander

All rights reserved

Printed in the United States of America on acid-free paper

This book may be available in an electronic edition.

21 20 19 18 17 16   6 5 4 3 2 1

First cloth printing, 2014
First paperback printing, 2016

Library of Congress Cataloging-in-Publication Data
Alexander, Simone A. James, 1967–
African diasporic women's narratives : politics of resistance, survival, and citizenship / Simone A. James Alexander.
pages cm
ISBN 978-0-8130-4982-3 (cloth)
ISBN 978-0-8130-6205-1 (pbk.)
1. American literature—African American authors—History and criticism.
2. African American women in literature. 3. Human body in literature.
4. American literature—20th century—History and criticism. I. Title.
PS153.N5A3986 2014
810.9'928708996073—dc23
2013047851

University Press of Florida
15 Northwest 15th Street
Gainesville, FL 32611-2079
http://www.upf.com

Contents

Acknowledgments vii

Introduction: Dis-Embodied Subjects Writing Fire 1

1 Captive Flesh No More: Saartjie Baartman, Quintessential Migratory Subject 20

2 "Crimes against the Flesh": Politics and Poetics of the Black Female Body 39

3 Framing Violence: Resistance, Redemption, and Recuperative Strategies in *I, Tituba, Black Witch of Salem* 68

4 Mothering the Nation: Women's Bodies as Nationalist Trope in Edwidge Danticat's *Breath, Eyes, Memory* 96

5 Performing the Body: Transgressive Doubles, Fatness and Blackness 127

6 Bodies and DisEase: Finding AlterNative Cure, Assuming AlterNative Identity 159

Notes 193

Bibliography 211

Index 227

Acknowledgments

I have relied on the good will and generosity of relatives, friends, and colleagues during the undertaking of this project.

Thanks to Carole Boyce Davies for her unwavering encouragement and endorsement. She was one of the first persons who underscored the manifest potential in my work on Grace Nichols. Sitting in on my conference presentation in Santo Domingo (Dominican Republic) that examined Nichols's *The Fat Black Woman's Poems*, she suggested afterward that I should "do something with this piece." I did!

Special thanks to Grace Nichols who I met at the conference of the Association of Caribbean Women Writers and Scholars in Grenada in 1998 where she graciously offered me a signed copy of *The Fat Black Woman's Poems*. In an act of unprecedented coincidence, I made a return trip to Grenada in June 2013 having just completed the final revisions of chapter 5 in which this poetry collection is analyzed.

I would like to thank the University Press of Florida and its incredible staff. Special thanks to my former senior acquisitions editor, Amy Gorelick, for her initial interest in this project. I would like to thank my current project editor, Marthe Walters, and the director and acting editor-in-chief, Meredith Babb. I also thank Ale Gasso, metadata manager/sales assistant, for her diligence. Elaine Otto deserves special mention for her efficient and careful copyediting of the manuscript. I am also grateful to the anonymous readers who evaluated the manuscript and offered useful and invaluable suggestions on revising it.

As a recipient of two consecutive fellowships from the Institute for Research on Women at Rutgers University, New Brunswick, I had the good fortune of engaging and brainstorming with an intellectual community of scholars. These seminarians challenged me to read the texts in multiple ways and from multiple perspectives. The residencies provided me with the intellectual space to work on and strengthen many of the ideas culled in chapters 2 and 4.

My dear friend and former Rutgers University librarian, Antoinette Peteet, has been a blessing, a true savior, lending her unwavering support and friendship. Expressing great interest in my project, Antoinette provided her expert assistance in locating important source materials. I have finally made it to the finish line, Antoinette! Thanks for cheering me on to the end!

I thank my dear friend and colleague, June Bobb, who has been a staunch supporter of both my academic and personal endeavors. Thanks to my girlfriend, Shondel Nero, for her continued support and for lending a listening ear whenever I needed one. My conference buddies, Renée Larrier, Brinda Mehta, and Adlai Murdoch have navigated the tides and terrains with me literally and figuratively. Your friendship and ongoing support has helped me to weather the storm. I am especially grateful to Abioseh Porter for his generosity and encouragement. A special thanks to my sister-friend, Winnifred Brown-Glaude, with whom I shared the rewards and challenges of maintaining a sensible balance between family obligations and academia. I am grateful to my childhood friend, Alana Holmes, who offered me her open arms, heart, and home (in Jamaica) whenever I required some needed rest and relaxation. I give special thanks to my girlfriends Karen King-Aribisala and Paula Walcott for their continued love, support, and friendship. Andre Nelson has been a patient and avid listener as I brainstormed some of the original ideas of this manuscript and as I tried to identify the proper placement—either chronologically or thematically—of the chapters.

I am indebted to my parents, Frank and Evadnie James, who planted the seed of desire and hope in me at a very young age. I, especially, thank my mother who stressed the relevance and rewards of hard work and determination. Mama, indeed, the "heights by great men reached and kept were not attained by sudden flight, but they, while their companions slept, were toiling upward in the night." Whenever I entertain the thought of retreat, I am reminded of your favorite and often repeated refrain. My siblings, Gregory and Dalero James, who cloak me in their unconditional love and support, are a blessing and an inspiration. To my nephew, Gregory James Jr., and niece, Gia James, who I hope will be truly inspired by this book. Aunty loves you!

To the wonderful and inspiring young men, Jason, Amani, and Akeem, in my life, who light up my life and give me hope to carry on. Mommy loves you! Negotiating between making numerous trips to and from basketball and soccer practices and games and working on the manuscript was both rewarding and challenging. These challenges were counterbalanced by my life companion, Aubrey, who saw me through the good and bad times, who bore witness to both my frustrations and celebrations, and who stayed the course of the long, and sometimes, tumultuous ride. This one is for you! Love and respect!

INTRODUCTION

Dis-Embodied Subjects Writing Fire

> They're treating my resistance to their diagnosis as a personal affront. But it's my body and my life and the goddess knows I'm paying enough for all this, I ought to have a say. I am going to write fire until it comes out of my ears, my eyes, my noseholes—everywhere. Until it's every breath I breathe. I'm going to go out like a fucking meteor!
>
> —Audre Lorde, *A Burst of Light*

> I am even more certain that to create dangerously is also to create fearlessly, boldly embracing the public and private terrors that would silence us, then bravely moving forward even when it feels as though we are chasing or being chased by ghosts.
>
> —Edwidge Danticat, *Create Dangerously*

A few years ago at a seminar on "Health and Bodies," I had the good fortune of sharing my work on Audre Lorde with fellow participants. By all accounts, the seminar was successful; the seminarians offered meaningful suggestions and feedback on ways to improve the work. One woman colleague or participant asked, "Who is the intended audience, and how will this project be accepted?" She further constructed "the audience as a class for black feminist theory in which case a discussion of Lorde's work would be appropriate." Other participants remarked, "Since you are using black bodies to speak about all bodies, the project fits within a canon of black, feminist political activists/authors." "If you had someone from another ethnic class, it would be quite different." "Use different authors so it doesn't appear as though they are coming from one community." Another concern raised was Lorde's relevance today having written her memoir so long ago.[1]

Even while alive, Lorde was extremely controversial, particularly among white feminists, whom she accused of perpetuating racism.[2] So it should be no surprise that even after her death, her work continues to evoke such emotional responses. These responses arguably stemmed from a sense of disease with the representation, occasioned by the choice of theorists and, by default, the theoretical framework.[3] Hortense Spillers remarks: "The charges leveled against Black Studies and Women's Studies, especially the former, in the initial period of their instauration—that the subject(s) were 'unresearched,' among other indictments—were blind to a material fact of discursive production—discourses do not spontaneously appear, but as writing, as an intellectual technology, they will follow the path and tide of generation" (*Black, White* x). She concludes, "An investigator will not 'find' what he or she is looking for, but will have to partially 'create' the differentiation against the stubbornness of tradition" (x). Furthermore, Lorde's personal embodied experiences did not fit, nor did she strive to fit, into the framework of the larger theoretical discourse. Rather, she unequivocally and unapologetically challenged the dominant mainstream discourse. Spillers ascertains that this perceived effortless challenge was occasioned because "the intransigent (and arbitrary) borders of the canonical were fragile to start with, predicated, as they were, on the reified properties of 'race' and 'gender'" (x).

Along these lines, one can safely argue that Lorde's success, or moreover her relevance, is manifested in her ability to "create dangerously." Concurring that "creating dangerously" is a corollary to "reading dangerously," Danticat surmises that this concept captures the essence of a writer: "Create dangerously, for people who read dangerously. This is what I've always thought it meant to be a writer" (*Create Dangerously* 10).[4] Spillers concretizes this concept, arguing that "Toni Morrison's *Sula* is a rebel idea, both for her creator and for Morrison's audience" (*Black, White* 93). In other words, "in bringing to light dark impulses no longer contraband in black American women's cultural address, the novel inscribes a new dimension of being, moving at last in contradistinction to the tide of virtue and pathos that tends to overwhelm black female characterization in a monolith of terms and possibilities" (93).

In keeping with this line of reasoning, Lorde (and fellow authors Grace

Nichols, Maryse Condé, and Danticat herself) did not fall short of "creating dangerously." Underscoring what she deems as Albert Camus's most viable interpretation of "creating dangerously," Danticat construes it as "creating as a revolt against silence, creating when both the creation and the reception, the writing and the reading, are dangerous undertakings, disobedience to a directive" (*Create Dangerously* 11). Boldly engaging the "dangerous undertakings," these women writers authenticate their experiences even as they refute the dominant discourse. The multiple physical and allegorical border crossings that the women and by default their protagonists undertake, in great part, constitute the "dangerous undertakings." Along similar lines, Lorde's strategic engendering of her varied lived experiences that underscore her transnational subjectivity become the legitimizing force in establishing her brand of theory (theorizing her illness) as a viable field of scholarship. Furthermore, the skewed question about her irrelevance finds resonance in the beautifully phrased Haitian proverb "Better that we are ugly, but we are here" (*Create Dangerously* 147).[5] Foregrounded in the phrase is conscious resistance and resilience.

In spite of having written her memoir more than three decades ago, both Lorde and her work continue to significantly impact women's lives, serving as a blueprint for women, regardless of age, race, creed, or location, tackling both personal and political disease. Lorde's influence is national, having inspired American feminists, lesbians, African Americans, and women of color during the 1970s and 1980s, but it also has international and transnational reach.[6] Thus Lorde explores the transnational through her own experiences. Underscoring the dynamism of transnationalism, Mary Friedman and Silvia Schultermandl reveal its crystallization of race and racial issues, establishing that it does "not obliterate the impact of 'race' as a shaping force on social power structures; on the contrary, [it] put[s] it into sharper focus" (9). Significantly, race matters to Lorde; subsequently, the racial subject occupies center stage in her discourse, a fact reiterated by Margaret Kissam Morris, who writes, "When Lorde names herself by identifying her multiple subject positions, she customarily begins with race; thus, she privileges the term that has been the source of her earliest experiences with prejudice" (169). Unequivocally, Lorde brought to the forefront breast cancer awareness, publicizing the disease, but more importantly, politicizing black women's health concerns. As a result, public awareness and public discussion of women's health increased greatly in the United States during the late twentieth century. Furthermore, Lorde's influence proliferated, extending beyond the United States' frontier, transcending border and race politics. Both discursively and physically, Lorde engenders a detour, a migration from mainstream gender-biased discourse as she unearths this (predominantly) female disease once shrouded in silence and secrecy.

In an attempt to articulate this book's transnational agenda, its engagement (or disengagement) with other texts/authors, the conversation that renowned black feminist critic Barbara Christian had with her daughter, Najuma, comes to mind.[7] Najuma asked her, "Why is it that you write mostly about black women's books? You read lots of other books. Is it because you like what they say best?" Christian surmises that the question her daughter asked had been asked before: "What is a literary critic, a black woman critic, a black feminist literary critic, a black feminist social literary critic?" (*Black Feminist Criticism* x). Not only was this question asked before, but it also has been answered. Addressing the importance and the comforting presence of black women writers in her life, Mary Helen Washington confesses: "Only they know my story. It is absolutely necessary that they be permitted to discover and interpret the entire range or spectrum of the experience of black women and not be stymied by preconceived conclusions. Because of these writers, there are models of how it is possible for us to live, there are more choices for black women to make, and there is a larger space in the universe for us" (xxxii). Giving voice to the challenges, the "stymied preconceived conclusions," Spillers remarks on the racist and sexist hurdles one has to surmount in attempting to "lay down discourse on aspects of African-American life and thought that did not conform to and replicate certain deeply held convictions" (*Black, White* xii). Arguably, these obstacles surfaced at the aforementioned seminar, resulting in the disqualification of Lorde's body as text and her body of work.

Although one may write mostly about black women's books, one is undoubtedly informed by other writers. Furthermore, interrogating this notion of a preconceived, intended, monolithic, or fixed audience, Christian underscores the presumptuousness of the writer inventing "a theory of how we *ought* to read." Instead she says, "We need to read the works of our writers in our various ways and remain open to the intricacies of the intersection of language, class, race, and gender in the literature. And it would help if we share our process, that is, our practice, as much as possible, since, finally, our work *is* a collective endeavor" ("Race for Theory"

42). Along these lines, Lorde's theorization is both far-reaching and all-encompassing, a fact that Alexis De Veaux underscores by ascertaining that Lorde's works were "firsts in . . . her literary career [in that they] established multiple dimensions of new terrain" (314).[8] "These multiple dimensions" lend themselves to Lorde's nonconformist stance, her embrace of multiple (flexible) identities. Even as Lorde discursively explores the manifold "dimensions of new terrains," her own body functioned as a terrain that disrupts and decenters the healthy, heterosexual body.

Aware that she is attempting to do something dangerous by normalizing the deviant body while simultaneously appropriating the literary canon, Lorde recuperates the female body from the male-dominated literary genres.[9] Similar to her embodied resistance to medical diagnosis, Lorde debunks the "discursive diagnosis" of a monolithic reader or writer. In keeping with this idea, she enacts Christian's statement that "theory is prescriptive [and] it ought to have some relationship to practice" ("Race for Theory" 42). Further illuminating the imperative of codependency between theory and practice, Christian remarks: "My fear is that when Theory is not rooted in practice, it becomes prescriptive, exclusive, elitist" (46). Consequently, she cautions that by succumbing to silence we run the risk of having our identities subsumed, allowing "Those who control the society [to] continue their cultural hegemony" (*Black Feminist Criticism* xiii).

Refusing to be silenced, Lorde, Danticat, Condé, and Nichols's body of work departs from "the western form of abstract logic," engaging instead "narrative forms, in the stories [they] create, in riddles and proverbs, in the play with language, since dynamic rather than fixed ideas seem more to [their] liking" (Christian, "Race for Theory" 41). This departure from fixity correlates with the fluidity of identity. Expounding on Christian's argument, Barbara Smith points out that "The use of Black women's language and cultural experience in books by Black women about Black women results in a miraculously rich coalescing of form and content and also takes their writing far beyond the confines of white/male literary structures" (7). Additionally, these women writers, advocates of transnational feminism, underscore the inextricability of the intersectional categories of sexual and racial politics in black women's writing. Specifically, Christian cautions about superimposing one's social history onto others without taking into consideration issues of race, class, and gender. Taking this argument a step further, Lorde stresses: "It is a particular academic arrogance to assume any discussion of feminist theory without examining our many differences, and without a significant input from poor women, Black and Third World women, and lesbians" ("Master's Tools" 110). Essentially, Lorde advocates for a transnational feminist agenda that challenges stereotypes and cultural imperialism.

Anthropologist Ifi Amadiume cautions: "One of the dangers of having our feet stuck in western-produced literature is the tendency to use European terms and expressions uncritically when addressing non-European cultures and experiences. The history of European imperialism and racism means that the language which aided that project is loaded with generalized terms which . . . serve a particularistic interest" (*Reinventing Africa* 1). Similar sentiments are echoed in the title of Lorde's insightful essay "The Master's Tools Will Never Dismantle the Master's House." Subsequently, she cautions that there is little or no hope for change when "the tools of a racist patriarchy are used to examine the fruits of that same patriarchy" (110–11). Operating within this feminist transnational continuum, this book problematizes black women's writings, ascertaining that it is not confining or should not be confined to a specific era, genre, or audience. Hence one can safely argue that the women writers discussed in this project refuse to engage mimicry against which Amadiume cautions. In giving voice to their experiences, they have in turn given voice to the experiences of countless other black women across the globe; they have given women the courage and language to reject and resist being silenced, to look at their "own antecedents for the sophisticated arguments upon which [they] can build in order to change the tendency of any established western idea to become hegemonic" (Christian, "Race for Theory" 43–44).[10]

Whereas this book employs western (feminist) theory, it does not do so uncritically or at the expense of black and Third World women's histories. Rather, it engages a transnational feminist agenda that debunks existing stereotypes and cultural hegemony. Underscoring the importance of avoiding these pitfalls, Inderpal Grewal and Caren Kaplan, quoting Fred Pfeil, address this oversight in feminist theories: "[E]ven among savvy and committed feminists, ahistorical relativism is in danger of replacing historical specificity as well as feminist solidarity. Feminist movements must be open to rethinking and self-reflexivity as an ongoing process if we are to avoid creating new orthodoxies that are exclusionary and reifying" (18). While this book is critical of white patriarchal structures, it reserves equal criticism and condemnation for patriarchal structures within black communities that espouse female oppression. These oversights have affected not only dialogue between black and white women but also representation. To counter these shortcomings, Grewal and Kaplan suggest "map[ping] these scattered hegemonies and link[ing] diverse local practices to formulate a transnational set of solidarities" (19). These "solidarities" facilitate diasporic consciousness and inclusion, engaging black women and their writings. Aware of the high cost of dismissing black women's realities, renowned feminist Adrienne Rich in conversation with Lorde candidly acknowledges: "What I can't afford is either to wipe out your perceptions or to pretend I understand you when I don't. And then, if it's a question of racism—and I don't mean just the overt violence out there but also all the differences in *our ways of seeing*—there's always the question: How do I use this? What do I do about it?" (Lorde, "Master's Tools" 106, italics mine). Rich's response directly addresses Barbara Smith's concern that "when white women look at Black women's works they are of course ill-equipped to deal with the subtleties of racial politics" (3). Rich has not only responded to Barbara Smith's challenge "to see in print white women's acknowledgement of who and what are being left out of their research and writing," (5) but she has also questioned "whether [white women's] perspective on women's reality is true to the lived experiences of women as a collective group" (hooks, *Feminist Theory* 3). Furthermore, her questioning is indicative of awareness, the above-mentioned oversight "of the extent to which [white women's] perspectives reflect race and class biases" (3).

Breaking away from the "academic practice of relying on disciplinary theories and conceptual debates originating in and dominated by the West" (Oyěwùmí, *Invention* ix), this work journeys away from established canonical structures and mainstream masculinist narratives, underscoring the importance of including the total sum—race, class, language, ethnicity—of the female subject. In other words, this work is informed by the theoretical reasoning of feminist scholars Amy Schulz and Leith Mullings, who insist on a holist approach in examining women's lives. Strong proponents of "intersectionality theory," Schulz and Mullings ascertain that "intersectionality theory was developed most prominently by Black feminist social scientists, emphasizing the simultaneous production of race, class, and gender inequality, such that in any given situation, the unique contribution of one factor might be difficult to measure" (5). Thus the mutual interdependence of race, class, and gender is pivotal in the articulation of women's experiences. As such, "The issue of who counts as a feminist is much less important than creating coalitions based on the practices that different women use in various locations to counter scattered hegemonies that affect their lives" (Grewal and Kaplan 18). The women writers herewith (Lorde explicitly) reveal the limits of a feminist discourse that does not take into account specific locations that construct the cultures that women negotiate in their daily lives. Amadiume's question about who should write a people's social history—"Is it others who should be telling Africans what they are?" (*Reinventing Africa* 5)—is adequately and articulately answered by Lorde: "It's my body and my life. I'm paying enough for all of this and I ought to have a say" (*Burst of Light* 76). Having their say, "writing and breathing fire," in other words "creating dangerously," black women give voice to their embodied experiences that not only destabilize and disengage the monolithic language of imperialism and racism but also fiercely interrogate Eurocentrism, thus dismantling the master's house. The coinage "writing fire" that echoes the cliché "playing with fire" engenders both danger and resistance.

Making a concerted effort not to "have [my] feet stuck in Western-produced literature," this book engages the theories of migration and diaspora, namely, migration flows and transnational movements within a gendered framework. In quoting Puerto Rican cultural critic Juan Flores, Duany writes: "The concept of diaspora evokes a wide range of connotations, including movement, travel, displacement, dislocation, uprooting, resettlement, hybridity, and nomadism" (2). This proliferation of definitions parallels the multiple transnational exchanges, a fact that is underscored by Duany, who observes that diaspora "overlaps substantially with current definitions of transnationalism" (3). Mindful of these overlaps, this book proposes that transnational ties occasion the birth of diasporas, blurring the congruence of geographic space and social space. While diaspora is imagined as a concrete locale in terms of destination, host countries, and home countries, it is also an imaginative space evoked through "collective memories, myths, and rituals" (3). In other words, it overlaps with Benedict Anderson's "imagined community." As Anderson puts it, a nation "is imagined because the members of the smallest nation will never know most of their fellow members, meet them, or even hear of them, yet in the minds of each lives the image of their communion" (15). This definition resonates powerfully in black diasporic communities where the "concept of the neighborhood," to echo Toni Morrison, takes on added significance. As Morrison intimates in her theorization of "the neighborhood" that strongly resonates with the current discourse of diaspora, an unspoken kinship exists among "folks," whose affection "for the city seems to be for the village within it: the neighborhoods and the population of those neighborhoods" ("City Limits" 37).[11] This implicit affinity alludes to a transnational sensibility among the residents of those neighborhoods who express "an urgent connection with and celebration of racial past" (38). Stuart Hall echoes similar sentiments whereby he defines this shared space or identity "as a collective, shared history among individuals affiliated by race or ethnicity" (233). In the same breath, Hall ascertains that "identity as a 'production' . . . is never complete, always in process, and always constituted within, not outside, representation" (234).

Furthermore, Vèvè Clark's theory on "diaspora literacy" crystallizes my claim to diasporic consciousness that resides in the imaginary, in the social and geographic spaces. According to Clark, "Diaspora literacy is the ability to read and comprehend the discourses of Africa, Afro-America, and the Caribbean from an informed, indigenous perspective. This type of literacy is more than an intellectual exercise. It is a skill for both narrator and reader that demands a knowledge of historical, social, cultural, and political development generated by lived and textual experience" ("Diaspora Literacy" 382). This ability to comprehend and interpret multilayered histories and folk stories beyond the reach of western ideology or "western or westernized specification," as Clark puts it, is celebrated by the "diasporically literate" (382). Indigeneity then is key in the materialization of these diasporic communities.

In like manner, Morrison's "neighborhood" resonates with current debates on citizenship. Detailing the varied conceptualizations of citizenship in the narrative by black artists as compared to mainstream (white) artists, Morrison calls attention to the sense of unbelonging experienced by black citizens, articulated by James Baldwin. Baldwin deliberates the critical question of "how a dispossessed people, a disenfranchised people, a people without orthodox power, views the cities it inhabits but does not have a claim to" ("City Limits" 35).[12] This sense of unbelonging crystallizes for women who are constructed as pawns in the national discourse and not as key players; as a result, their migrant status, their peripheral (fluid) existence becomes fodder for excluding them from the ranks of citizenship.

Addressing the exclusionary practices inherent in the national discourse of citizenship, this book promotes collective consciousness even as it argues in favor of flexible identity. In essence, the "mandates of individualism" do not dictate one's identity (Morrison, "City Limits" 36). These "imagined communities" therefore give rise to transnational alliances, diasporic kinship, and sensibility as Anderson calls attention to the "finite, elastic boundaries" of nation (15). In turn, this elasticity engenders female mobility, or "fluid migration," to quote Meredith Gadsby, and the attendant flexible definitions of home, identity, and citizenship.

Migration theorists share different views on the "feminization of migration." Some argue that despite the recent pervasive use of the term, the migratory flow of women is not novel, and as such the term is misleading, "insofar that it suggests an absolute increase in the proportion of women migrants, when in fact by 1960 women made up nearly 47% of all international migrants, a percentage that increased by only two points during the next four decades."[13] Nevertheless, underscoring how critical it is in understanding gender in the context of migration, Monica Boyd and Elizabeth Grieco remind us: "Traditional theory fails to help us to understand the circumstances that encourage women to become transnational migrants."[14] These circumstances, in other words, the politics and economics of migratory movements, are wide-ranging and include quest for employment, escape from abusive relationships, and better educational opportunities for their children. Calling added attention to women's calculated erasure from the discourse of migration, Boyd and Grieco are quick to point out that in the "1960s and 1970s the phrase 'migrants and their families' was a code for male migrants and their wives and children." This oversight therefore accounts for the "near invisibility of women as migrants, their presumed passivity in the migration process, and their assumed place in the home."

What has unequivocally changed is women's role in migratory processes. Whereas they once accompanied their spouses or partners, they now travel as independent subjects in search of jobs and better living conditions. However, as autonomous subjects, many women find themselves at the mercy of host countries that reinforce and reproduce "pre-existing gender patterns that oppress women."[15] These oppressive patterns result in the formation of a diaspora within a diaspora, or a "country within a country," to borrow Danticat's coinage. Addressing the configuration of Haitians as the abject "other," Danticat pontificates that their precarious subject position serves as fodder for the denial of citizenship.[16] In furthering her critique, Danticat, referencing Hurricane Katrina, says that the United States tries to erase its "poor," thereby intimating that such atrocities do not happen here, but they do in other countries, primarily in Haiti. This denial creates a "country within a country." Women in particular are victims, doubly affected and defined by their subjugated positions within the nation-state.

In this study's engagement with cultural studies and critical race theory, Stuart Hall's theorization of migration and diaspora informs the ways in which identity is constructed in relationship to history, race, and culture. In its pathologization of the black female subject (body), the hegemonic discourse "pens" women as diseased, passive, and docile, an assumption derived from the continued, controversial relation between biomedical science and race. By the same token, women are hypersexualized and racialized, constructed as sexual deviants.[17] This trend leads to the black female subject being denied ownership of her body; meanwhile, her worth is defined by the profits that can be had from her body, even as the body's worthlessness, its vulgarity, is underscored. Hall's poignant articulation that "the place of the Other fixes us, not only in its violence, hostility, and aggression, but in the ambivalence of its desire" rings true (234). Interrogating this "othering" of the subject in western discourse, Carole Boyce Davies initiates a counter discourse: "Boyce Davies's work introduces a new way of imagining migrations by situating one's own family history as point of departure for theoretical work instead of those dominant discourses (such as postcoloniality, postmodernism, masculinist Western theorizations of 'third world' peoples, and deconstruction)" (Gadsby 16). Thus Boyce Davies's theorization of migration through lived (bodily) experiences informs this study. Furthermore, this study frames migratory experiences that take place both in the real and the imaginary and that are physical as well as allegorical.

Defying the monolithic national discourse and by default the national body, *African Diasporic Women's Narratives: Politics of Resistance, Survival, and Citizenship* fiercely interrogates sexual deviance embodied in the diseased, disabled, and hypersexualized body. This cross-examination destabilizes gender, sexuality, and racial parameters, postulating that women's bodies not only engage subversive theory but also challenge hierarchical constructs and disrupt normative standards. In other words, they engender a politics of resistance, a detour from normative (western) categorizations and ideologies, a migration from and challenge of single, fixed (heteronormative, heterosexual) definitions of self.

Operating within this theoretical framework of reference, this book seeks to answer several questions: How does female bodily presence complicate and/or challenge the once "male constructed" migratory process? How is the framework of migratory experiences redefined and reappropriated by female travels? Along these lines, how do women's experiences of migration differ from men's, psychologically and somatically? How do these migrating bodies experience the new diasporas they inhabit? In other words, how do these women use their much oppressed bodies to reconfigure the discourse on migration, diaspora, citizenship, and identity? How do transnational exchanges engender resistance, even as they expand the definition of diaspora via diasporic encounters and relations? How does the circulation of black female identities and sexualities discursively engender a parallel "migration" that disrupts and debunks hierarchical structures? Further, how do these women employ their "migrating" bodies as sites of resistance to male hegemony? How do bodies mobilize and destabilize the meaning of race, class, and gender?

Evaluating the migration of the subject, Hall remarks that "the displacements of slavery, colonization, and conquest . . . stand for the endless ways in which Caribbean people have been destined to 'migrate'; it is the signifier of migration itself—of travelling, voyaging, and return as fate, as destiny" (243). In the above articulation, Hall reveals the politics of displacement that accompanies migration. At the same time, he captures the complexity of both voluntary and involuntary migration that defines the ensuing discussion. Borrowing Hall's phrase "the signifier of migration," this book ascertains that the body as signifier functions discursively as text. All the female characters in the texts either discursively or literally write the body as political resistance.

African Diasporic Women's Narratives is an in-depth study of selective texts of four migrant women writers: Audre Lorde, Edwidge Danticat, Maryse Condé, and Grace Nichols.[18] This grouping of diaspora writers presents a literary cocktail of sorts, providing a comparative and analytical study of fiction, poetry, autobiographical writing, memoir, and travel narratives from the Francophone and Anglophone worlds.[19]

This study is divided into six chapters. Chapter 1, "Captive Flesh No More: Saartjie Baartman, Quintessential Migratory Subject," chronicles Baartman's journey as captive flesh to free subject, ascertaining that her story is one of recovery and recuperation that culminated in her posthumous attainment of citizenship. Citizenship for black South Africans was a tenuous subject, due in great part to the country's racist apartheid politics. This racial division manifested in black South Africans forming that "country within the country." Furthermore, the unmitigated and uninhibited "theft" of Baartman was the direct result of her noncitizen status, for the most part determined by her race, class, and gender. As a Khoisan woman, Baartman's body fell significantly short of the set standards for the national (read white) body. Consequently, this presumed anomaly resulted in her being placed on the axis of deviance, wherein she was constructed as subhuman and exploited to deny her citizenship. Baartman's "healthy" body is therefore pathologized (analogous to Lorde's ill body seeking health on her own terms) as she becomes the object of the white patriarchal gaze. Furthermore, Baartman's rise from humble "servant" to esteemed stateswoman witnessed not only the debunking of established hierarchical structures but also the insertion of the woman in the national discourse. Consequently, Baartman's being granted citizenship provides a discursive and political space, an invaluable framework for women not only to articulate resistance but also to ascertain their role in nation-building. Woman becomes "nation and narration," to borrow Homi Bhabha's famous phrase, as the nation is (subversively) reimagined through Baartman's body, constituting a migration from traditional masculinist discourses that imagine a "distinctly gendered nation through the representation of the female body" (Grewal and Kaplan 22).[20] Appropriating Toni Morrison's powerful coinage about self-affirmation, the chapter concludes that the "deeply loved flesh" is antidotal to the captive flesh.

Similar to Baartman, Lorde defies the nation's configuration of propriety, normalcy, and legitimate sexuality. As Faith Smith succinctly articulates: "Notions of sexuality are deeply inflicted by colonial and imperial inheritances that have framed nationalism's discourses and silences" (2). Attending to these silences, chapter 2, "'Crimes against the Flesh': Politics and Poetics of the Black Female Body," politicizes the female body using Lorde's personal, embodied experiences with breast cancer to articulate that the erasure of the female body constitutes "high crimes against the flesh." The assault on Lorde's flesh is twofold: first, the state's (the Cancer Society) requirement that she normalize her diseased body by donning prosthetic breasts after her mastectomy, and second, the obliteration of her lesbian identity, positing compulsory heterosexuality as the norm.

Lorde's deviance, manifested in her sexual orientation, is criminalized even as she challenges the concept of the "deviant or criminalized body." As a transnational subject, Lorde not only traverses multiple borders but she also embodies multiple "incompatible" identities. In equal manner, Lorde's lesbian identity calls into question her right to citizenship, as M. Jacqui Alexander, illuminating the nation-state's criminalization of the queer body, dutifully reminds us in her phenomenal essay "Not Just (Any) Body Can Be a Citizen." In keeping with Alexander's theorization, Lorde is an "outlaw" in multiple ways, engaging in "queering the nation" and self-identifying as a black lesbian feminist writer, activist, and mother of two. Her refusal to wear a prosthesis therefore becomes an additional "transgressive" (read treasonous) act.

Furthermore, Lorde's autobiographical inquiry into selfhood operates within the framework of transnationalism as it fiercely interrogates the Eurocentric literary tradition.[21] In essence, Lorde's biographical rendition of her personal experiences subverts and deconstructs hegemonic discourses. In deconstructing the body politic, Lorde links the domestic politics of the United States to its foreign policies, exposing the common oppression that the United States and South Africa unleash on their citizens. This connection reinforces Morrison's observation about the neighborhood/the black diaspora whose residents are excluded from the nation's discourse.

Chapter 3, "Framing Violence: Resistance, Redemption, and Recuperative Strategies in *I, Tituba, Black Witch of Salem,*" recuperates the black female subject, Tituba, from obscurity, reinstating her and her story in the national discourse. Tituba's story is one of migration and repatriation. She accomplishes circuitous journeys, exemplary of enslavement in reverse, traveling from Barbados back into slavery to Salem, Massachusetts, and then back home again to Barbados. Tituba's migrations chronicle the (gendered) violence that is often deemed too horrific to tell, within which the diasporic subject is fixed, to echo Hall. However, revealing these horrors facilitates the scripting of an alternative discourse that resists the masculinist narrative and redeems and reinstates the subject. Alternatively, Tituba's mobility lends itself to transnational alliances. Therefore, her travels challenge the concept of place and belonging, whereby she resists fixity in favor of transnational citizenship.[22] Similarly, Tituba advocates for transnational feminism, which operates within an "antiracist and anti-imperialist ideological framework and a vocabulary that articulates differences in power and location as accurately as possible" (quoted in Friedman and Schultermandl 8–9).

Furthermore, Tituba's "transgressions," her denunciation of culturally normalized and tenuous expectations of motherhood and mothering, scripted female identity, and sexuality, disqualify her as a suitable candidate for citizenship.

Addressing the masculinist guise embedded in the phrase "mothers of the nation," chapter 4, "Mothering the Nation: Women's Bodies as Nationalist Trope in Edwidge Danticat's *Breath, Eyes, Memory*," demonstrates how Danticat confronts hegemonic masculinity and nationalism by decoding the nationalist language of the phrase "mothers of the nation." The chapter examines how the woman was politicized as "a wife and mother of the nation," prerequisites for good citizenship, and saddled with the duty of taking care of her children as well as her country. Not surprisingly, the language within which women are scripted is articulated and dominated by men, similar to the dominance they exercise in state institutions and present in hegemonic masculinity and nationalism. As such, men are projected on the national scene as protectors/defenders of women and the state and enforcers of state-regulated laws. The chapter demonstrates how the language of nationalism is used to restrict or limit women's public roles or appearances, denying them the ability to "practice citizenship." It also requires them to control their sexuality by espousing and practicing proper womanhood. Therefore, the nationalist language functions as an approved language through which sexual control and repression are justified and masculine prowess is expressed and exercised. As a result, women's bodies undergo a form of militarization (as citizenship is exclusionary), subject to militaristic scrutiny by the nationalist regime. Further, examining the relationship between gender and the state, this book demonstrates that despite the conferral of the state title "mothers of the nation," women are perceived and accordingly treated as second-class citizens. The label "mothers of the nation" that purportedly functions as a qualifier for "good" citizenship has strong historical and cultural resonance for black women who have been socialized or pathologized as deviant, corrupt, and unfit.

While women are seen as passive supporters of men/the state, the desire for land/woman's body is constructed as masculine desire. The study establishes that women are used to promote ethnic mobilization, to advocate "good" citizenship, and that policies are put in place to regulate women's experiences (of motherhood) in defense of state interests. Reasonably concurring that some women are complicit in espousing the nationalist agenda, the study nonetheless identifies how women in Danticat's novel get pigeonholed into certain stereotypical roles. Nevertheless, in framing a counter discourse, these very women operate within the existing (patriarchal) structures of state violence, using their mutilated, abused bodies as weapons to resist and rebel against the nationalist agenda and state-mandated directives as a whole.

Further, in chapter 4 we witness a palpable case of gender-specific migration as the mother-protagonist Martine's migration to the new host country, America, takes her on a completely different route from that of her lover, Marc. Whereas Marc's acquisition of statesmanship or statehood is seamless, Martine's migrant status palpably manifests in the new home country. Similarly, Martine's quest for citizenship is circuitous, if not contentious.

In chapter 5, "Performing the Body: Transgressive Doubles, Fatness and Blackness," Grace Nichols renders her eponymous heroine, the Fat Black Woman, visible making her the site/sight of public, political debates as her fat black body functions as a platform, a discursive strategy so to speak that permits and validates alternative identity or subjectivity. This alternative subjectivity challenges the concept of fixed identity and ideal citizenship. The chapter establishes that the ideal body translates to the ideal citizen; as such, fatness and blackness do not qualify and need not apply. Whilst advocating for fluid identity, the Fat Black Woman critiques monolithic construction of race, sexuality, and national identity. Along these lines, Nichols engages an interesting confluence of fatness and laziness in her poetry collections, *The Fat Black Woman's Poems* and *Lazy Thoughts of a Lazy Woman*, drawing on the age-old racist stereotypes of the Sambo and the Mammy archetypes assigned to black subjects. These very archetypes rendered blacks nonpersons, noncitizens. Reclassifying the "vulgar," Nichols exposes that "vulgarity" is innately present in the promotion of "gender- and body-conformity," fiercely interrogating the practice of exclusionary citizenship. Along these lines, acceptance of the body in all its formation—deviant, outcast, othered, grotesque—signals rejection of Victorian ideals of femininity, decency, and the ideal citizen. Drawing on Carolyn Cooper's theory of the "vulgar" and Mikhail Bakhtin's theory of the "grotesque and the classical body" that respectively correspond to low and high culture (lowbrow and highbrow), the study assesses concrete examples of the demonization and devaluation of the black female body. This theory deconstructs hegemonic discourses manifest in the concept of vulgarity that challenges the principle of decency and propriety and dispels the myth of normalization. The dismantling of propriety and heteronormativity deconstructs hierarchical structures. Similarly, the "crisscrossing of cultural borders and legal boundaries by migrants, disturbs the conventional dichotomy between 'us' and 'them'" (Duany 1). In other words, Nichols's Fat Black Woman collapses the boundaries between "good" and "bad" citizenship, fiercely interrogating the politics of identity and belonging. The convergence of high and low culture equally collapses this dichotomy.

Further, Nichols's invocation of the Frankenstein persona calls attention to the attempted cannibalization cum erasure of the black female body. Substantiating that Nichols's *Fat Black Woman's Poems* is a transnational text that spans the black diaspora as it responds to Saartjie Baartman's exploitation that culminated in her orchestrated and staged performances across Europe, the study traces how the fat black woman "performs her excess flesh," presenting a formidable challenge to black women's denial of citizenship and their assumed hypervisibility and hypersexuality. In short, the Fat Black Woman "performs her fatness and blackness" not only as a counter discourse to hegemony but also as critique to Baartman's sexual exploitation.

Operating from the theoretical standpoint that bodily experiences are sociosomatic and therefore closely tied to one's social or socioeconomic position in society, chapter 6, "Bodies and DisEase: Finding AlterNative Cure, Assuming AlterNative Identity," through a close reading of texts by Toni Morrison, Edwidge Danticat, Maryse Condé, Jamaica Kincaid, and Paule Marshall, details how women's experiences of their bodies and illness carry traits of denationalization. In other words, the unhealthy body is constructed within the framework of difference and deviance and therefore is not in line with the nation's definition of citizenship. In view of this, whiteness and able-bodiedness are the transcendental norm. Abhorred and unwelcome, the sick female body occupies a peripheral position beyond the nation-state that renders it stateless and therefore lawless. As Yancy contends: "Those on the outside are rejected because they are deemed suspicious, vile, unclean, infestations of the (white) social body" (xix). While being attentive to the fact that different diseases affect different communities dissimilarly (in the ensuing discussion, Paul Farmer exposes this health disparity cum discrimination in regards to Haitian citizens); this chapter ascertains that one's socioeconomic condition determines access to health and citizen rights, as articulated by Danticat and Morrison. It is this blatant disparity that impelled Angela Davis to politicize black women's health, equating the personal struggle with the quest for "social, economic, and political emancipation" ("Sick and Tired" 18). By the same token, the locus of socioeconomic settings is raced and gendered; this diasporic locale, the "country within the country," inhabited by the "infested" body is the focus of this chapter. Along these lines, the chapter draws heavily on Paul Farmer's theorization of disease as a means to reveal the disparities (us versus them, the country within the country) in immigrant and/or black communities. The residents of this impoverished diaspora are rendered refugees in their own country.

Reinforcing the line of reasoning advanced by several theorists that disease is often symptomatic of societal ills, the study explores how manifest disease—bulimia, breast cancer, tuberculosis, "testing," skin bleaching—is experienced and dealt with by female characters. The societal ills include isolation, exile, discrimination, and racism. The alienation from home/self and body forces characters to link disease with geographic location; for example, bulimia is labeled as an American disease (not Haitian), illuminating socioeconomic inequality. Noticeably, these "ailing" female characters are predominantly immigrant women whose migratory experiences are mired in (body) alienation and estrangement. Moreover, their current condition imperils their migratory quest for betterment, even as it bars them from the path to citizenship. This social and political unbelonging is quieted by reminders of home, of indigeneity, and in resorting to alternative cure administered by midwives and female healers to combat marginalization and alienation. Thus the female figure that challenges western medical authority is the *ol'higue* or the *soucouyant*, who is bestowed with the power of "flight." Bestowal of agency and power to this "renegade" woman manifests transgression in the masculine world in which she is demonized and ridiculed. To counter her demonization, the study argues that female mobility is key to her empowerment as she routinely enacts a reverse or return journey to the initial source and force: her past, the world inhabited by the ancestors. This ability to traverse both worlds with ease leads to her elusiveness, her ambiguity, a fact endorsed by Duany, who ascertains: "Peoples that span national borders are ambiguous in that they in some ways partake of both nations and in other ways partake of neither" (1–2).

In "birthing an alternative nation,"[23] the midwives and female healers constitute an abounding female-centered diaspora and also establish their own criteria for citizenship, independent of western medicine. This rejection cum migration from western medicine that manifests in crisscrossing boundaries and borders in favor of homeopathic remedies, not only accentuates medicine's limits but it also challenges pervasive western medical authority. Consequently, Lorde invariably made her body available to various (nonwestern) sources of medicine, accomplishing several trips to Germany, among other places, for alternative treatments. Similarly, Ma Chess miraculously appears on the island of Antigua to cure her granddaughter. Herein, the numerous journeys and transnational alliances that function as linkages to various diasporic communities come full circle as the chapter's focus on healing and reconciliation brings this book and the women's migrations to a triumphant close. Championing the cause of mutual interdependence between folk remedy and western medicine advanced by these women writers, the experiences herewith are experimental as well as experiential. Strengthening this black feminist tradition by theorizing and politicizing personal embodied experiences, this book reflects the reality of the politics of black women's lives, writing their experiences into existence.

1 Captive Flesh No More

Saartjie Baartman, Quintessential Migratory Subject

South African Saartjie Baartman has been the focus of much scholarly publication and ongoing academic debate over the past few years.[1] Specifically, her migratory journey from Africa to Europe and then her posthumous return to Africa have garnered much attention, gracing the pages of academic books and discourses at conferences and symposia. Whereas Baartman's initial journeys from South Africa to London and Paris were accomplished through coercion and deception, her journey home was a national homecoming. Hence her travels are manifested both in (symbolic) voluntary and forced migration. This renewed focus that reconstructs her narrative as one of recovery and recuperation fittingly heralds her survival and eventual attainment of citizenship. Suffice it to say this undivided attention accorded Baartman is long overdue.

Addressing race and erasure, Hortense Spillers examines the visibility/invisibility dichotomy within which the black woman/body is ensnared. To echo Spillers, Baartman is a "marked woman, but not everybody knows [her] name." Yet her "country needs [her], and if [she] were not here, [she] would have to be invented" (Mama's Baby 65). Consequently, Baartman is invented within white racist ideology as primitive, as exotic—dubious characteristics that justify her denial of citizenship and freedom. George Yancy succinctly frames this white invention as expressed within the white imaginary:

> The history of the Black body . . . is fundamentally linked to the history of whiteness, primarily as whiteness is expressed in the form of fear, sadism,

hatred, brutality, terror, avoidance, desire, denial, solipsism, madness, policing, politics, and the production and projection of white fantasies. From the perspective of whiteness, the Black body is criminality itself. It is the monstrous; it is that which is to be feared and yet desired, sought out in forbidden white sexual adventures and fantasies; it is constructed as a source of white despair and anguish, an anomaly of nature, the essence of vulgarity and immorality. (xvi)[2]

Even Baartman's performance was appropriated to appeal to the white imagination: "Sara Baartman had to learn to act the part of the Hottentot Venus. On stage, Baartman had to erase aspects of her personal history, experience, and identity in order to make her performance of the Venus credible to the audience that was staring at her" (Scully and Crais 304). Expanding the discourse of the white imagination, Toni Morrison reminds us that the United States' culture along with the cultures of "South America, England, France, Germany, Spain . . . have participated in and contributed to some aspect of an 'invented Africa'" (*Playing* 7). Articulating "the continuing significance of race," Yancy underscores that the "black body has endured a history of more than symbolic white violence" (xvi). Addressing the pervasive historical silencing of black bodies, Morrison remarks that "in matters of race, silence and evasion have historically ruled literary discourse. Evasion has fostered another, substitute language in which the issues are encoded, foreclosing open debate." She adds: "Silence became an unbearable violence" (*Playing* 9, 23).

The silencing of Baartman and fellow South Africans through the denial of citizenship is not a new phenomenon for those who reside in Continental Africa.[3] Human rights activist Bronwen Manby substantiates this line of reasoning. Assessing the poignant articulation of a fighter for the rebel "new forces" in Côte d'Ivoire: "We needed a war because we needed our identity cards. Without an identity card you are nothing in this country." Manby ascertains "that the denial of a right to citizenship has been at the heart of many of the conflicts of post-colonial Africa, and that it is time to change the rules" (1). Historicizing the selective denial of citizenship to black people, Saidiya Hartman articulates: "The selective recognition of humanity that undergirded the relations of chattel slavery had not considered them . . . deserving of rights or freedom" (*Scenes* 5). Baartman is at the center of this conflict of denial of citizenship wherein not only is her civic right violated, but she is also deemed an outcast, a deviant. Besides, she suffers from bodily violation through "theft," an act that engenders her physical and psychological abuse.[4] Thus the attainment of citizenship for women takes on an added challenge as women are habitually erased from the national discourse.

A victim of this new world order, Baartman's "New-World, diasporic plight marked a *theft of the body*" (Spillers, Mama's Baby 67). Envisioned as the quintessential migratory subject—she traveled from Africa to Europe, England and France, and back to Africa—Baartman paradoxically exemplifies the captive female body to which Spillers makes reference. These forced multiple journeys that Baartman accomplished epitomize the African diaspora which is defined as "any group that has been dispersed outside its traditional homeland, especially involuntarily, as Africans during the Atlantic slave trade."[5] Clifton Crais and Pamela Scully intimate that Baartman's "theft" was inevitable, evidenced by her tenuous citizenship: "She was born at a time when the Gonaqua were losing their independence as a people and effectively being hunted out or subjugated and turned into indentured laborers on white farms" (quoted in Frith). Furthermore, Baartman's sense of unbelonging is crystalized by her relentless objectification, her exilic existence in the colonial spaces (England and France) to which she migrated. Unequivocally, Baartman's denial of personhood is occasioned by her race, class, and gender. Scully and Crais, to some extent, corroborate this fact in noting that "as a poor woman, and as a woman, the parameters of her being able to control her life were quite narrow" (quoted in Frith). Evidently, Baartman's initial migration from her homeland on the Eastern Cape to England was motivated by her quest to ameliorate her socioeconomic condition as she was expecting to profit from her performances. However, it remains questionable whether Baartman saw any proceeds from her performances. What is unequivocal is that Baartman was deceived by British naval surgeon Alexander Dunlop into thinking that she would garner a formidable fortune in Europe by placing her "deviant, anomalous" body on public display before a curious and voyeuristic European audience.[6] She became "an object of unbridled medical curiosity and physical lust" (Washington, *Medical Apartheid* 83), and Dunlop was able "to pad his paltry wages and create some insurance for his pending retirement" (Frith).

Baartman's migration to improve her socioeconomic condition did not serve her well; actually, it became a double-edged sword. Instead, her subject position changed from economic migrant to commercialized migrant. Furthermore, Baartman's coercive migration resonates with trafficking of women for labor and sexual exploitation. Andrea Marie Bertone affirms that the International Organization for Migration (IOM) defines human trafficking as when "a migrant is illicitly engaged (recruited, kidnapped, sold, etc.) and/or moved, either within national or across international borders; [when] intermediaries (traffickers) during any part of this process obtain economic or other profits by means of deception, coercion, and/or any other forms of exploitation under conditions that violate the fundamental rights of migrants" (quoted in Bertone 6). Despite Crais's claim that Baartman "in a sense knew what she was getting into" (quoted in Frith), her "theft" nevertheless constitutes human trafficking, as the definition includes "those cases where the woman is aware of the nature of the work at the point of leaving but on arrival finds herself in a situation where her fundamental human rights and freedoms are violated" (quoted in Bertone 6).

Hence Baartman's migrant status is complicated, shrouded in ambivalence. Yuval-Davis and Stoetzler address this conundrum in the following manner: "In crossing the borders a woman can get away from constraints within her society and become constructed via the double-edged sexualized 'othering' processes that make her into the 'exotic woman'" (338). Essentially, Baartman's exoticization becomes fodder for her unattainment of citizenship. Despite the "migrations of the subject,"[7] the female body is "irreversibly" encoded within racist assumptions and presumptions, a testament to Spillers's observation that the "othering" of the female body is "so loaded with mythical prepossession that there is no easy way for the agents buried beneath them to come clean" (65).

Although "borders and boundaries can be imagined as a way out of traditional gender roles," in the given scenario they perform a different function: they enchain, paralleling Baartman's proverbial shackling within the nation-states as her captors functioned both as the impenetrable border and the border patrols that restrict her movement (Yuval-Davis and Stoetzler 339). Thus the imperial powers, England and France, reinforce border politics to substantiate the instating of geographic borders in an effort to restrict movement of certain bodies. In essence, Baartman's performance manifests in disciplinary control of the black female body that is literally and proverbially entombed within boundaries and borders. Her encasement is rendered most palpable in her mummification.[8] Moreover, Baartman's involuntary migration is exemplified by fixed departures and destinations; her restricted mobility manifests in the restraint of her identity and space. This regimental policing leads to racial categorizations that in turn foster the creation of a "country within the country."

Baartman is ensnared within the European imagination of the black woman's "exoticism and primitivism"; this fixity is entrenched in "violence, hostility, and aggression" as Hall observes, even as the female body is a locus of desire (234). Baartman's public exhibition of her body advanced from her being semi-nude to being completely nude, an act that literally and figuratively stripped her of her basic rights as a citizen. She was also made to impersonate a captured animal and later completed the bestial, jungle image as she was forced into a cage. Furthermore, Baartman's nudity reinforces her bestiality, her promiscuity. For almost two hundred years Baartman was displayed both in flesh and posthumously on the European world stage as a freak of nature.

A member of the Khoisan herder tribe, Baartman, as a result of her endowed figure—her fleshly buttocks—her "excess flesh," became the object of desire and derision, fear and adoration.[9] Baartman's inability to attain citizenship was a foregone conclusion, since her body, in many ways, did not correspond to the national (read white) body. Reputedly Khoi women are known for their large buttocks (steatopygia) and elongated labia. Placed on the "axis of deviance," Baartman's "presumed" hypervisibility and hypersexuality attest to her subhuman characteristics, serving as the impetus for her exploitation and attendant denial of citizenship. In keeping with this agenda, Baartman's ethnic difference is manipulated to establish her inferiority or deficiency, a fact brought to light by Sumi Colligan: "Bodies that were put on display were objectified and stripped of all their humanity, frequently viewed as samples of inferior evolutionary forms" (47). Calling attention to the fact that the underclass is routinely pathologized, Terry remarks that "the bodies—and particularly the brains and nervous systems—of the poor, of women, of criminals and nonwhite peoples were assumed to be primitive, fundamentally degenerate, or neurotically diseased" (131). As established earlier, Baartman had been showcased to European audiences as an anomaly, a freak of nature because of her protruding posterior and her elongated labia; her body, of course, was read through western eyes.

As part of the entertainment, Baartman, seductively clad in a tribal skintight brown dress that bore the semblance of nudity to emphasize her large breasts and buttocks, was forced to gyrate provocatively in front of a gaping white audience. This performance further serves as an attestation to her degeneracy. The undeniable fact that Baartman's public display attests to Eurocentric and androcentric bias is no mystery. Shedding light on this culture of consumption, sociologist Oyèrónkẹ́ Oyěwùmí puts it best as she assertively opines "that though Saartje was displayed for European consumption because her parts were *hyper-sexual* from a Western perspective, the African woman today is displayed for the *hyposexuality* caused by her presumed missing parts" (*African Woman* 160–61). Oyěwùmí concludes that more often than not, such portrayals are misidentified, uninformed "by African realities [and] instead they reflect the Western culture [and] Westerners' voyeuristic and groin-centered preoccupations with Africa[ns]." Even in the absence of factual evidence, Oyěwùmí substantiates that "Westerners have been known to create persons, events, and customs that affirm their voyeuristic preoccupations with Africa" (160). Further, Oyěwùmí provides a plausible explanation for the objectification and exploitation of Baartman's alleged "excess," exposing the excesses embodied in the prurience of the European audiences that remain unnoticed or unchecked. Calling attention to European audiences' unbridled fascination with the black female body, Oyěwùmí reminds us that not only did they find Baartman's "protruding buttocks" riveting, but the "alleged large size of her labia and nymphae, labeled the 'Hottentot apron,' was also of immense fascination in scientific circles" (160). Baartman therefore existed only as "a collection of sexual body parts" (160).

Baartman's "wounded" flesh finds resonance in the disgraceful display of her body parts for public consumption, at the same time that it underwent a form of carnivalization or cannibalization by her European exploiters. Even though Carole Boyce Davies analyzes the carnivalized Caribbean woman body within the context of Trinidad carnivals, her findings are relevant and applicable to Baartman's body and the black woman's body in general. Drawing on Davies's careful analysis, the reprehensible display of Baartman's body (parts) amounts to pornographic exposure, for Davies reasons that "in pornography one of the standard tropes is that women's bodies are dismembered, reduced to parts for easy consumption" ("Carnivalized" 334). Revealing the patriarchal cum imperialistic agenda that fuels the pornographic display of women's bodies, Davies points out that "female genitalia are pornographically exposed, identified in ways so detailed and objectified that no amount of women reversing the terms of pornography by exposing males' sexuality is equivalent" (334). Baartman's exposure serves as evidence that "it is the women who are reduced to nakedness, making them objects for male consumption and reinforcing the central messages of female subordination" (336). Hence subordination manifests in her almost-naked display that posits her body as a site of both revulsion and containment, "naked and prostituted and willfully performing for the pleasure of the voyeur" (337).[10] Davies additionally remarks: "for black female bodies, the link between violence and rape are mapped onto the historical meanings of the voyeuristic gaze" (338). This proverbial disfiguration and disrobing of Baartman's body, evocative in Cuvier's dissecting of her parts, resonates with human trafficking. As such, Baartman's performances and her subsequent experimentation manifest in sexual bondage, which is "analogous to erasing one's identity and blurs the lines of where slavery begins and economics ends" (Bertone 12). This form of female disempowerment is reductionist as it keeps women "in economic and social bondage" (12).

Dismantling this bigoted postulation of the pathological black female body, South African's esteemed paleoanthropologist and anatomist Philip Tobias provides a clear-cut context for Baartman's commodification, referring to the attraction of the black body by Europeans as an "international symbol of colonial and imperial excesses" (Holmes 104). Oyĕwùmí concurs: "The bottom line (pun intended) is that whatever the realities of African and African bodies, they are liable to be exhibited to soothe the western mind/body of its sexual predilections *du jour*" (*African Woman* 161). Jennifer Morgan lends her voice to this discussion in arguing that "Europe has a long tradition of identifying Others through the monstrous physiognomy or sexual behavior of women" (16).

Furthering this argument, President Thabo Mbeki, in eulogizing Baartman, unreservedly identifies scientific racism as the source of her exploitation. Rachel Holmes captures his sentiment: "Saartjie was exploited by leading European scientists to prove their xenophobic notions of white superiority" (109). In a similar vein, Baartman's "excess flesh" becomes the barometer by which her implied lascivious and licentious characteristics are measured. By the same measure, her "excess" punctuates her sexual availability. This measurement of bodies or body parts, premised on the theory of eugenics as a way to reinforce black inferiority and promote white supremacy, brings to bear the scene in Morrison's *Beloved*, where Schoolteacher measures the animal characteristics of his slaves, accentuating their propertied possession and provoking angst in the main protagonist, Sethe. Instructing his pupils/nephews on the proper measuring requirements in assessing Sethe's humanity, or lack thereof, Schoolteacher coaches them: "No, no. That's not the way. I told you to put her human characteristics on the left; her animal ones on the right. And don't forget to *line them up*" (193; emphasis added). Up until this moment when she overhears the conversation between Schoolteacher and his nephews, Sethe is unable to decipher the calculated reasoning that occasions her physical measurement, a fact to which she herself attests:

> I didn't care nothing about the measuring string. We all laughed about that—except Sixo. But I didn't care. Schoolteacher'd wrap that string all over my head, 'cross my nose, around my behind. Number my teeth. I thought he was a fool. And the questions he asked was the biggest foolishness of all. (*Beloved* 191)[11]

In a later scene, Paul D is rudely awakened to reality, reminded of his worth (or lack thereof) in this profit-making market economy:

> Shackled, walking through the perfumed things honeybees love, Paul D hears the men talking and for the first time learns his worth. He has always known, or believed he did, his value—as a hand, a laborer who could make profit on a fare—but now he discovers his worth, which is to say he learns his price. The dollar value of his weight, his strength, his heart, his brain, his penis, and his future. (*Beloved* 226)

Upon gaining access to the (master) script, Sethe comes to the stark realization that the measurement was intended to establish her assumed difference, to relegate her to subhuman status. She records her reaction to this startling revelation in the following manner:

> I commenced to walk backward, didn't even look behind me to find out where I was headed. I just kept lifting my feet and pushing back. My head itched like the devil. Like somebody was sticking fine needles in my scalp. (*Beloved* 193)

Endeavoring to identify a morsel of humanity in her white masters, Sethe attempts to distinguish Schoolteacher from their former master, Mr. Garner, who in her summation accomplished a humane act by permitting her husband, Halle, to purchase his mother's freedom, but is duly reminded by Halle that "he's white. It don't matter. What they say is the same. Loud or soft" (195). In conversation with Halle, Sethe finds out that he bought his mother's freedom in exchange for his own, hers, and that of their three children, significantly increasing Schoolteacher's wealth: "He got you, me and three more coming up" (196). She additionally learns that Halle's mother's advanced age no longer provided Schoolteacher the profits that her youthful years guaranteed. Furthermore, the trope "line them up" invokes the scene in which black bodies are being auctioned off at will (a parallel to Baartman's theft and subsequent commodification), instilling unimaginable but justifiable fear in Sethe of her children being taken from her and becoming chattel. This fear is legitimized in Halle's recapping Schoolteacher's advice that it "don't pay to have [his] labor somewhere else while the boys is small" (196). Sethe recalls that the chilling phrase "while the boys is small, woke [her] up," putting her on the course to action that resulted in the triumphant articulation: "No notebook for my babies and no measuring string neither" (198). Hence Sethe resists the nation-state's construction of her and her children's identity and personhood, challenging the nation's definition of "black citizenship," even as she refuses to belong to that "country within the country."

As with Sethe, President Mbeki accentuates a parallel racist, supremacist tactic employed in the way Baartman was treated and her willful assignment in that "country within the country." Calling attention to the racist, sexist, and classist tactics employed in Baartman's exploitation as she became the icon of supposed black racial inferiority and black female hypersexuality, President Mbeki expressed indignation and disgust with the deplorable treatment of one of Africa's daughters. In essence, in chronicling the injustices that Baartman experienced, he takes up what Saidiya Hartman calls "the language of humanism, seiz[ing] upon that which had been used against and denied" enslaved Africans (*Scenes* 5). Articulating the multiple forms of oppression that Baartman experienced, he reveals that "Baartman was firstly a victim of the exploitation suffered by South African ethnic groups during colonisation. Secondly, Saartjie Baartman was the victim of colonialism and sexism because her dignity as a woman and her rights were denied. Thirdly, she was also the victim of racism which was the characteristic of anthropology at the time, the latter being very much turned to ethnocentrism." Furthermore, establishing that perversion is not innate to Baartman's sexuality but rather stems from white supremacist beliefs, Mbeki unapologetically pontificates: "Even scientific inquiry was perverted to serve the cause of racism and the domination of human beings by other human beings."[12]

Ironically, Baartman who was consumed by the white audience allegedly died from alcohol consumption.[13] Despite obvious health concerns, the consumptive and codified labels encoded within the black female body render obscure dire health concerns (this point is reinforced in the successive chapter on Lorde). Furthermore, this discourse of pathology that is employed to frame Baartman is strategic in that it attempts to deflect from the mercantile and voyeuristic goals of her captors. However, it remains undebatable that Baartman's presumed difference was exploited, profiting Europe and Europeans twofold: reinforcing their erroneous claim to racial superiority and increasing her exploiters' monetary acquisition. Deemed propertied possession, her story epitomized the devaluation of the black female body that resulted in an identity crisis, a discursive erasure. Even so, Baartman's physical and psychological abuse at the hands of her European exploiters serves as evidence that coerced migration was manipulated for both profit and voyeuristic means, substantiating George Yancy's earlier claim that the monstrous body that is both feared and desired is still sought out in the corridors of white sexual exploits and fantasies (xvi). Linking Baartman's exploitation to the slave (profit-making) enterprise, Spillers equates public consumption with "body erasure," since one's identity gets obfuscated, reduced to cargo or merchandise (65). This reductionism lends itself to Baartman's new role as commercialized migrant. Spillers duly reminds us that as merchandise, the female subject is quantifiable despite her "smaller physical mass [that] occupies 'less room' in a directly translatable money economy" (72). Stephen Gould concurs that the "predominantly female market" that showcased "the exhibition of unusual humans (referring to Baartman) became a profitable business both in upper-class salons and in street-side stalls" (292).

Amy Schulz and Leith Mullings concur that labeling certain bodies deficient or unhealthy is premised on a racially motivated and biased criteria: "Physician scientists have played key roles in producing race, class, and gender hierarchies by 'seeing' differences in the bodies of presumably inferior groups" (28). Pointing out how black sexuality was exploited in affirming difference, Sander Gilman says that "an attempt to establish that the races were inherently different rested to no little extent on the sexual difference of the black" (*Difference* 112). In the same vein,

Rosemarie Garland-Thomson demonstrates how reading Baartman's body through the lens of western hegemonic discourse lends itself to easy "pathologiz[ation] and exoticiz[ation]" ("Integrating Disability" 78). The black body then is located contradictorily as "diseased yet attractive Other" (Gilman, *Difference* 110).

Identifying the critical and crippling factor of race that is used as a barometer for measuring Baartman's dehumanization, Zine Magubane reveals that the idea of blackness lacks historicity in the works that address Baartman's "racial representativeness." She argues that this blatant omission resulted from the "fact that many of Baartman's scholars have unthinkingly reproduced commonsense understandings of Blackness as it exists in the contemporary United States" (822). This essentializing further results in the denial of Baartman's personhood. Magubane cites "two historically untenable assumptions [scholars] make about race. The first assumption is that Baartman's color and sexual difference not only marked her as different but also rendered her fundamentally the same as all other Black people. The second assumption is that ideas about what constitutes Africanity and Blackness have remained relatively unchanged over time" (822).[14] Mugabane's assertion about the fixity of Africanness and blackness resonates with Morrison's earlier declaration of an imaginary Africa invented by imperialist powers.

Despite that, Baartman has risen above her humble station to become the symbol of hope and freedom for disenfranchised women. In the same vein, her tragic story serves as the catalyst for resistance embedded in the counter narrative articulated by fellow South African women (this resistance transcends boundaries and borders), who refused to be silenced or to submit to the apartheid regime, the "country within the country." Instead, they demanded to be recognized as equal citizens under the law. The narrative of courage and perseverance unfolds that on August 9, 1956, twenty thousand black South African women protested the law that required that they carry passbooks as proof of citizenship, marching to the Union Buildings in Pretoria, the site of the apartheid government at the time. Although women of all races took part in this protest march, Khanyi Mugabane reminds us that the flames of protest ignited decades earlier, in 1913, when black women formed the Bantu's Women League, which later became known as the ANC Women's League, to oppose the state's attempt to force women to carry passbooks. While the league was successful in overturning the law, it was reinstated in 1952 with the "introduction of the

Abolition of Passes and Coordination of Documents Act [that] required all black people over the age of 16 to carry a passbook at all times" and that required the signature of an employer each month to verify proof of citizenship, granting them the right to be within specific areas and to pay taxes. The law was eventually repealed in 1956, but only after the formation of the Federation of South African Women that mobilized around a united anti-apartheid front, and two momentous anti-pass marches, the first, two thousand members strong in October 1955, and the second in August 1956 that boasted over twenty thousand. This resistance to the pass laws ignited the Sharpeville Massacre on March 21, 1970, which left 180 black Africans injured and 69 dead at the hands of the South African police. The 1996 Bill of Rights that purportedly recognizes South African women as equal citizens is deserving of scrutiny because these state laws and policies do not represent women's interests. According to Mugabane, black women are disproportionately economically disadvantaged as they continually find themselves in low-paying jobs as domestic workers and farm laborers. Additionally, they are confronted with high incidents of rape and domestic violence. In this fashion, women are routinely constructed and/or imagined as commodity or disposable consumers. Migrant communities of women experience similar forms of oppressions; in this regard, South African women are given immigrant status. Even within their own nation-state, black women are likened to illegal, undocumented immigrants.

Drawing attention to the existence of global apartheid, Patricia J. Williams identifies a compelling parallel between the United States' and South Africa's practice and implementation of segregationist and racist policies. Although the succeeding incident involves three men, this narrative nonetheless informs this discourse. Furthermore, it reveals a shared identity politics characteristic of a diaspora. Recapitulating the infamous 1986 beating of three black men whose car broke down in Howard Beach, Queens, New York, Williams explains: "They needed documented reason for excursioning into neighborhoods where they do not live, for venturing beyond the bounds of the zones to which they are supposedly confined" (68). As Yancy is quick to point out: "The space of the white neighborhood has already been polarized into 'inside and outside' in such a way that 'curtails black people's inhabiting of [that] space'" (xix). Furthermore, Howard Beach's residents were antagonized by the trespassing by these black men, their transgressing and transcending of the invisible and "impermeable" borders. In essence, the young men required a proverbial passbook to show or claim legitimacy, similar to their South African compatriots.

The march that signaled the reclamation of personhood culminated with South African women being at the forefront of the political struggle against apartheid, an act that occasioned the rewriting of the masculinist narrative. This amending of the nationalist agenda was already in progress, exemplified by female resistance and resilience ensconced in the march's motto: "You strike a woman, you strike a rock." The burning of the passbooks by the women—a legally issued government document—ironically underscores the illegality of the practice of "conditional" citizenship. The above-mentioned acts of tremendous courage accomplished by the women give voice to transnational feminism. Baartman's exploitation induced outrage, producing a transnational feminist agenda that brought about the unification of women globally and specifically in South Africa where women forged a new diaspora of empowered citizens. This feminist coalition advocated for transnational alliances and partnerships. Addressing the importance of transnational coalitions as a means to expose the histories that have occasioned such oppressive practices, Grewal and Kaplan remind us: "We need to articulate the relationship of gender to scattered hegemonies such as global economic structures, patriarchal nationalisms, 'authentic' forms of tradition, local structures of domination, and legal-juridical oppression on multiple levels" (17). As we are reminded by Crais and Scully: "Baartman's funeral was an exercise in producing history from the other side, from the vantage point of the poor and the oppressed" (165). Emphasizing further the wholesome feminist agenda, Catherine Ndinda and Korwa Adar argue that "women's protest against pass laws was a feminist endeavor in that it united them in the fight against their own oppression as women regardless of their class differences."

Furthermore, President Mbeki renders potent the cliché that women's rights are human rights whereby he precisely categorizes Baartman's exploitation as a "crime against humanity" or, to invoke Spillers's more poignant phrase, "crimes against the flesh." He reminds the nation that apartheid was "based on the criminal notion that some had been called upon to enlighten the hordes of barbarians, as Sarah Bartmann was enlightened and tamed" (Holmes 109). Mbeki's wide-ranging and far-reaching critique of apartheid to American racism and slavery, to colonial legacies, to gender disparity and discrimination, alludes to a pervasive criminalization of black subjects carried out in the name of imperial expansionism. On the other hand, this transnational partnership transcended gender as Presidents Nelson Mandela and Thabo Mbeki partook in this feminist discourse. In actuality, they are the architects of the discourse, signaling a challenge to the white masculinist national discourse and hegemony and debunking the myth of white supremacy.

Accordingly, South African women engendered a new diaspora premised on inclusion and solidarity. Vèvè Clark is quick to point out that the "recognition of an African diaspora in part reclaimed [demographic, cultural and class] differences and rhetorically redefined unity in transnational terms" ("Diaspora Literacy" 382). More importantly, South African women's protracted struggle and protest against the apartheid regime effected Baartman's return home to freedom and her conferral of citizenship.

Both Clifton Crais and Rachel Holmes express some disagreement with the solemnization of Baartman. Whereas Crais focuses on the predominance of men speaking on behalf of Baartman, Holmes takes issue with the intermittent patronizing tone employed in her homecoming tribute (Holmes 110; Crais and Scully 164).[15] Choosing instead to focus on Baartman's momentous return home, especially given South Africa's racist history, namely, its protracted criminalization of its black citizens, I emphasize the visible shift in the national discourse. National discourses have been routinely characterized by either the absence or the marginalization of the woman (question) on the nationalist agenda. This fact has strong resonance for African nations that, according to Indrawatie Biseswar, increasingly reflect "autocratic tendencies and control and aggressive forms of repression." She stresses further that in "the absence of a comprehensive radical gender discourse" stands "a rigorous focus on a depoliticized national women's discourse" (405).[16] Although Biseswar's article specifically addresses the Ethiopian nationalist agenda, the concerns raised are extremely relevant to this discourse. Biseswar prefaces her argument by identifying that Ethiopia has adopted the prevailing gender discourse practices on the continent, whereby "it does not feel compelled to follow global trends on gender discursive practices." At the same time, Ndinda and Adar call our attention to the fact that in addition to having different kinds of nationalism in South Africa, nationalism is defined along racial lines.

Nationalism in South Africa took a racial character in that Afrikaner nationalism aimed at liberation from British dominance and the need to achieve white privilege at the expense of the rights of the African majority. With the formation of the Union of South Africa in which the British and Boer Republics united to form the Republic of South Africa, all Blacks (Africans, Coloureds and Indians) lost the remaining political rights they had. This saw the formation of various Black organisations all fighting for the liberation of their people from white supremacist rule. African nationalism was driven by the need to repossess what had been illegally appropriated by the white minority. In the pursuit of nationalist goals feminist goals were also articulated though their achievement seems to have come after the nationalist goals.

The shift from despotic rule—deep-rooted apartheid ideology—to democratic rule was heralded in various black nationalist groups with the African National Congress (ANC) as the representative group of South African black nationalism.[17] Despite the ANC's various shortcomings, including its marginal view of the feminist agenda as cited by Ndinda and Adar, one would be equally negligent or blind-sighted to overlook the shift (albeit slight) from a predominant masculinist agenda to the inclusion of the woman question, namely, women's contribution to the nationalist discourse and nation-building.[18] This shift is commendable and should be regarded as such, especially considering that South Africa had just recently emerged from the yoke of apartheid and colonialism. The esteemed Nelson Mandela played an integral role in implementing this shift, resulting in the inclusion of the woman within the highly charged masculine nationalist agenda. Shortly after assuming the presidency of South Africa in 1994, one of the first acts that Mandela accomplished was to invite Mrs. P. W. Botha and the widows of the other old apartheid leaders to have lunch with some women of the black community.[19] Assessing this historic moment, Frene Ginwala illuminates the need for female alliances: "It's not theatre. It's not symbolic. It is this view that [women] have got to see this new South Africa as something in which they have a place, that we don't allow whatever gains we've got to be washed away.[20] In keeping with this feminist agenda, on his first visit to France, Mandela broached the subject of Baartman's return home to South Africa with French president, François Mitterrand.[21] As a long-standing member and president of the ANC, the Black Nationalist movement that explicitly fought against the apartheid government, Mandela's record on human rights is commendable.[22] In keeping with his comprehensive political agenda, he was accordingly certified as a ceremonial president and nation builder. Drawing on Mandela's human rights activism and lead, his successor, Thabo Mbeki, continued to add fuel to the flame for Baartman's repatriation.[23]

Baartman's repatriation was marked by national celebration. Lydie Moudelino chronicles this event best as she explains that "ultimately the dismembered, exiled colonial ghost of the Hottentot Venus is re-historicised, re-named and re-patriated into a collective imaginary" (206). Refreshingly, Baartman was not portrayed as "the suffering mother" of the South African nation, a notable and welcome detour from Gaitskell and Underhalter's, Chancy's and Charles's insightful assessment that whenever women are figured in the nationalist discourse, they are portrayed as being like infants and dependent, "suffering mothers of the nation" (see chapter 4). As such, the national identity that Baartman inhabits is not that of victim.[24]

Furthermore, the emotive portrayal of pain is not relegated to the female (personal or domestic) domain nor rendered "welfarist rather than political" (Ndinda and Adar). Instead, Baartman's suffering is transnational in scope, transcending gender and class barrier and consequently resulting in a celebratory moment of national identity and belonging. In Mbeki's own words, "The story of Sarah Baartman [is not simply] the story of the African people,"[25] but moreover the "nation identified with the burden of Saartjie's pain and intolerable misery" (Crais and Scully 110). We witness a nation in pain, in national (public) mourning as a result of the personal pain experienced by one of its daughters, mothers. As mother (Africa), Baartman is metonymically representative of the motherland.[26] Baartman's metonymic parallel to the nation is rendered most palpable when President Mbeki intimates that the exploitation and violation that she suffered at the hands of the white colonial masters mirror the exploitation, the plundering, and the rape of the motherland, Africa. Urging the exploiters and violators of humankind to make amends for the wrong done, to ask penance for the crimes committed against humanity, Mbeki calls for restitution and reconciliation: "Those who sought to dehumanise Saartjie Baartman also have the responsibility to join hands with the millions whose fate she exemplified, to help rebuild South Africa and Africa, in a common effort to give meaning to the vision that all of us, regardless of race or colour, were created in the image of God."[27] At the same time, he cautions the citizens that while mourning encompasses celebration and forgiveness, forgetting (the past) is not optional. President Mbeki's cautionary message powerfully resonates with Toni Morrison's memorable phrase in *Beloved*: "This is not a story to pass on" (275). Calling on fellow South Africans to refrain from engaging in a politics of forgetting or denial that lends itself to an identity crisis, he exposes slavery and colonial violence as the root cause of Baartman's demonization: "[Baartman's story] is the story of the loss of our ancient freedom. . . . It is the story of our reduction to the state of objects who could be owned, used, and discarded by others."[28]

In equal manner, Morrison's sage grandmother and woman preacher, Baby Suggs, joins Mbeki's lament about black subjects being "owned, used, and discarded by others," severely cautioning against forgetting, self-denial, and self-denigration. Issuing an equivalent cautionary message about the detriments of forgetting, Debra Walker King demonstrates how it is tantamount to self-erasure, as she establishes how we have become complicit with popular culture's "denial of and collusion with a value-laden social hierarchy that commodifies the pained black body" (6). Furthering her argument, she writes, "Denial can be emotionally, spiritually, and even physically wounding. Engaging in denial means accepting the assumptions and personal assaults . . . that the black body is always a memorial to African and African American historical pain" (6). In the same breath, Baby Suggs's exhortation of self-love and communal kinship and responsibility is triumphant, as she insists that it is imperative to reclaim the flesh: "Love it. Love it hard. Yonder they do not love your flesh. They despise it. Yonder they flay it" (Morrison, *Beloved* 88). "Deeply loved flesh" (89) serves as an antidote to the commodification of the "pained black body" to which King refers. Hence the recapture and recuperation of Baartman's captive flesh lends itself to exercising control of one's body, being, and agency.

Baartman's final journey epitomizes Hall's "return as fate, as destiny," as she was finally and respectfully interred in her birthplace, the Gamtoos River valley in the Eastern Cape, 187 years after her fateful journey from Cape Town to London and Paris (234). This return engenders recontextualization, "transforming [her story] from the exclusive narrative of an exhibition into a story of migration" (Moudelino 206).

Baartman's personal identity is not co-opted by the national identity because she is constructed outside the nation-state, outside the categories of domination, as an agent of her own discourse. This autonomy culminated in the recovery and recuperation of the injured female body. Baartman's return home culminated in her conferral of citizenship and provided both a discursive and physical space to pay tribute to women, to commemorate their invaluable contribution to nation-building and to the struggle for freedom and democracy. Significantly, Baartman's bestowal of citizenship is realized by the South African government brokering a deal with France that granted the French government amnesty, absolving it completely from charges of kidnapping, slavery, or indentureship. This role reversal exemplifies a noticeable shift of power whereby the amnesty-granting institution is the newly democratic South Africa and not the colonial state of France. Incidentally, it was the new state under the leadership of the noble statesman Nelson Mandela that reinstated Baartman into the nation-state and restored her citizenship. Fittingly, she was interred on August 9, 2002, National Women's Day in South Africa, a day marked by jubilant celebrations of the advancement of women's rights.[29]

The reimagination of the nation through Baartman's body is exemplified by her being coronated as Mother Africa in the coinage "Mama Sarah!" At her funeral, chants of "Mama Sarah! Mama Sarah!" rang out from South Africans, reinstating her into the annals of history.[30] Completing her reinstatement, President Mbeki fittingly and reverentially solemnized Baartman: "This is our grandmother. This is the nation's grandmother, South Africa's great mother and ancestor" (Holmes 107, 108–9). Bestowed ancestral status, celebrated as and crowned a national heroine, a title once reserved exclusively for men, Baartman shares the spotlight, the national stage, so to speak, with "great men," South African heroes in the likes of Oliver Tambo, Walter Sisulu, and Nelson Mandela himself. Once predominantly constructed as masculine, the nation-state now honors women/mothers, acknowledging their invaluable contribution to nation-building by resurrecting and reinstating them as key players and contributors to the national discourse and not basically as pawns.

The simultaneity—personal and historical—of Baartman's narrative is transformative, having transcended the private, personal sphere and become a narrative of international impact and magnitude that resonates far beyond the continent. Thus love of the flesh, according to Morrison's Baby Suggs, epitomizes the power to heal, save, and redeem; the flesh must be reclaimed in order to actualize freedom. As Baartman lies in eternal peace in the bosom of Mother Africa, one can safely surmise that she is "captive flesh no more."

Championing the cause for self-ownership, President Mbeki readily discloses extant gender disparity and discrimination, articulating the unfair, imbalanced treatment meted out to women who are twice as likely as their male counterparts to be impoverished, abused, and victims of violence. To counter these social and economic ills, he calls for a speedy creation of a nonsexist society (Holmes 109). A paradox nevertheless, Baartman's life/living years did not give rise to the political and social changes that her death occasioned. In this regard, Baartman's migrations decisively culminated in her ultimate journey to her final resting place.

2 "Crimes against the Flesh"

Politics and Poetics of the Black Female Body

> The European hegemonies stole bodies—some of them female—we regard this human and social irreparability as high crimes against the flesh, as the person of African females ... registered the wounding.
> —Hortense Spillers, "Mama's Baby, Papa's Maybe: An American Grammar Book"

> All too often the enemies of our physical and emotional well-being are social and political. That is why we must strive to understand the complex politics of Black women's health.
> —Angela Davis, "Sick and Tired of Being Sick and Tired"

Addressing the downward spiral of black women induced by various ailments, including cancer and drug addiction, Evelyn C. White bemoans that illnesses have rendered them powerless, resulting not only in their lack of citizen rights but also in their ultimate erasure. She remarks: "Ironically, this downward trend has occurred at a time when this country has developed state-of-the-art medical technology that is envied around the world. Without a sound body and mind, it is impossible for black women to attain personal goals or to provide the leadership our community needs" (xiv). On one hand, White's comment reveals that medicine has an innate hierarchy that marginalizes certain bodies, thereby creating a community or diaspora of "diseased" bodies. On the other hand, she interrogates the discriminatory policy of the medical establishment/the state, performing a cross-examination of the state's obligation in ensuring the well-being of all of its citizens. It is therefore no mere coincidence that Angela Davis politicizes black women's health concerns, underscoring the struggles women have endured in their quest for health: "the pursuit of health in body, mind and spirit weaves in and out of every major struggle women have ever waged in our quest for social, economic and political emancipation" ("Sick and Tired" 18). Hence the pursuit of health should be unquestionable, a necessary requirement that engages the politics of belonging and identity. One's health, that is, the personal well-being of the individual, determines the welfare of the community, the black diaspora. Alternatively, an unhealthy body further engenders patterns of oppression.

Audre Lorde reveals how the concept of health is exploited to appeal to the national white body, intimating that the medical establishment is complicit in reinforcing and perpetuating disease among patients in its goal to "normalize" the body. Health is deeply politicized, a fact that Lorde exposes in ascertaining that the ills are preconditioned by a racist, heterosexist, hegemonic society. Consequently, Lorde rejects homogeneous categorization of female patients, imploring that women empower themselves by rejecting "body conformity" and the "theft" of the body. Responding to the "theft," Lorde repudiates the essentialist approach in treating all female bodies. Addressing how certain bodies are stigmatized, M. Jacqui Alexander duly reminds us in her informative essay "Not Just Any (Body) Can Be a Citizen: The Politics of Law, Sexuality, and Postcoloniality in Trinidad and Tobago and the Bahamas" that some bodies imperil the nation.[1] Straddling multiple borders and embodying multiple "incompatible" identities, including gay, black, woman, feminist, lesbian, and mother, Lorde qualifies as an "outlaw" of the state, to borrow Alexander's term. Addressing the criminalization of certain bodies, Alexander argues that those bodies that have refused the nation's "heterosexual imperative for citizenship" have been stigmatized, rendered deviant and defiant. She writes:

> Although policing the sexual (stigmatizing and outlawing several kinds of non-procreative sex, particularly lesbian and gay sex, and prostitution) has something to do with sex, it is also more than sex. Embedded here are powerful signifiers of appropriate sexuality, about the kind of sexuality that presumably imperils the nation, and about the kind of sexuality that

promotes citizenship. Not just (any) *body* can be a citizen anymore, for some bodies have been marked by the state as non-procreative, in pursuit of sex only for pleasure, a sex that is non-productive of babies and of no economic gain. ("Not Just [Any] Body" 6)

Drawing on Alexander's theoretical insight, Lorde is figuratively positioned between borderlands, partaking in sex for both procreative—she is a mother of two—and non-procreative reasons—she is a professed lesbian. Furthermore, Lorde's deviance (and attendant defiance) is exemplified through her lesbian identity and her sick, diseased body. Accordingly, Lorde's "queering the nation" is dualistic. Engaging the act of "queering," Lorde further challenges hegemonic conceptions of family and nation by destabilizing fixed, "normative" gender categories and the definition of the good citizen and ideal mother. Alexander substantiates this line of reasoning when she intimates that Lorde inhabits the kind of sexuality that does not promote citizenship.

Furthermore, Lorde's queer or deviant body challenges the medical industry's "one size fits all" method, demanding reassessment of the approach to healing the sick. In other words, she challenges the medical industry to implement a more extensive and inclusive plan of action to accurately reflect women's varied experiences. This call for an end to injustice in medical "malpractice" is representative of her larger campaign to end racial discrimination and specifically female oppression cum marginalization globally. To this end, she reinterprets the national (medical) discourse, creating new spaces of female subjectivity. In line with this, locating the discourse in a militaristic zone, Lorde not only reveals the causalities of the proverbial war, but she simultaneously challenges the notion of women as victims, women as preservers of the nation's health. Thus, drawing a parallel of her personal experiences with oppression within the black female diaspora, namely, with South African women's experiences of oppression (and by default other "Third World Women"), is no mere coincidence; rather, it illustrates her transnational sensibility. Further, her solidarity with South African women who register their disgust and defiance with the nation-state denying them citizenship signals her desire for transnational citizenship. In line with this claim, Lorde's personal diary promotes a transnational agenda in that it functions as a public, political document that fosters the flow of ideas. Lorde literally writes (on) her body, creating a new text that supplants the master narrative, the Eurocentric literary tradition. This self-examination creates a new theoretical framework that fiercely interrogates the labeling of certain bodies as diseased and deviant. By the same accord, Lorde's staunch advocacy for the working class and the disenfranchised (the diaspora within the diaspora) establishes a detour, as it sets her discourse apart from hegemonic, elitist discourses. Moreover, this "body text" challenges the static, normative body by crisscrossing literal and metaphorical borders and boundaries. These transnational undertakings become a challenge to the nation-state, as Dzenita Hrelja Hasecic is quick to point out that "women who travelled and described the travelling experiences transgress the boundaries between private and public challenging such naturalization (namely the private, pre-political and domestic spheres) of women" (2).

Lorde's "sick" body migrates from normative representations of female bodies, of health, and able-bodiedness. Her experience with the American Cancer Society, especially during her post-mastectomy recovery, is likened to a profit-seeking and voyeuristic mission that entraps women within the masculine gaze or narrative. Sharing a coveted spot on the axis of female deviance with her female compatriot, Baartman, Lorde's "hypervisibility" and "hypovisibility" are simultaneously the object of public consumption and the subject of fierce scrutiny and debate. All the same, this coalition engenders diasporic connections. "Performing deviance" engenders an alternative female body politic that challenges and subverts the status quo as it functions as a site for articulating resistance.

Lorde's skillful juxtaposition of the ill engendered by South Africa's apartheid regime and America's highly charged racist policies calls attention to a global phenomenon that affects the diasporic community, specifically the female diaspora. This adept "troping" of her disease finds resonance in her analogous reading of her battle with breast cancer and her continued fight against racism embodied by the bigoted leaders, South African's President P. W. Botha and Public Safety Commissioner Bull Connor. This analogy exposes globalized forms of oppressions meted out to certain bodies that transcend borders and boundaries, as it realizes Angela Davis's appeal to "place our battle for universally accessible health care in its larger social and political context" ("Sick and Tired" 25). Revealing the "apartheid-like" relation and dismissal of the black (female) body, Lorde convincingly articulates that social or societal ills impact negatively on women's health. Thus she serves as a conduit between the female diaspora and the medical establishment.

We bear witness to Lorde's indictment of the American Cancer Society for promoting and practicing what she fittingly alludes to as "medical profiling," which bears a strong resemblance to racial profiling. Similar to what many scholars and political activists classify as routinized "policing" of the black body, the heightened "intrusive" characteristics of medicine, as Lorde observes, are becoming increasingly naturalized or normalized.[2] Consequently, this normalizing process lends itself to codification and commodification—where certain bodies are deemed more worthy than others—of the female body. Along these lines, Lorde's lesbian identity is predetermined, categorized as "deviant," rendering Alexander's declaration that not "any body can be a citizen" potent. In line with this, Yancy ascertains that "the Black body is condemned before it even acts; it has always already committed a crime" (xxi). Even so, Lorde's fierce interrogation of the masculinist, heterosexist philosophy finds resonance in her objecting to female commodification and challenging the concept of deviance. In other words, she rejects the state's "sexual inscriptions on [her] body" (J. Alexander, "Not Just (Any) Body" 5). So her refusal to wear a prosthesis is an act of transgression that engenders the interplay of deviance and defiance, obvious disqualifiers of a (model) citizen. Politicizing the body within the framework of race, class, and gender politics, Lorde challenges the established heteronormative/heterosexual order and objects to the blanketed deviance and pathology within which black women are encoded; "scripting" instead an alternative discourse that subversively exposes the inherent "deviance" of racism. Lorde's cancer-affected body becomes a site for articulating resistance, functioning as a battlefield on which the battle for social justice and equality is waged. Consequently, her body "defies the fixed fantasies and distorted images projected upon it through the white gaze, and, hence, through the episteme of whiteness" (Yancy xxii).

Arguably best known for politicizing her personal battle with breast cancer in her memoir *The Cancer Journals*, Lorde demonstrates that the personal is political.[3] De Veaux concurs that "no earlier work had explored the impact of breast cancer on a black feminist lesbian's life. *The Cancer Journals* pioneered wider public discourse on the disease within feminist circles. It gave women a precedent to speak about both the disease and their fear of it" (269). And so Lorde's memoir becomes a manifesto for promoting transnational feminism. Written seven years before Hortense Spillers's groundbreaking article "Mama's Baby, Papa's Maybe," Lorde's memoir serves as a precursor to the "war" against silence.

Chronicling the sociopolitical order of the New World, Spillers points out how silencing, in the guise of dismemberment and mutilation, has affected generations. This diasporic plight has left an indelible imprint on the bodies and psyches of the violated individuals. Acknowledging that the colossal damage inflicted upon the captive slave body is criminal in intent, Spillers offers the following description of the heinous act: "We regard this human and social irreparability as high crimes against the flesh, as the person of African females . . . registered the wounding" (67). Rendering the phrase "high crimes against the flesh" effective, Lorde focuses on how silence about breast cancer renders the female body captive. Captive, the body is prevented from traversing boundaries or borders. It also bears illegitimacy. The "torture" that the body experiences, namely, the unspeakable crimes committed against the flesh that are tantamount to "human and social irreparability" (Spillers 67), is not simply a result of the pain engendered by surgery. It is exacerbated by the pretense of normalcy, the disguise or erasure of difference. This erasure amounts to a literal and symbolic "theft of the body." Furthermore, surgery displays physical scarring of the already psychologically scarred black female body. Scarred, the body does not fit the definition of the ideal body, and so the scarred subject is not an ideal citizen. Serving as an advocate for what Spillers refers to as the "wounded," Lorde offers her cancer-affected body as primary text, inducing a simultaneous "registering of the wounds" and resistance to the pain that bears the imprint of silencing (67). Lorde's articulation of her pain is an empowering act that results in her transitioning from object (of pain) to subject/citizen of the state.

Disputing biology as the sole determinant of black women's illness, Angela Davis is quick to draw attention to the socially determined factor of illness. Her unequivocal statement that "all too often the enemies of our physical and emotional well-being are social and political" establishes the challenge. Lorde was one of many African American writers during the 1970s and '80s who demonstrated that "individual disease is inextricably bound up with broader social ills" (Stanford, "Mechanisms" 28).[4] Her acute awareness of the (obligatory) politicization of women's health manifests in her visualizing her battle with breast cancer in "very political terms." In *A Litany for Survival: The Life and Work of Audre Lorde*, the film that offers a snapshot of her life and work, she confesses that battling cancer is similar to battling racism and sexism. While she visualizes the "cancer cells as white South African policemen," she envisions her battle with the disease as "a sea of black faces marching over P. W. Botha and stamping apartheid into the ground." She then poignantly and persuasively expounds on her statement:

> I visualize daily winning the battles going on inside my body.... In those visualizations, the cancer at times takes on the face and shape of my most implacable enemies, those I fight and resist most fiercely. Sometimes the wanton cells in my liver become Bull Connor and his police dogs completely smothered, rendered impotent in Birmingham, Alabama, by a mighty avalanche of young, determined Black marchers moving across him toward their future. P. W. Botha's bloated face of apartheid squashed into the earth beneath an onslaught of the slow rhythmic advance of furious Blackness. Black South African women moving through my blood destroying passbooks. (*Burst of Light* 132–33)

The seamless parallel that Lorde envisions between Bull Connor and Botha signals the ease with which she discursively traverses borders. In a symbolic gesture she locates her battle with cancer within a racialized context, reemphasizing on one hand the shift of illness from a "biomedical to a biopsychosocial model" and on the other hand underscoring that racism is as virulent as the cancer cells (Stanford, *Bodies* 2). This racial dimension is rendered most palpable in the discursive indictment of Bull Connor and P. W. Botha, agents of racial, segregationist politics. This common racial politics points to global "scattered hegemonies," to borrow Grewal's and Kaplan's coinage. The cancerous, bigoted message (of hate) espoused and reinforced by these purveyors of race politics is matched only by the virulent invasive nature of cancer. Cancer's attack on the body that results in restricted body movement bears resemblance to the militarization—substantiated further by the menacing presence of the police and their dogs—imposed by both Connor and Botha on the black citizens of Birmingham and South Africa. Despite the fact that the black citizens of Birmingham are passport holders, unlike their South African counterparts, they are still policed and restricted from inhabiting certain spaces. The conflation of Botha and Connor with apartheid and segregation calls attention to a shared politics of racial ideology, but most importantly, it exposes the complicit relation that the United States maintained with South Africa. In her biography of Lorde, Alexis De Veaux captures this (global) historical moment fraught with tension:

> The wanton killings of black South Africans, the killings of Americans, government neglect of the social needs of black communities, the precarious nature of black survival against the backdrop of struggles for power on the world stage, were all emblematic of connecting political realities. (350)

De Veaux underscores that Lorde felt "the urgency to unearth the connections between these assaults" that culminated in the composition of the poem "Apartheid U.S.A." (350). The poem is a reiteration of a shared politics of oppression, but more directly, it serves as "a stinging condemnation of those and other connections maintained by white supremacy in America and South Africa" (350).

These racist laws frame and enable the politics of exclusion, resulting in a crisis of citizenship. Furthermore, the militarization or the disciplining of these black bodies mimics captivity or enslavement, as it renders the flesh captive, to echo Spillers. The captive flesh is denied all citizen rights and is rendered a non-person. Fiercely challenging and interrogating this shared white supremacist vision, Lorde equally engenders transnational solidarity between the black underclasses of America and South Africa. She calls for collective mobilization against global discrimination and oppression. Staging a proverbial war in response to the call to action to bear arms by the Côte d'Ivoirian "fighter for the rebel 'new forces,'" who illuminates the gravity of those denied citizenship, Lorde draws attention to the importance of transnational alliances that challenge borderland politics (Manby 1). Specifically, she calls for a unified female diaspora, for South African women's struggle resonates with the struggles of women worldwide. In like manner, their unyielding demand for citizenship is a fight against female oppression globally.

Envisioning her fight with cancer as if engaged in war on a battlefield, Lorde consequently employs the language of protest, suggesting that practicing a corresponding militancy may be the only available tool to disarm and dismantle racist and sexist ideologies. By the same token, Lorde's centering of race and racial tensions in her personal narratives substantiates her claim about the racial politics embedded in medicine and medical practices. This viewpoint becomes manifest in Harriet A. Washington's *Medical Apartheid* in which she offers an in-depth examination of racially biased medical practices conducted in the United States for centuries. Lorde's likening of medical malfeasance to racial profiling of black citizens is authenticated by the historical records. A perfect example, as discussed in chapter 1, is the medical exploitation of Saartjie Baartman. The object of derision and European voyeurism, Baartman, considered grotesquely hideous because of her physical difference, was put on display by a naval surgeon before a European audience in London's Piccadilly Circus and subsequently in France at a zoo and posthumously at the Musée de l'Homme. Furthermore, one may recall the unethical practice used by the Tuskegee Syphilis Study. This medical breach was so horrific that it has left an indelible mark on successive generations, fueling continued fear and suspicion of the medical establishment.[5] This dehumanization renders blacks invisible and serves as fodder for their denial of citizenship. Furthering the argument that the racialization of medicine is no enigma, Dorothy Roberts offers another classic historical example of racial cum medical profiling. Citing the biological or reproductive control of black women's bodies, she convincingly argues that this obvious practice of racial oppression serves the interests of white supremacy. Paralleling Roberts's line of reasoning, Lorde demonstrates how the racist and sexist masculinist medical discourse serves as a regulatory force in its execution of care to the medically disenfranchised.

By invoking South African women's rejection of the state-mandated policy to carry passbooks as verification of citizenship, Lorde calls attention to female resistance transnationally to securitization. The first Pass Laws were introduced in 1760 to regulate the movement of slaves in the Cape. Later, Pass Laws were reinforced to suppress the liberation struggles. Specifically, they were designed to control the movement of Africans under apartheid; initially, only males over the age of sixteen were expected to carry passbooks. Illuminating Lorde's promotion and practice of transnational citizenship, Alexis De Veaux reveals that in her support of South African women's political resistance to apartheid, Lorde developed relationships with two significant "sister grassroots organizations, the Zamani Soweto Sisters and the Maggie Magaba Trust." These relationships not only spoke to the shared identity politics between black South African women and African American women as they embarked on a common quest for black liberation, but it also facilitated African American women sharing economic and political resources with their less fortunate sisters of the African diaspora (280).[6]

Baartman is the embodiment of this sisterhood of shared politics of oppression and exploitation of women under colonial domination. Similar to South African women who were once deemed second-class citizens and therefore placed under legal control of husbands and fathers, Lorde demonstrates that a parallel designation of second-class citizenship is conferred to underprivileged American women, most of whom are black and in dire need of medical attention; they are (surgically) infantilized as they remain dependent on the male-dominated medical industry.[7] Davis observes that black women's health is inextricably intertwined with social welfare. One can therefore safely surmise that Lorde's refusal to wear a prosthesis is a call for social justice and equality, a show of female solidarity. More importantly, Lorde's engagement in a feminist politics of liberation brings to bear that her personal battle with breast cancer has larger political and global ramifications. Apart from shedding light on the devastating characteristic of the disease—an act intended to demand better care and to attend to the specific needs of those affected—it calls overdue attention to the question of access or lack thereof. Lorde's memoir is a rallying call for change within the medical industry.

Lorde finds most objectionable the profit-seeking and profit-making craze that the medical industry has implemented in its agenda, resulting in the practice of politics of exclusion. In her response to this medical "malpractice," Lorde pontificates: "Institutionalized rejection of difference is an absolute necessity in a profit economy which needs outsiders as surplus people" (*Sister Outsider* 115). President Mbeki concurred as he earlier expressed that surplus is attained by reducing human beings to objects to be used, abused, and discarded at will. As surplus, humans become expendable and "are taken into 'account' as quantities" (Spillers 72). Surplus (subhuman) people are easily identifiable most often by race and the attendant class stratification, resulting in the creation of a "country within the country." Spillers adds to this (race-class) equation, intimating that the decipherable markings are gendered as she unfalteringly points out that the slave market was dominated by females despite the documented fact that men at all ages outnumbered women on the slave ships (72). This predominance of enslaved female bodies gestures toward their disproportionate mistreatment as non-citizens.

Lorde reveals that the commercialization of health has forced women to regard difference with fear and intolerance, often at our own detriment. She critically observes that difference is not the primary contributor to our discord, but the dismissal or negation of those differences has dire consequences, resulting in female isolation and the attendant relinquishing of freedom that affects us psychologically and somatically. Serving up equal criticism for the profit-seeking medical industry, Davis demonstrates how the body has been compromised, held captive by health or lack thereof, in that it has been unscrupulously transformed into a commodity whereby the highest bidder gets the best care/cure. She writes: "In this society, dominated as it is by the profit-seeking ventures of monopoly corporations, health has been callously transformed into a commodity—a commodity that those with means are able to afford, but that is too often entirely beyond the reach of others" (19). Davis's "others" is Lorde's "surplus people" and Spillers's "marked women," whose bodies have *registered the wounding*.

In attempting to heal the wounds, Davis joins Lorde in campaigning for individual as well as state responsibility and accountability to its citizens, the first step of which is to better understand the *complex politics of black women's health* ("Sick and Tired" 20–24). The need for accountability becomes manifest in Lorde's relentless investigation of the medical industry that serves as impetus for her decisively situating women's battles with and survival of breast cancer in a militarized zone. Discursively, her "preemptive strike" disarms the master narrative as she beats them at their own game of militancy and violence. Lorde employs a politics of militancy or more specifically a militaristic language that becomes a rallying cry for women's corresponding militancy and aggression in dealing with (and reclaiming) their health and their bodies. She declares that the battle for self-determinacy and self-preservation must unabatedly continue in spite of the survival statistics of breast cancer (*Cancer Journals* 60). Her missile-laden language approximates the militaristic tactics that Botha employed to safeguard his country from foreign invasion and internal subversion. In like manner, Lorde embraces a militarized focus against the infringement of women's rights, rejecting the narration of the nation on the female body. In this regard, her battle cry is symptomatic of the mammoth military contingents that nation-states maintain "for the purpose of protecting and maintaining the boundaries of the Self against encroachment, conquest, invasion and intrusion by the 'enemy'" (Saigol). In the given scenario, cancer is the crowned enemy; silence is the runner-up. Lorde's strategic alignment of the war on cancer with military warfare as a means to elucidate the dreadful nature of this disease has its historical context. Thatcher Carter reminds us that in 1969 during Richard Nixon's presidency, prominent advocates and fund-raisers for cancer research "fought for federal recognition and funding, relat[ing] their cause directly to the unsupported war in Vietnam, stating that the money available for research was being depleted by the federal spending in Vietnam" (656). Along similar lines, Cynthia Wu points out that the medical establishment relied on this militaristic image to bolster its proclaimed commitment to "fighting" cancer (245). It is against this backdrop of heightened awareness of breast cancer that Lorde published her *Cancer Journals*.[8]

Thus Lorde tactically locates disease within a militaristic zone to script an alternative discourse, one that does not portray women/mothers as sacrificing citizens who suffer in silence. Wu's argument that Lorde "focuses on addressing the breast cancer patient" and not "the medical establishment" is not entirely accurate (249). While it is true that Lorde's use of military metaphors empowers the patients, she nevertheless unleashes severe criticism of the medical industry that promotes normalization to patients irrespective of race, class, and ethnicity. In this regard, Lorde's agenda, which has as its primary goal the empowerment of female patients, is not only limited to those with (medical) access but also extends to the uninsured and the disenfranchised. In essence, she is genuinely concerned about the "surplus" patients, the "ill-gotten" and forgotten diaspora. This concern becomes manifest in Lorde routinely and consciously "accepting lower fees for events organized by grassroots women" (De Veaux 353). Therefore Lorde's deliberate attention to class/race structure remains incontestable and is strategic. While I support Wu's line of reasoning that Lorde's women-centered sensibility "allows her to form a different set of assumptions about femininity," it should be emphasized that Lorde's appropriation of white femininity is premised on race and class consciousness. From time to time in her campaign for citizenship for black subjects, Lorde was at odds with white feminists. De Veaux notes that whenever the opportunity arose, Lorde, even at the risk of her popularity among white feminists, "seized the moment to air the difficult truth: racism within the women's movement perpetuated black women's invisibility, and had links to the failure to bridge differences between women in spite of notions of 'sisterhood'" (192).

By the same token, Lorde's unrelenting crusade against replicating patriarchal notions of (black) women and their bodies should be accorded greater importance. Wu's theorization of Lorde's super-feminization of her body "into that of a 'super-woman'" is interesting, although I don't completely buy the idea that Lorde's intention was to set herself apart from and above the masses. I would venture to say that Lorde is not even remotely invested in exceptionalism, especially given her history with grassroots women's organizations. It should be noted that apart from the defeminization that Lorde experiences as a result of her mastectomy, she also undergoes deracialization, insofar as her race is seen as marginal and is detached from her identity (Wu 250). All the same, Wu persuasively ascertains that the removal of one of Lorde's breasts makes her "seem less sexually desirable" in keeping with the western ideal of beauty and femininity (250). Adding to this discourse, Saywell writes, "Iconic both of female sexuality and maternity, breasts are often the currency through which feminine value is attributed" (39). Moreover, asserting that the sexiness of breasts is used to sell breast cancer, Cherise Saywell argues that mastectomies are regarded as a violation of femininity and an assault on beauty and perceptions of normality. In her effort to de-normalize scripted feminine values, Lorde reappropriates the confines of femininity, lessening the undue burden placed upon the female subject. Moreover, standing in "violation of femininity," she engages the process of defeminization by refusing a prosthetic breast, which in turn signals her refusal to approximate the idealized feminine body.

Lorde's identification with the women warriors, the legendary Amazon women of Dahomey, signals her refutation of the notion of ideal womanhood and ideal citizen. Accordingly, the women warriors engender and embody her militaristic engagement in achieving unconditional citizenship. The Dahomey women wielded power outside traditional boundaries beyond the nation-state's definition of citizenship. Known for building their bodies into lethal weapons from a young age and removing one breast so as to become better archers, they were known for their "deviance" and therefore were labeled unmanageable as wives and daughters.[9] Consequently, the Amazonian women do not conform to the gender roles assigned to members of their anatomical sex. Rather, they challenge sexually defined or prescribed female roles. In effect, they resist being defined by their body parts; they resist the commodification and glamorization that accompany the ideal female body. In this sense, their rejection of compulsory normalcy poses a direct challenge to heterosexuality and heteronormativity.[10] The one-breasted female body that the Amazonian women boast signals departure or migration from normative categorization. As the living embodiment of these rebel women, Lorde's resistance and resilience is epitomized in her refusal to wear a prosthesis after her mastectomy. By the same measure, her queerness manifests in her rejection of prostheses and her nonnormative body. This act of resistance crystallizes the limitations of state control and surveillance over citizens, signaling reappropriation of the neat masculinist narrative.

The classed and raced parameters that abound in the medical discourse and establishment are fiercely interrogated by Lorde. She cites one of the major oversights of the medical establishment as enforced homogenization that aspires to regularize or normalize the "deviant" body. Providing a historical context of the regularization of "embodied deviance," Jennifer Terry and Jacqueline Urla remark: "The somatic territorializing of deviance, since the nineteenth century, has been part and parcel of a larger effort to organize social relations according to categories denoting normality versus aberration, health versus pathology, and national security versus social danger" (1). Taking the American Cancer Society to task, Lorde alleges that it hands out (to unsuspecting patients) a blueprint for normalcy in its recovery agenda. Assessing her postmastectomy visit by a female representative of the American Cancer Society's Reach for Recovery Program, Lorde almost immediately senses a discord between her and the representative. She articulates this dissonance in the following manner: "The woman from Reach for Recovery while quite admirable and impressive in her own right, did not speak to my experience or my concerns" (*Cancer Journals* 56). Thus Lorde is written out of the national narrative as a desirable citizen. As J. Alexander succinctly puts it, "the state marked these sexual inscriptions on [her] body" ("Not Just [Any] Body" 5). She further reasons that the construction of the ideal citizen/body involves its "racializ[ation] and sexualiz[ation], which also meant the naturaliz[ation] of whiteness. There could be no psycho-social codices of sexuality that were not simultaneously raced" (11–12). Further exposing the industry's complicity in silencing women, Lorde remarks:

> I believe that socially sanctioned prosthesis is merely another way of keeping women with breast cancer silent and separate from each other. The emphasis upon wearing a prosthesis is a way of avoiding having women come to terms with their own pain and loss, and thereby, with their own strength. (*Cancer Journals* 16, 49)

Socially sanctioned prosthesis therefore falls into the category of what Susan Bordo refers to as the "ideological construction of femininity" that is "always homogenizing and normalizing, erasing racial, class, and other differences and insisting that all women aspire to a coercive, standardized ideal" ("The Body" 94). Subscribing to this "ideological construct of femininity," the Reach for Recovery representative vigorously supports and promotes homogenization. Rather than address the post-recovery process, namely, possible recurring cancer and the transition into society, the representative offered advice on inhabiting a "normal" body and on regaining the body (sex) appeal, namely, its reinsertion into society as a highly commercialized, sexualized (able) body. Significantly, this able body is not "any body," but a heterosexual body for the state has "naturalized heterosexuality by criminalizing lesbian and other forms of non-procreative sex" (J. Alexander, "Not Just [Any] Body" 5). Indisputably, compulsory heterosexuality is exemplary of the normative body, and Lorde's nonconformity renders her body nonreproductive in that it does not reproduce the normative body of the nation. In other words, it does not reproduce the ideal female citizen. This presumption of compulsory heterosexuality leaves no doubt that "women are attributed value via bodies which are sexualized and commodified for the male gaze and masculine consumption" (Saywell 39). Alternatively, Evelynn M. Hammonds sheds light on the problematic aspect of the "politics of silence," offering a cautionary message that "choosing silence, black women have also lost the ability to articulate any conception of their sexuality" (174).

Lorde's indictment of the Cancer Society for reproducing while maintaining systems of oppression is just and justifiable. Completely astounded by the representative's presumption, Lorde is quick to register her indignation:

> As a 44 year old Black Lesbian Feminist, I knew there were very few role models around for me in this situation, but my primary concerns two days after mastectomy were hardly about what man I could capture in the future, whether or not my old boyfriend would still find me attractive enough, and even less about whether my two children would be embarrassed by me around their friends. (*Cancer Journals* 56)

In rejecting the "ideal" body, Lorde shares Bordo's position that we must view "our bodies as a site of struggle, where we must work to keep our daily practices in the service of resistance to gender domination, not in the service of docility and gender normalization" ("The Body" 105). In line with this, Lorde's unequivocal disaffection with gender conformity engenders a "determinedly skeptical attitude toward the routes of seeming liberation and pleasure offered by our culture" (105). In refusing the "heterosexual imperative of citizenship, [Lorde's body], according to the state, pose[s] a profound threat to the very survival of the nation" (J. Alexander, "Not Just [Any] Body" 6).

Addressing gender conformity and its implied self-erasure, Lorde arrives at the conclusion that literal and figurative (surgical) transformation signals proverbial amputation of the black female self. From this vantage point, the surgical appropriation of Lorde's body as a means to reproducing and reconstructing normalcy can be likened to an act of violence, which is tantamount to crimes committed "against the flesh." Thus bell hooks locates this amputation of identity—the attempt to eradicate the difference Lorde inhabits—within the framework of a cannibalistic, consumerist culture, intimating that it is a form of exchange by a "consumer cannibalism that not only displaces the Other but denies the significance of that Other's history through a process of decontextualization" (*Black Looks* 31). Furthering this line of reasoning by illuminating the disembodiment that occurs within a "cannibalistic, consumerist culture," Bordo declares: "Female bodies become docile bodies—bodies whose forces and energies are habituated to external regulation, subjection, transformation, 'improvement'" ("The Body" 91). In this regard, the prosthetic, glamorized body fits the profile of a docile body, one that does not act but is acted upon. Invoking racial difference as a major factor in the process of "decontextualization," Lorde opines that it is conveniently used as a weapon to depersonalize black women, rendering them invisible non-citizens:

> Within this country where racial difference creates a constant, if unspoken, distortion of vision, black women have on one hand always been highly visible, and so, on the other hand, have been rendered invisible through the depersonalization of racism. (*Cancer Journals* 21)

J. Alexander cautions against state deployment of power and the boundaries "it draws around sexual difference" ("Not Just [Any] Body" 6). To this I add racial difference. The fact that "black women's sexuality has been constructed in a binary opposition to that of white women" is no mystery, as Hammonds reveals, adding that the result is the black female who "is rendered simultaneously invisible, visible (exposed), hypervisible, and pathologized in dominant discourses" (170). Besides, Hammonds's assertion that the misrepresentation of black women's sexuality "demonstrate[s] the disciplinary practices of the state against black women" is relevant to my argument here in the sense that the extreme commercialization of medicine contributes to the depersonalization of its patients and functions as a regulatory force that disciplines the "unruly" body (179).[11]

Making specific reference to her attempted erasure, Lorde shares an anecdote. Outfitted with a prosthetic breast, she calls attention to her experience of double alienation: on one hand she is silenced because of the lack of a mirrored representation—black, lesbian, and feminist—and on the other hand, the prosthesis creates a false sense of self that lends itself to the estrangement of the body. Of this separation of body and self, she writes:

> [I] stuffed *the thing* into the wrinkled folds of the right side of my bra where my right breast should have been. *It perched* on my chest *askew, awkwardly inert and lifeless*, and having nothing to do with any me I could possibly conceive of. Besides, *it was the wrong color*, and looked *grotesquely pale* through the cloth of my bra. (*Cancer Journals* 44; emphasis added)

Lorde's body destabilizes the meaning of race and gender as determined by the nation-state. Frustrated with the pretentious nature of the false breast, Lorde ultimately arrives at self-acceptance as she reclaims her citizen rights: without it, "I looked strange and uneven and peculiar to myself, but somehow, ever so much more myself, and therefore so much more acceptable than I looked with *that thing* stuck inside my clothes. For not even the most skillful prosthesis in the world could undo that reality, or feel the way my breast had felt, and either I would love my body one-breasted now, or *remain forever alien* to myself" (*Cancer Journals* 44; emphasis mine).

Lorde's inability to articulate this medical in(ter)vention, prosthesis, bears the imprint of disapproval but also hints at a cosmetic incursion. Instead, "it" remains nondescript; its lack of definition equals symbolic laceration and serves as a retaliatory measure for Lorde's erasure and alienation.[12] Interchangeably referred to as "it," "the thing," and "that thing," Lorde places emphasis on the im/materiality of the prosthesis even as she underscores the misappropriation of the body. Along these lines, her exclusion from the nation-state, epitomized by the cosmetic and misappropriated prosthesis, renders her invisible and illegitimate, a non-citizen.

Misappropriated, the body is constructed as homogeneous within the confines of normalization. Emphasizing the inherent dissemblance in prosthesis, Lorde arrives at the foregone conclusion that the normalized (state) body is always (perceived as) heterosexual and white. J. Alexander concurs in articulating that the state's interpretation of a reconfigured nation is a resuscitated heterosexual nation ("Not Just [Any] Body" 6). The expressions "wrong color" and "grotesquely pale" support this allegation of a white, heterosexual nation. Undeniably, the prosthesis was tailor-made (special emphasis is placed here on the gendered construct) for a white "standardized" body. Legitimizing this point of view, Kimberly Wallace-Sanders demonstrates that whiteness or the white female body has been routinely imagined or constructed as the standard, whereby the black female body is always measured in opposition to or in competition with the white female body. In other words, deification of the white female body comes at the expense of (demonization of) the black female body. Consequently, the white body is a marker of the ideal citizen in ways that the black female body is not. Wallace-Sanders takes to task Laurence Goldstein and Charles Johnson, challenging their monolithic and skewed misrepresentation of the (black) female body. Goldstein, who offers high acclaim for the (generic) female body as erotic object, writing that "'a naked woman' is, for most men, one of the most beautiful things they will ever see," was duly reminded of the sad history of Saartjie Baartman, who was considered so hideous that she was likened to and treated like an animal (Wallace-Sanders 2).

Committing an equally egregious sin, Johnson puts forth the erroneous hypothesis that while black men were subjected to repetitious characterization "in literature and media images from the news to music as the 'Negro beast'—violent, sex-obsessed, irresponsible, and stupid," black women were spared this vilification (Wallace-Sanders 3). Given no other recourse but to discursively confront these manifest inaccuracies, Wallace-Sanders sets the record straight, bringing to light the fact that Johnson had conveniently ignored the fact that in addition to many other denigrating types including "the long-suffering desexualized Mammy, the primitive Topsy, the exotic Jezebel, and the evil, emasculating Sapphire, Black women have historically been represented as hypersexual, ignorant, and violent female 'Negro beasts'" (3). As follows, black women have a long history of being denied citizenship. Paying additional attention to the pervasive and predetermined attributes that are ascribed to these cultural definitions, she insists that "these well-known stereotypes are of pathologized bodies that are specifically Black and female, and they are also found in literature and in media images from the news to contemporary music" (3). Along these lines, the female body to which Goldstein refers is "undoubtedly a healthy able-bodied, white woman, her body rendered free of any identifiable markers of class or ethnicity" (2). Along similar lines, King's insightful analysis of the infamous murder of Laci Peterson by her husband, Scott Peterson, exemplifies that black bodies are expendable, cannibalized in the media.[13] This expendability of black bodies is powerfully manifested by the brilliant comparison she makes between the media coverage of Laci's death and James Byrd Jr.'s death.[14] She opines that in an effort "to humanize [Laci] of murder and mutilation while normalizing her public image," the media performed a surgical transformation of sorts, removing Laci's ethnicity to complete the process of whitening. She further discerns that as Byrd's "image is overcome by bodily wounding so that any semblance of his humanity vanishes, Peterson's wounds fade beneath the healing images that embrace her humanity" (2). King fittingly concludes that "whether imposed, assumed, or adopted, whiteness masks difference" (3).

The enforced imposition of an all-encompassing, pervasive whiteness resuscitates a conventional white heterosexual (male) order. Revealing that the (white) male order is alive and well, Lorde recounts how the performative features of the prosthesis guarantee the masking of differences, resulting in self-distortion of the female subject. Shedding light on the damaging effects of self-censorship, Lorde issues a cautionary message to those women who become complicit in their own undoing:

> When other one-breasted women hide behind the mask of prosthesis or the dangerous fantasy of reconstruction, I find little support in the broader female environment for my rejection of what feels like a cosmetic sham. (Lorde, *Cancer Journals* 16)

Hence prosthesis functions as a blueprint for women's marginalization, their relegation as subalterns, as unworthy of citizenship. Women therefore are defined by the worthiness of their bodies at the expense of their health and are consequently socialized as objects, as a commodity for male consumption, as wards of the state and not as participants. Investigating how women are constructed within the tenets of femininity, Bordo writes that "female subjectivity is normalized and subordinated by the everyday bodily requirements and vulnerabilities of 'femininity'" ("Feminism" 249). Remaining within the confines of white femininity lends itself to female respectability, a required criterion for the ideal state representative. However, this limited definition does not lend itself to transnational coalitions (it is racially and socially charged), but instead promotes the politics of exclusion. Lorde alternatively demystifies this so-called ideal, subverting the notion of female "bodily requirements" or conformity by fiercely challenging the tenets of femininity. Since the woman's breast is regarded as an indicator of womanhood and an important criterion for evaluating femininity,[15] Lorde's missing breast and her "incomprehensible" decision not to wear a prosthesis render her (body) deviant and transgressive. In an interesting perception of difference, while Lorde's so-called deviance is understood as a threat to the dominant heterosexual culture, her missing breast links her to the one-breasted Amazonian women, as it registers her resilience and resistance. As previously mentioned, the point of reference for the Amazonian women is not beauty as defined and valued by Eurocentric ideology but self-autonomy, agency, and female empowerment. Further, Lorde's "deviance" is manifested further by her sexual orientation as a lesbian. Therefore, her body not only threatens the social and political order as a result of its "imagined" deficiency but also collapses the boundaries of "true" femininity and the attendant citizenship, while adding to the historical and cultural extremities for which the lesbian body has become known, despite its indistinguishable features from the female body (Creed 122).[16]

The heterosexual (male) order is equally at play in the aforementioned scene where the Reach for Recovery representative prophesized Lorde's reemergence into society with her imagined boyfriend's categorical acceptance of her "prosthesized" albeit ideal body. During subsequent visits, the representative shared anecdotes about the success of her own recovery, which resulted in two marriages and an existing romantic relationship with "a wonderful friend" (*Cancer Journals* 43). More importantly, the unchecked presumption here is that Lorde's romantic interest resides in the (conventional) heterosexual realm. As Lorde herself admits: "The absence of any consideration of lesbian consciousness or the consciousness of Third World Women leaves a serious gap" ("Master's Tools" 111). Drawing on the "prefabricated" norm of heterosexuality and the attendant requirement of femininity, Lorde invokes a third alternative space that directly opposes encoded standards of heterosexual and feminine norms. In short, Lorde resuscitates the nation as homosexual. Satirically musing over the representative's narrative of idyllic recovery, Lorde articulates: "What a shame such a gutsy woman wasn't a dyke, but they had gotten to her too early, and her grey hair was dyed blond and heavily teased" (*Cancer Journals* 43). The "prosthesized" body, coupled with the heavily teased blond hair, complements the European standard of beauty and epitomizes white femininity, established requirements for citizenship. A question begs to be asked: Since the female body is already constructed as "other," how does the black lesbian (body) that is multiple "othered" negotiate difference within differences? Or as Hammonds puts it, how does a black lesbian "whose 'deviant' sexuality is framed within an already existing deviant sexuality" (181) negotiate her identity within a highly infused heterosexual world?

Shedding light on this complex politics of negotiation, De Veaux informs us that although in the late 1960s white-owned lesbian bars became a space "for articulating lesbian resistance, they offered complicated arenas, in which black women who were lesbians traded sexual ease with other lesbians for racial solidarity with each other" (56). She adds that Lorde soon discovered that "the few black lesbians she encountered in white bars rarely related to each other on the level of their shared racial reality; and they subsumed their identities as black women with their identities as 'gay-girls'" (56). Despite not being able to identify racially with each other, their sexual orientation stands in as a breach and threat to "homo-hetero sexual binary and remakes gender as not simply performance but also as fiction . . . of a body taking its own shape" (Halberstam 125). In likening the body taking its own shape to fiction, Halberstam captures the heterogeneous, elastic makeup of identity as a "cut-up genre that mixes and matches body parts, sexual acts [that emblematize] postmodern articulations of the impossibility of identity" (125). Alternatively, there is a demand for flexible identity, for unconditional citizenship, for a ban on restricted movements across borders and boundaries. Chronicling Lorde's relentless challenge to compulsory heterosexuality, and more specifically to scripted definitions of female sexuality, De Veaux contends: "Lorde wanted to believe in, and practice, loving without boundaries— a philosophy and behavior she found consistent with rebellion against heterosexually scripted models of monogamy" (57). Lorde certainly challenges the criteria for citizenship by disrupting the neat narrative of ideal femininity, personified as the guardian of the state. She also fiercely interrogates the concept of female deviance. In an interesting moment of subversive play in which she destabilizes race, the grotesque (as in "grotesquely pale") is not elicited by or linked to the black female body. Instead, Lorde de-normalizes the chaste white national body. By the same token, the male heterosexual order is demystified.

One can safely argue that Lorde's challenge to "compulsory" heterosexuality necessitates her deconstructing the norm, which on one level resulted in the inscription of lesbian (gender), race and class-related issues at the center of the dominant discourse. Even as she endorses Lorde's celebration of her difference, Hammonds nevertheless maintains that the "specificity of black lesbian experience has to be explored and historicized" (181). Besides, she writes, "I want to suggest here that if we accept the existence of 'the politics of silence' as an historical legacy shared by all black women, then certain expressions of black female sexuality will be rendered as dangerous, for individuals and for the collectivity" (181). Black lesbians' experiences open up/add another paradigm to the discourse on the female body politics. Making a relevant observation that knowledge and power are tantamount to female empowerment, Lorde underscores that "Breast cancer with its mortal awareness and the amputation which it entails, can still be a gateway, however cruelly won, into the tapping and expansion of . . . power and knowing" (*Cancer Journals* 53–54). Debunking the myth of black women's deviant sexuality, Lorde rescues and recuperates the stolen black female body from oblivion, reinstating the woman as a desirable citizen. In so doing, she performs a migration of sorts from the state's definition of citizenship which, in J. Alexander's words, "continues to be premised within heterosexuality and principally within heteromasculinity" ("Not Just [Any] Body" 7).

Appalled by the prevailing theme of disembodiment and disarmament that characterized the discourse on recovery, Lorde is justifiably enraged as she is being coerced by the representative into believing that once she applies a good prosthesis, "you'll never know the difference." Shocked by the language of coercion, as in "you'll never know" and "nobody'll ever know," Lorde retaliates: "She lost me right there, because I knew sure as hell *I'd* know the difference (*Cancer Journals* 42). The representative also reassures Lorde that although breast reconstruction (augmentation) may not be a perfect replica of the lost breast, it will, nonetheless, enable her "to wear a *normal bra or bikini*" (69). In Lorde's careful assessment, "normal" functions as a homogenizing agent where "'normal' means the 'right' color, shape, size, or number of breasts" (64). It becomes quite evident to Lorde that prosthesis, in the given situation, is illustrative of "body-posturing," or as she calls it, a "cosmetic sham," which is a skillful pretense of normality, as it not only promotes the masking and masquerading of women and their bodies but also offers the empty comfort of "nobody will know the difference." This rejection of difference masks the "false complacency of a society which would rather not face the results of its own insanities" (61). She cautions that by treating breast cancer as a cosmetic problem that can be "solved by a prosthetic pretense," the medical institutions in cahoots with the cosmetic industries are culpable of disarming and disempowering women (55). Consequently, she opines that the pressure to conform and the loneliness of difference leave women emotionally anesthetized (10, 66).

Bringing additional attention to the anesthetizing effect of the dominant (white) culture, Halberstam remarks that "dominant ideologies of beauty and power can undermine completely the fixedness of race, class, and gender by making each one surgically or sartorially reproducible" (131). Strongly opposing the marginalization, if not downright dismissal, of race and class in the bid for normalization, Lorde emphatically voices her objection: "But it is that very difference which I wish to affirm, because I have lived it, and survived it, and wish to share that strength with other women" (*Cancer Journals* 61). One can therefore unreservedly draw the conclusion that Lorde's previous tongue-in-cheek statement about regretting that the representative was not a dyke is in actuality her instinctive desire for a mirrored self-image or reflection. This desire is captured in the following pronouncement: "Where were the dykes who had had mastectomies? I wanted to talk to a lesbian, to sit down and start from a common language, no matter how diverse. I wanted to share dyke-insight, so to speak" (49). Herein, Lorde advocates for a politics of inclusion, a more realistic and inclusive representation of the nation-state, a broader definition of citizenship. Earlier, experiencing a heightened sense of alienation, she wonders out loud whether there were any black lesbian feminists in Reach for Recovery "who shared at least some of [her] major concerns and beliefs and visions [and] at least some of her language" (42). Asked by the tightly clad, full-bosomed representative to identify her real breast from her false one, Lorde reserves judgment momentarily.

Notwithstanding, she inwardly draws the conclusion that both breasts appear unreal, admitting that as a connoisseur of women's breasts, she was never overly fond of stiff uplifts. All the same, Lorde is understandably infuriated by this calculated denial of difference as she quizzically ponders whether a conspiracy is at play. Determinedly using her embodied experience as articulation of her reality, Lorde, following in Sumi Colligan's footsteps, comes to the realization that "the promise and benefits of normalization are, at best, partial, and at worst, downright deceptive and contradictory" (53).

Illuminating Lorde's primary objection to the glamorization of prosthesis and the attendant commodification and commercialization of the female body, De Veaux ascertains that not only was wearing a prosthesis in Lorde's mind "a signifier of pretense, but it also meant succumbing to market-driven standards of the feminine and female beauty" (229). Establishing a clear distinction between cosmetic surgery and surgery that requires the use of prosthetic devices, and at the same time underscoring the functionality of the latter, Lorde reveals the sexism that lends itself to women being regarded as mere commodity, as victims: "Emphasis upon the cosmetic after surgery re-enforces this society's stereotype of women, that we are only what we look or appear, so this is the only aspect of our existence we need to address" (*Cancer Journals* 57).[17] In keeping with this male-centric agenda, women are strategically denied "psychic time and space" to reflect upon the body transformation after surgery. Yet, with quick precision, they are "cosmetically reassured that [their] feelings are not important, appearance is all, the sum total of self" (57). Unremitting promotion of cosmetic surgery therefore deflects from the real concerns at hand, and as a result "the necessity for nutritional vigilance and psychic armament to prevent recurrence" is dangerously brushed aside in favor of (keeping up) appearances (57). "Sanctioned" prosthesis, conditioned by a consumptive, consumerist, market-driven economy, reinforces women's worth, or lack thereof, as decorative sex objects, as non-beings. In the final analysis, "women just are their bodies in a way that men are not, biologically destined to inferior status in all spheres that privilege rationality" (Price and Shildrick 3).

Lorde's allegation that the commercial benefit of cancer lies in treatment and not in prevention bears weight. By the same token, illness is depersonalized, depoliticized. Accosted by a usually supportive nurse for being "a threat to the 'morale'" of the surgeon's office because of her refusal to wear a prosthesis, Lorde is made to feel immoral (*Cancer Journals* 59). Following this, her "sexual decadence [is blamed] for the dissolution of the nation [the surgeon's office]" (J. Alexander, "Not Just [Any] Body 6). More importantly, Lorde's sexual orientation poses a danger to respectability. We witness an interesting moment of "role-reversal" cum devaluation. While Lorde experiences de-personification, the surgeon's office undergoes a proverbial facelift as the female patients are programmed to be paragons of virtue. Ensuring the maintenance and execution of the "heterosexual norm," the nurse gives Lorde a double dose of rebuke and caution: "We really like you to wear something, at least when you come in [the office]" (*Cancer Journals* 59). It seems rather paradoxical that in the given situation that the question of morality would surface, especially since ethics rarely made it to the medical agenda in relation to the treatment of certain bodies. We are appropriately reminded by Cheryl Mwaria that when it comes to medical research involving human experimentation, "imperialist, Eurocentric, and patriarchal goals have been inflicted on women of color with little or no regard to ethics" (188). Baartman readily comes to mind. Shedding light on the distrust that medical practices have occasioned, Susan Sherwin writes that one of the problems that feminist critics have with current medical practice is that it serves "as an instrument in the continuing disempowerment of women and thrives on hierarchical power structures," while it "strengthen[s] patterns of stereotyping and reinforce[s] existing power inequalities" (22).

By exposing the innate glamorization of prosthesis, Lorde unearths an interesting parallel between her hyposexuality and Baartman's hypersexuality. Similar to Baartman, who is subject to scrutiny resulting from her "excess," so too is Lorde for her missing (prosthetic) breast. As Baartman's "excess flesh" becomes the object of western consumption, Lorde's lack is read similarly in consumer terms. Ironically, the very excess for which Baartman is ridiculed becomes laudatory in the realm of cosmetic surgery. While hypertrophy is regarded as an anomalous body trait in describing Baartman's genitalia, it is normalized in relation to European standards of beauty. Rachel Holmes elucidates this fact in the following articulation: "At the beginning of the twenty-first century, buttock augmentation surgery became the fastest-growing cosmetic procedure in America and Europe. In Britain, the demand for the 'plump rump' increased tenfold, while across the Atlantic, there was a fivefold increase" (102).[18] It is indeed paradoxical that the buttocks, once a symbol of the grotesque body and sexuality, have become a hot commodity for European consumption (of convenience).

Along these lines, Lorde's post-mastectomy recovery is premised on Eurocentric values and designed for male consumption. In like fashion, both Baartman and Lorde are objects of the voyeuristic gaze, clearly evident in Baartman's case and more subtle in Lorde's. As a consequence, Baartman's reputed anatomical abnormalities, similar to Lorde's "oddity," are regarded as grotesque. At the same time, their excess and lack ironically punctuate their presumed deficiency, disqualifying them as ideal citizens. Colligan's clear-cut analysis of "the ritual staging of freakdom" bolsters this line of reasoning as she points to the fact that "it entailed an underscoring of lack and excess, in which malformations of bodies and sexuality became significantly entwined" (47).

Drawing a parallel with Cuvier's dissecting of Baartman's body (discussed in chapter 1), the dismembering of Baartman parallels the amputation and attendant disfigurement characteristic of a mastectomy. For Lorde, nevertheless, the real body disfigurement occurs in the desire for sameness, in the proverbial surgical erasure of difference.

Whereas Baartman's healthy body is medicalized as deviant on account of her assumed grotesque hypersexuality, Lorde's identification as a lesbian, her sexual otherness, is equally rendered pathological and undesirable. Furthermore, her sexual orientation lends itself to pornographic exposure of her body, placing it/her on the axis of the grotesque. In summation, the intense scrutiny that lesbian sexuality suffers is symptomatic of dismemberment, a fact that J. Alexander underscores when she writes about the conundrum in according "lesbians and gay men the respect of fully embodied human beings, not reduced to a perfunctory mind/body dichotomy, in which the dismembered body could be imagined only as a dangerous sexual organ" (*Pedagogies* 43). Further, drawing attention to the skewed medical assessment of Hottentots' genitals and its implied link to lesbian sexuality, Garland-Thomson remarks that "Hottentot genitals were being described in the gynecological handbooks as a 'congenital error' involving a 'malformation' of the clitoris associated with excessive sexuality that led to lesbianism" (*Extraordinary Bodies* 76). Along similar lines, Gilman points out that the "Hottentot apron" was labeled a congenital error, a "malformation [linked] to the overdevelopment of the clitoris" that leads to "those 'excesses'" defined as "lesbian love" (89). Thus, despite her hyposexuality, in the given analysis Lorde's predisposition to hypersexuality increases twofold: as a black woman and as a lesbian. In essence, being black and lesbian, she "articulated identities that remained marginal and problematic to the mainstream agenda" (De Veaux 252). More importantly, lesbian identity is problematic to the nation's agenda, in light of the fact that

> Women's sexual agency and erotic autonomy have always been troublesome for the state. They pose a challenge to the ideology of an originary nuclear heterosexual family that perpetuates the fiction that the family is the cornerstone of society. Erotic autonomy signals danger to the heterosexual family and to the nation. And because loyalty to the nation as citizen is perennially colonized within reproduction and heterosexuality, erotic autonomy brings with it the potential of undoing the nation entirely. (J. Alexander, *Pedagogies* 23)

Quite cognizant of societal fear of difference and the accompanying denouncement and rejection of nonconventionality, Lorde articulates the following statement:

> Most Black lesbians were closeted, correctly recognizing the Black community's lack of interest in our position, as well as the many more immediate threats to our survival as Black people in a racist society. It was hard enough to be Black, to be Black and female, to be Black, female, and gay. To be Black, female, and gay, and out of the closet in a white environment . . . was considered by many Black lesbians to be simply suicidal. (*Zami* 224)

In spite of the threats, Lorde sees "living 'subversive' as an immutable aspect of her being" (De Veaux 120).

Lorde's presumed abnormality and her animal characteristics become manifest in her "excess." Creed corroborates that equating lesbianism with bestiality is an age-old practice (119). Alexander corroborates, asserting that "homosexuality could only be imagined as residing at the pinnacle of perverted heterosexualized violence" (*Pedagogies* 40). Noting that "perverted heterosexual violence" is routinely (not to mention unfairly) conflated "with same-sex desire," Alexander concludes that "the psyche of criminality *is* the psyche of homosexuality" (*Pedagogies* 41). Price and Shildrick bolster and expand this argument in articulating that "the association of the body with gross, unthinking physicality marks a further set of linkages—to black people, to working class people, to animals, and to slaves" (2).[19] Creed additionally points out that the lesbian (body) "signifies an irremediable lack," exemplified by the rampant stereotypes that abound in describing lesbian sexuality: the masculine lesbian, the "animalistic lesbian," and the "narcissistic lesbian body" (112, 115). Yet, despite this anomalous difference, we witness the (continued) tendency to normalize the lesbian (genital) by likening or regularizing her (anatomy) to the masculine for public consumption: "One woman was said to possess a clitoris that 'equalled the length of half a finger and in its stiffness was not unlike a boy's member'" (quoted in Creed 113). This description bears a striking similarity to the "Hottentot apron." Normalization of the lesbian genital attests to and "arise[s] from the nature of the threat lesbianism offers to patriarchal heterosexual culture" (Creed 112). As follows, the lesbian body is one of transgression that threatens the heterosexual order because it disrupts the boundaries of normalcy and imposed decency. It defies the fixed dichotomous delineation of male/female, undermining while destroying rigid (yet fragile) patriarchal gender boundaries. Further, underscoring the threat that the lesbian poses to the nation-state, J. Alexander surmises: "Heterosexuality still appears more conducive to nation-building than does same-sex desire, which appears hostile to it—for women cannot presumably love themselves, love other women, and love the nation simultaneously" (*Pedagogies* 46).

Lorde further expresses that defeminization of the lesbian (body) has forced some lesbians to play right into the hands of the patriarchy, believing that the only alternative available to them was to adopt an overtly masculine persona. Rather, this adoption/adaptation of an "alternative" identity that Lorde labels as "heavy roles [that] frightened [her]" as the women appeared to be "dressed in enemy clothing" (*Zami* 224) inadvertently reinforces the stereotype of the lesbian "as pseudo male ... as a man trapped in a woman's body" (Creed 112). Shedding light on the all-pervasive and perverted white patriarchal notions of female beauty and conduct, Lorde remarks that "white america's racist distortions of beauty"[20] did not accommodate black lesbians playing the role of "femme," thereby engendering "competition among butches to have the most 'gorgeous femme' on their arm. And gorgeous was defined by a white male world's standard" (*Zami* 224). In furthering Lorde's argument, Price and Shildrick contend that "all women are positioned in relation to and measured against an inaccessible body, in part determined by a universalised male body" (434).

Similar to the lesbian body that functions as a site of resistance, Baartman's body poses a threat to the dominant heterosexual culture. In essence, the deviant body reconfigures the discourse on citizenship. A palpable threat to the social and political order, her "deviant" body collapses the boundaries of white femininity and the ideal citizen. Analogously, by reconfiguring the black female body within the framework of the national body, which is imagined as white, middle class, and always heterosexual, Lorde threatens the "neat" heterosexual order. Charlotte Bunch puts it best when she remarks that "lesbian-feminist politics is a political critique of the institution and ideology of heterosexuality" (55). By offering all women exclusive rights to and insights into her personal struggle, Lorde identifies with a "positive woman-identified identity," proving that "lesbian-feminism is not a political analysis 'for lesbians only'" (57). Consequently, Lorde's personal embodied experiences become community property.

3 Framing Violence

Resistance, Redemption, and Recuperative Strategies in *I, Tituba, Black Witch of Salem*

One cannot help but notice the manifest violence in Caribbean women's writing and black women's writing in general that renders the cliché "violence begets violence" effective. Stuart Hall, among other theorists, historicizes this violence, locating it in the colossal disruptions created by colonization and slavery that have "distributed [black people] across the African diaspora" (235). Consequently, Hall establishes that "the displacements of slavery, colonization, and conquest . . . stand for the endless ways in which Caribbean people have been destined to 'migrate'" (243). This severance from one's origin registers unspeakable violence. Addressing the pervasive violence in women's narrative as representative of their lived experiences, M. Giulia Fabi writes: "The awareness of how human bodies can be systematically reduced to the total objectification of captive flesh, the practice of breaking the silence on female-specific experiences of sexual and racial abuse, the insistence that racial violence is always 'en-gendered': these issues characterize the narrative tradition of African American women and dominate [their] literary works" (229). Fabi's accurate assessment rings true for Guadeloupian-born writer and scholar Maryse Condé, whose body of work engages even as it fiercely interrogates the aforementioned themes.

An invaluable contributor to this narrative tradition, Condé joins the band of black female writers who break the silence often deemed too horrific to tell. Capturing the "initial" violence as intimated by Hall, Condé demonstrates how black women's lives are shrouded in violence that becomes encoded on their bodies, resulting in their silencing and their denial of personhood and attendant citizenship. Tituba's opening statement captures the unspeakable violence, "the experience of dispersal and fragmentation, which is the history of all enforced diasporas" (Hall 235). The telling statement reads: "Abena, my mother, was raped by an English sailor on the deck of *Christ the King* one day in the year 16** while the ship was sailing for Barbados. I was born from this act of aggression. From this act of hatred and contempt" (*Tituba* 1). Achieving its intended objective, this abrupt opening paragraph captures the brutality of slavery and the inhumanity of the enslaver. In other words, brevity encapsulates the severity of the act of rape that has both literal and symbolic resonance. Abena's rape coincides with the rape of the mother, Africa. The denial of personhood—Abena's rape has rendered her a non-person, a non-citizen—which was initially caused by her separation from her mother (land), Africa, is complicated by her separation from the self, personified through the rape.[1] Along these lines, Abena's captivity is twofold, first, as "captive flesh," her body is restrained in the bowels of the ship, and second, her "body violation" further manifests in her being raped, resulting in "silencing" of the flesh. Abena's denial of personhood transfers onto her daughter, Tituba, who, the product and victim of rape herself, experiences dual victimization. Tituba also doubles as witness to her mother being hanged and as subject of lynching that bears resonance with her mother's lynching. Hence Tituba literally (somatically) relives the catastrophic events her mother experienced. On a grander scale, Tituba's narrative qualifies as a reenactment of the Middle Passage, as we are presented with images of ships that in Paul Gilroy's careful assessment "immediately focus attention on the middle passage, on the various projects for redemptive return to an African homeland, on the circulation of ideas and activists as well as the movement of key cultural and political artefacts: tracts, books, gramophone records, and choirs" (4). This reenactment engenders resistance and repatriation of the severed subject. By the same token, it fosters "the circulation of ideas and activists," to echo Gilroy, promoting transnational alliances.

"This redemptive return to an African homeland" to which Gilroy alludes is crucial in the quest for (or redemption of) citizenship, as Hall reminds us: "Africa is the name of the missing term, the great aporia, which lies at the center of our cultural identity and gives it meaning which, until recently, it lacked" (235). Acutely aware of the need to accomplish a redemptive return to give meaning to one's cultural identity, Condé rescues

Tituba from obscurity, confessing in the epigraph: "Tituba and I lived for a year on the closest of terms. During our endless conversations she told me things she had confided to nobody else." Tituba and Condé's unbroken friendship alludes to unspoken kinship, reminiscent of Morrison's neighborhood. Furthermore, Tituba regains her stolen voice, and this accentuates her humanity, her citizen rights, and her coveted role in history. Tituba's repatriation parallels Baartman's reinstated citizenship, indicating female solidarity, which in turn engenders a transnational female diaspora. Condé's writing itself transcends borders and boundaries as Tituba navigates various geographic and social spaces. This unrestricted border crossing is rendered most palpable in Condé's recounting of an event that occurred in the seventeenth century. This conflation and intersecting of chronological time signal the need for adaptable identities and elastic borders, resulting in the practice of transnationalism.

In keeping with her demand for flexible, adaptable identity, the "peculiar" institution of slavery does not circumscribe Tituba's ability to love and nurture or effectively mother. Along these lines, Condé constructs Tituba, Abena, and her othermothers, Mama Yaya and Yao, outside the nation-state beyond patriarchal dictates.[2] As such, they are able to navigate geographic and spiritual boundaries and borders with relative ease; this ability to straddle both worlds allows them to practice transnational citizenship. Tituba's practice of transnationalism manifests in her finding the "missing term—Africa," as Hall argues above. Despite the fact that Tituba's "radicalism," which draws heavily on forms of resistance employed by slave women, is revealed through the embrace and practice of abortions and infanticide as means of resistance, she nevertheless re-visions motherhood and mothering (as viable options) beyond the dictates of enslavement and patriarchy.[3] The practice of abortions and infanticides challenges the nation's design for population increase in the form of chattel, which promotes exclusionary citizenship, as slaves do not qualify as citizens; instead, they are property. On the other hand, Tituba destabilizes this masculinist narrative. This re-visioning in turn delegitimizes the pathological discourse that condemns Tituba as a witch and further labels her as suffering from mental illness. Furthermore, demonization of Tituba as a witch is emblematic of western cultural imperialism, a staged antiwoman, antifeminist campaign, a clear condemnation of female power and an attempt to circumscribe women's roles in society, limiting them spatially, diasporically, and creatively.

Alternatively, the maroon woman—the maroons resisted the nation-state's definition of citizenship, residing in diasporic enclaves outside the boundaries and borders of the nation—is a combatant revolutionary figure that fiercely resists female subjugation and oppression. In line with this, by empowering Tituba with magical and spiritual powers, Condé is reconstituting the principles of (first-wave) feminism, advocating instead for a transnational feminist agenda that includes the "transgressive" black female subject, or the "antislavery rebel," to borrow Davis's coinage ("Reflections" 9).

As both the subject and narrator of unspeakable violence, Tituba's trauma takes on astronomical proportions, appearing mythical as a consequence of the ruthless brutality. Notwithstanding, Tituba's narrative does not fall into the category of "unclaimed experience," to borrow the title of Cathy Caruth's book; rather, it signals her-story (her body) reclaimed and recuperated.[4] Or to echo Gilroy, it is a call for a redemptive return home. To say the least, Tituba took a circuitous redemptive return to Barbados, leaving its warmth and freedom to follow her lover, John Indian, to New England where she experiences the brutal puritanical customs that mirror many aspects of slavery and enslavement. Herein, Tituba challenges the concept of fixed place and belonging as she resists fixity in favor of transnational citizenship.

In her characterization of trauma and traumatic experiences, Caruth ascertains that "the story of trauma, as the narrative of a belated experience, far from telling of an escape from reality—the escape from a death, or from its referential force—rather attests to its endless impact on a life" (7). Along these lines, the traumas Tituba experienced vicariously through Abena, compounded by her own personal traumatic experiences, have profoundly impacted her existence. As both witness and victim, or more poignantly as both "the wound and the voice," Tituba's narrative is one of extraordinary survival, a testimony to her resilience and indomitable spirit (Caruth 4). It is also a narrative of migration and repatriation. Thus by becoming the agent of her narrative, Tituba not only bears witness but she also refuses to allow the unforgotten wounds of slavery to remain obscure, to go unheard or unseen. As a consequence, Condé rescues this wounded, invisible subject, the only black female victim of the Salem witch trials, from oblivion.

Addressing the diasporic dialogue that Tituba's invisibility occasioned, Angela Davis is quick to point out that "Tituba's impassioned efforts to revoke her own disappearance from history . . . is Tituba's revenge" (Foreword ix).⁵ Davis concludes that by adopting the "retelling of history" as her tool of revenge, Tituba saves herself by not "taking on the historical characteristics of the colonizers and the slaveholders she detested" (ix). A cautionary message, not to mimic the enslavers, was echoed repeatedly by Mama Yaya to Tituba, who wanted to exact revenge on her master, Susanna Endicott. Mimicry in the given situation is reductive, entailing recolonization of the subject and therefore equated with perversion: "You will have perverted your heart into the bargain. You will have become like them, knowing only how to kill and destroy" (30).

Thus Tituba's conception coincides with and mirrors the violent, forced beginning of the diaspora, the New World. Rape of the female body strongly resonates with land occupation. One can safely argue that brutality finds its most efficacious moment when inflicted upon the black female body. Nevertheless, in framing violence Tituba/Condé "scripts" an alternative discourse, one that resists, redeems, and recuperates the black female subject from obscurity. In line with this, Tituba/Condé rejects culturally normalized and tenuous expectations of motherhood and mothering, female identity and sexuality. In Condé's revision of history, (slave) women who are routinely depicted as docile and lacking agency are granted authorial presence and agency. As both midwife and witch, Tituba is a combatant revolutionary figure. Condé concurs: "I wanted to turn Tituba into a sort of female hero, an epic heroine, like the legendary Nanny of the maroons" (201). Significantly, Tituba's magical powers are expressed via her independence of mind and body. Consequently, her body, as text, functions as a site of social dissent, for she challenges the circumscribed roles of black women. It is equally a locus of political and sexual dissent as she fiercely interrogates patriarchal control of black female sexuality. Furthermore, as transgressive female subject, Tituba's challenge to slavery manifests in several ways, the most prominent being the practice of abortions and infanticide.

Despite the numerous images of death, destruction, mutilation, and (body) violation, Tituba does not embody the iconic suffering woman or mother. Even as Tituba or Abena battles with racism and sexism, Condé shatters the "reified images or stereotypes" of women as "aggressive, matriarchal or castrating female" (Davis, Foreword 3) Davis refutes the "designation of the black woman as a matriarch," labeling it a "cruel misnomer because it implies stable kinship structures within which the mother exercises decisive authority" (3). Revealing the deceptiveness of this alias, she conclusively ascertains that "it is cruel because it ignores the profound traumas the black woman must have experienced when she had to surrender her child-bearing authority to alien and predatory economic interests" (3).

Deborah Gray White reinforces this argument as she reminds us that slave women have had to destroy the myths and the stereotypes that starkly contradicted their realties, their lived experiences. Further assessing how they dealt with their imperiled state, she remarks, "They did not see aggression and independent behavior as unfeminine, but a means to 'protect their most fundamental claims to womanhood; . . . their female sexuality and physicality, and their roles as mothers and wives'" (8). This insightful assessment holds true for Abena, whose resistance to her master's sexual advances is premised on her defending her honor, her female sexuality and physicality, and her role as mother and wife to Yao.[6] Even in light of this fact, Abena's resistance is regarded as dishonorable, attesting to White's claim that "some were convinced that slave women were lewd and lascivious, that they invited sexual overtures from white men, and that any resistance they displayed was mere feigning" (30). By this account, Abena was likened to the Jezebel character. At the same time, her subversion of this hypersexualized role facilitates her self-reclamation and autonomy.

In her subversion of the Jezebel character, Condé skillfully creates Abena as an empowered subject who was purchased by Darnell not as a Mammy but as a companion to his wife, Jennifer. Owing to the fact that black women were not constructed within the framework of respectability, Abena, as companion, as inferior "other" to the white woman, by default assumed the role of Jezebel, Mammy's foil, her "other." This argument gets reinforced by the anger Darnell expressed when he realized that Abena was pregnant and subsequently by his unwarranted sexual advances. White offers a timely and appropriate reminder: "The image of Jezebel excused . . . the sexual exploitation of black women" (61). Apart from being lewd and lascivious, Jezebel is conceived as emasculating. This character trait palpably manifests in Abena slashing Darnell's flesh with a cutlass, a phallic symbol to say the least, in retaliation to his sexual advances (*Tituba* 8). At the same time, the cutting of his flesh emblematizes her performing proverbial rape on him rather than allowing him to possess her body. She attacks not only her current master and attempted rapist but also the English sailor who raped and impregnated her. The implication here is that the men are cut from the same cloth: white patriarchy. Even if Darnell might have erroneously interpreted Abena's resistance to his sexual advances as feigning, her subsequent attack on him leaves no doubt. Furthermore, inhabiting the role of Jezebel reinforces Abena's resistance to the patriarchal institution, for she does not fit the profile of the idealized slave and woman, nor is she an ideal citizen.

Darnell's attempted rape of Abena that imitates "an animal-like act" exemplifies his endeavor not only to manipulate her body but also to "conquer the resistance" that she consequently unleashes (Davis, "Reflections" 13). Davis adds that one of the strategies of oppression employed by the white master against the slave woman was "to reestablish her femaleness by reducing her to the level of her biological being. Aspiring with his sexual assaults to establish her as a female *animal*, he would be striving to destroy her proclivities towards resistance" (13) We bear witness to Darnell's attempted dehumanization of Abena in the ensuing public scene that Tituba recounts: "When I turned back toward my mother, she was standing up against a calabash tree, breathing hard. Darnell stood less than three feet away. He had taken off his shirt, undone his trousers and I could see his very white underclothes. His left hand was groping for his penis" (*Tituba* 8). In self-defense Abena struck him twice with a cutlass. Not only does Tituba bear witness to this heroic act of resistance that reveals slave women's "reverence for heroism and their celebration of it as a feminine trait," but she is also an accomplice, an accessory to attempted murder,[7] providing her mother with the assault weapon (D. White 8). All the same, while it is safe to conclude that Darnell's objective was not to control Abena's reproductive ability for profit, his unmistakable goal was to reaffirm her propertied existence by controlling her sexuality.[8] Davis is quick to point out that the slave is "particularly vulnerable in her sexual existence" as female ("Reflections" 12). Further, relegating Abena to propertied possession complements the "animal-like act" that rape engenders.

Unequivocally, Abena's disaffection stems from the inhumane, oppressive conditions under which black women found themselves during slavery. She voices the unparalleled plight of black women as she laments about the equivalent life of servitude that awaits her daughter, Tituba, wishing instead that she was born a boy. Tituba articulates her mother's regret: "My mother sorely regretted that I was not a boy. It seemed to her that a woman's fate was even more painful than a man's. In order to free themselves from their condition, didn't they have to submit to the will of those very men who kept them in bondage and to sleep with them?" (6). The lament underscores the contradictory lives of black women even as it exposes the double oppression, that of race and gender. D. White contextualizes this dichotomous relationship as the "nexus of America's sex and race mythology," which inextricably binds the slave woman making it "most difficult for her to escape the mythology" (28).[9] All the same, Abena refuses entrapment by sparing her body continued violation, rejecting unauthorized access to it.

Slave women's bodies, specifically their procreative capacity, were considered prime real estate capital and accordingly they were marketed for maximum profit. D. White reiterates that once it caught on that the "reproductive function of the female slave could yield a profit, the manipulation of procreative sexual relations became an integral part of the sexual exploitation of female slaves" (68). Seemingly the subject of uninterrupted public attention and debates,[10] this visibility simultaneously rendered black women invisible. Black female sexuality is constructed within the framework of bestiality, a fact underscored by Davis, who argues that being "pressed into the mold of beasts of burden in the area of production, the slaves were forcibly deprived of their humanity" ("Reflections" 6). We are offered a glimpse of the black woman's value in terms of her procreative ability when John Indian, Tituba's lover, instructs her shortly after she was raped by the Puritans to save herself for him and their unborn offspring (*Tituba* 92). John Indian's manipulative intent mirrors or, more pointedly, rivals the slave master's scheming tactics. However, this manipulation becomes muted as Tituba is the one who palpably and with marked precision manipulates their sexual relations, remaining in control, if not at all times then most of the time, of her sexuality and her sexual desires. Along these lines, Tituba's refusal to procreate, to assume the role of biological mother, registers her avoidance of sexual exploitation and female subjugation. In other words, she dexterously refuses to have motherhood structure her behavior (D. White 75).

In reconstituting Tituba's history, Condé informs us that her main objective was to unearth her from oblivion, to render her visible, "to offer her her revenge by inventing a life such as she might perhaps wished it to be told" (*Tituba* 199). This self-invention or self-reclamation fiercely interrogates even as it negates women's predestined role as commodity for male consumption and their bodies as procreative vessels. Thus by having Tituba willfully and intentionally inhabit the role of "othermother" instead of biological mother, Condé proposes an alternative course to motherhood and mothering, one that exists beyond the dictates of enslavement and patriarchy. This alternative path not only disrupts but also challenges the maternal ideal of womanhood. As follows, in refuting the mere biological role of mothers, Tituba in turn resists the devaluation of the female body as laboring object and as reproductive vessel. She refuses to reproduce the nation. Correspondingly, she subverts the notion that the female body functions as a receptacle for male sexual gratification.

Alternatively, refuting the role of sexual "other," Tituba rejects culturally normalized and tenuous expectations of female sexuality. Therefore, not only does Tituba maintain autonomy over her decision not to become a mother, but she also exerts control of her sexuality whereby it cannot be directly claimed by the oppressor. Even so, Tituba subverts the prescribed role of the female as an object of desire, becoming the desirous subject as she "preys" on John Indian. It is rather telling that Howard Frank Mosher analyzes Tituba's sexual attraction to John Indian as her "shortcoming, [a] blind passionate sexual dependence." Noticeably his criticism of John Indian is somewhat muted as he describes him as "feckless," who in spite of his own "shortcomings" makes Tituba "a fully believable and very appealing character."[11] John Indian's fecklessness is apparently attributed to his "uncontrollable" masculine desires that not only compel him to join the Puritans, noticeably an all-male group, in accusing Tituba of being a practitioner of witchcraft and subsequently raping her, but he also ultimately deserts her for the widow of a Puritan minister. Since Mosher credits John Indian for making Tituba "a fully believable and very appealing character," it is safe to argue that John Indian is naturally appealing, a claim that the widowed Goodwife Sarah Porter will endorse. Whereas John Indian's maleness allows him access to the patriarchal world where he engages in black female subjugation, Mosher is unable to perceive Tituba as a sexually autonomous subject, as an agent outside the discourse of the nation. Rather, Mosher restrains Tituba's sex and sexuality within the discourse of the nation and within the framework of nationalism. Furthermore, Tituba is "languaged by sex," to echo Faith Smith (2). Similar to John Indian, who reads Tituba's body as a profitable commodity, as a site for reproducing the nation, Mosher renders her body docile. In other words, he is oblivious to the fact that she inhabits a transgressive body, one that acts out, retaliates, and migrates both physically and socially, as it deviates from patriarchal norm, from prescribed notions of Victorian (white) womanhood.

Tituba's transgression most powerfully resonates in her practice of witchcraft. This practice becomes an empowering female pursuit that engenders diasporic and transnational affiliations. These affiliations palpably manifest in the scene where Judah White, a friend of Mama Yaya (unknown to Tituba) and a native Bostonian who never left Boston, unexpectedly approaches Tituba in the forest, cautioning her about the wrath of Peter Parris and the Puritans and subsequently reintroducing and reacclimatizing her to the properties of herbs.[12] This unmitigated kinship realizes a transnational feminist agenda. Thus Judah White, also a practitioner of witchcraft, belongs to the diaspora of empowered women who inhabit the coveted role as "citizens of the world." This female diaspora operates beyond the dictates of patriarchy. Subsequently, witchcraft becomes a counter discourse that challenges female oppressions.

As a transmigratory subject whose journeys take her from Barbados to Puritanical New England and back to Barbados, Tituba engenders female mobility. In so doing she engages in a politics of resistance, survival, and citizenship.[13] Moreover, as a witch, Tituba is the consummate figure of transgression. Rejecting Mosher's characterization, Tituba's relationship with John Indian is merely sexual and not one of sexual dependency. In this manner, Tituba defies "conventional notions of passive female sexuality" (hooks, *Black Looks* 48). In spite of Mosher's indictment, Tituba is very much aware and in control of her sexual identity, which she unabashedly assumes and skillfully employs as the situation demands. Even after having acquired ancestral status, Tituba fondly reminisces about her former sexually imbued life: "I have loved men too much and shall continue to do so. Sometimes I get the urge to slip into someone's bed to satisfy a bit of leftover desire" (178). This carefully crafted pronouncement unequivocally drives home the fact that Tituba's desire is not linked specifically or exclusively to John Indian, negating any assumption of blind sexual dependence.

Tituba's self-possession, particularly her celebration of sexual autonomy, contrasts and at the same time challenges slave women's dispossessed and disembodied status, their treatment as property. As the aggressive pursuer of John Indian, Tituba subverts the masculine gaze, transforming him into an object of her carnal desire. His objectification cum insignificance is made more palpable wherein Tituba aborts his child, an act that demonstrates her refusal to procreate, namely, to reproduce the nation. She thereby relegates and reduces their sexual escapades to the mere recreational. As he repeatedly refers to their unborn children, Tituba warns: "John Indian, don't talk about our children, for I shall never bring children into this dark and gloomy world" (92). Although Tituba subsequently became pregnant for John Indian, she nevertheless made the conscious decision to discontinue her pregnancy, refusing to be coerced into premature and obligatory (institutionalized) motherhood as Abena was. This resolute decision or "gynecological revolt," to borrow Jennifer Morgan's fitting phrase, reveals Tituba exercising control of her body and her procreative ability (11).

Although Tituba momentarily relinquishes her freedom and follows John Indian into slavery in Puritanical New England, she nonetheless does not allow him to manipulate her (body), candidly confessing that the attraction was related to the sexual pleasures he provides. As I have argued earlier, Tituba realizes transnationalism through these noncoercive migrations. Even so, Tituba's decision to follow John Indian to Boston is an autonomous one, occasioned by her strong sexual interest in him. In the following passage, she offers a candid assessment of their relationship that is noticeably sexual:

> What was there about John Indian to make me sick with love for him? Not very tall, average height, five feet seven, not very big, not ugly, not handsome either. I must confess it was downright hypocritical of me to ask such a question, since I knew too well where his main asset lay and I dared not look below the jute cord that held up his short, tight-fitting *konoko* to the huge bump of his penis. (19)

Tituba later reinforces John Indian's objectification: "He'd never been very brave or very intelligent or honest, but loving, yes!" (109). Parodying the iconic Jezebel character, Tituba both challenges and subverts the black female stereotype. Her unrelenting pursuit, objectification, and manipulation of John Indian bear the imprint of emasculation. In the given situation, she assumes the male role as pursuer, relegating John Indian as the hunted, a non-person. Furthermore, she subverts the notion of the female (slave) body as a site of continued oppression, appropriating it as the locus of desire and pleasure. But more importantly, she exerts self-ownership, becoming the agent of her (body) discourse. This fervent desire for autonomy manifests in Tituba's decision to become pregnant for her maroon lover, Christopher. This decision has symbolic resonance for the reason that there exists a subtle reference to infertility, another effective mode of resistance employed by slave women.[14] Notably, Tituba's sexual relationship with her Jewish owner and eventual lover, Benjamin d'Azevedo, is marked by a period of self-imposed sterility. The analogy Tituba draws between Christopher and d'Azevedo is telling: "Christopher's brutal embraces had conceived what the love of my Jew had been unable to do" (158). In the given situation, "induced infertility" is employed as a means to obstruct reproducing violence and oppression, for despite the humane relationship that d'Azevedo and Tituba shared, she nonetheless was his propertied possession. As his property, Tituba is problematically constructed or, more pointedly, reinstated within the nation-state.[15] In this way, d'Azevedo's refusal to grant Tituba her freedom symbolizes his denying her citizenship and prohibiting her pursuit of liberty.

Moreover, Tituba's calculated attempt at embracing biological motherhood is predicated on the possibility of giving birth in freedom in the maroon community, a viable diasporic community. Further, the combativeness that this pregnancy engendered, motivating Tituba to conclude that it was a girl, is characteristic of the resistance that maroons embody (158). Tituba's consequent questioning of the condemned life that awaits her daughter forebodes Christopher's betrayal. Thus his presence (and ultimately the presence of his unborn child) is short-lived as Tituba replaces him with a much younger lover, Iphigene.

Tituba's seamless transfer of desire from John Indian to d'Azevedo to Christopher to Iphigene finds expression in hooks's compelling assessment of Sula, Toni Morrison's radical black female subject. In "refusing standard sexist notions of the exchange of female bodies, Tituba, like Sula, engages in the exchange of male bodies as part of a defiant effort to displace their importance" (hooks, *Black Looks* 48). This displacement has special resonance for Christopher. Although he makes a futile attempt to assert his importance, his insignificance is discernible through his reverence to Tituba. A self-professed, powerful maroon leader, he sought Tituba's assistance in acquiring supernatural power for evil purposes.[16] By exposing Christopher's peripheral existence as an impostor in the maroon community, Condé debatably re-creates Tituba and Christopher in the likeness of the maroon duo Nanny and her brother, Cudjoe. This role-play mirrors the historical narrative as Condé engages transhistorical play in keeping with the transnational agenda. Christopher usurped the role of

Cudjoe, who was regarded as the leader of the maroons despite the fact that Nanny was the one who valiantly led the revolution.[17]

Apart from assuming Nanny's heroism, Tituba shares her combativeness and her gift as a spiritual healer. Additionally, Tituba's resemblance to Nanny is no mere coincidence, as Condé herself earlier acknowledges. Lucille Mathurin paints a sensual, maternal side of the mother of the Maroons, who had no children of her own (36). By the same token, Karla Gottlieb focuses on Nanny's nurturing qualities as "first mother" and how she is tied to legends of fertility and food (6). As nurturer, surrogate mother, and healer, Tituba breaks with the traditional patriarchal definition of womanhood and the attendant definition of citizenship. At the same time, her embrace and celebration of her sexuality challenges white male notions of black women's promiscuity.

Reappropriating the narrative of the "respectable" white woman, Hester, Tituba's prison mate, engages female resistance by indulging in carnal pleasure at the expense of the Puritans. This fact is often overlooked or dismissed by critics.[18] While I will return to Hester's "indulgence" and the common goal that she and Tituba share in challenging and dismantling existing patriarchal structures, it is fitting that I pause to analyze Robert H. McCormick Jr.'s analysis of a conversation that the two women share about feminism. Engrossed in a private moment, Hester reveals to Tituba her desire to write a book in which she will portray a model society governed by women who will pass on their names to their children. At this point, Tituba interjects, reminding Hester that men will have to be a part of the procreative process, to which Hester counters: "You're too fond of love, Tituba! I'll never make a feminist out of you!" (101). Whereas Hester's pronouncement to have children carry their mothers' names induces the dismantling of patriarchy, Tituba's declaration calls attention to the intricate and complex relationship between feminism and men.

Intimating that being in love or being involved in male-female relationships is not a pastime of "sound-thinking" feminists unearths the age-old stereotype that feminists and the feminist agenda are opposed to men. Olga Benoit recounts that her embrace of feminism elicited the following response: "Well, feminists are just women leading struggles against men" (86). Further directing our attention to the preconceived racialized assumption of feminism, Johnnetta Betsch Cole and Beverly Guy-Sheftall inform us that "speculation about sexual orientation is fueled by the homophobic assumption that any Black woman who is a feminist is also a lesbian" (23). We witness a strategic erosion of the assumption that feminism is a euphemism for lesbianism in the character of Tituba. As Davis readily points out, Tituba's acceptance and embrace of her sexuality and her strong sexual attraction to men do not "dilute her solidarity with women, black as well as white" (Foreword x).

Even so, Davis reveals Tituba's ambivalence, ascertaining that she is "reluctant to call herself a feminist" because of her strong "defense of her sexuality" (Foreword x). Along these lines, Tituba's defense of her sexuality necessitates that she practice or perform fluid sexuality that exists beyond the boundaries and dictates of imposed patriarchal heterosexuality. As I have argued in chapter 2, compulsory heterosexuality is a determining criteria for citizenship. Tituba's questioning of a probable sexual attraction to Hester destabilizes the rigid, conventional definition and practice of compulsory heterosexuality:

> Can you feel pleasure from hugging a body similar to your own? For me, pleasure had always been in the shape of another body whose hollows fitted my curves and whose swellings nestled in the tender flatlands of my flesh. Was Hester showing me another kind of bodily pleasure? (122)

By suggesting that Hester, the self-professed feminist, introduced Tituba to same-sex relationships, Condé further interrogates patriarchal ideals of proper womanhood. This ideal is earlier interrogated by Hester's indulgence in an extramarital affair. Rendering the relationship insignificant, McCormick reduces the exchange between Tituba and Hester to a mere play of words or ideas. He establishes that "Hester is part of the 'joke' in that her exaggerated and self-destructive behavior is contrasted with Tituba's more real cowardice" (278). Both of these women are imagined as docile, rendered inactive and invisible. One is not sure whether the self-destructive behavior refers to the charge of adultery leveled against Hester or her committing suicide/infanticide. Furthermore, while the charge of self-destructive behavior was intended to reveal the "joke," the evident irony in the conversation between Tituba and Hester about feminism goes unnoticed. As Condé herself admonishes, "if one misses the parody in Tituba, one will not understand, for example, why she meets Hester Prynne in jail and why they discuss feminism in modern terms" (212). This symbolic female-to-female exchange is a subtle call for the revision of feminism to truthfully and adequately attend to and reflect the varied needs and concerns of women across economic, social, racial, geographic, and political spectra. In other words, this is a call for a transnational feminist agenda. Furthermore, Condé's call to modernize or revolutionize the feminist discourse falls on (Mosher's) deaf ears. Mosher's incomprehension is best explained by Mary Friedman and Silvia Schultermandl, who articulate that "transnational feminism tilts common perceptions of identity, nationhood, and family: perceptions that in the past operated along essentialist criteria and thus failed to offer meaningful and satisfactory definitions of lives that are marked by increased global flow and the new challenges it poses for society. Transnational feminism operates within an 'antiracist and anti-imperialist' ideological framework" (9).

Reemphasizing the need for restructuring and reconfiguring feminism, Condé reiterates in an interview that Hester and Tituba "both talk about feminism in very modern language" (Pfaff 60). Appropriating a "modern language" within the extant feminist discourse is undeniably a concerted move to eliminate the biases and injustices within the movement. In calling attention to these biases, bell hooks reminds us that "the women's liberation movement has not only been structured on a narrow platform, it primarily called attention to issues relevant primarily to women (mostly white) with class privilege" (*Feminist Theory* xii). Therefore, one can reasonably conclude that even though Hester might be indirectly the "butt of the joke" in keeping with McCormick's assumption, the gist of the joke is evidently a jab at first-wave feminism, signaling Condé's departure or migration from essentialist, biased, blind-sighted notions of feminism.

Furthering this line of reasoning, having Hester and Tituba locked in a jail cell signals a needed "change in the direction of feminist thought," one that accommodates the "interlocking nature of gender, race and class" (hooks, *Feminist Theory* xii). As a result, we have a white woman and a black woman literally face-to-face, dialoguing on somewhat "equal" terms; identifying on common grounds (in a jail cell), in a common language, that of female oppression and its attendant resistance. Reemphasizing this female identity politics, Hester not only violently interrupts Tituba when she attempts to explain that her demonization results from white racist attitudes, but she also categorically denounces the white society to which Tituba claims she belongs: "It's not my society. Aren't I an outcast like yourself? Locked up between these walls?" (96). A few pages later, she directly indicts the patriarchy, unequivocally identifying both white and black men as the oppressors of women: "Don't talk to me about your wretched husband! He's no better than mine. Shouldn't he be here to share your sorrow? Life is too kind to men, whatever their color" (100). In a contemplative moment, Tituba agrees that "the color of John Indian's skin had not caused him half the trouble mine had caused me" (101). Tituba's pronouncement reinforces the ease with which John Indian accesses the patriarchal order, pointing to his unequivocal citizenship status. Condé further validates this line of reasoning as she ascertains that "racism is very important in Tituba. She was forgotten by history because she was black. She was a black woman" (210). While Condé/Tituba is mindful of the female condition, she nevertheless cautions that despite the fact that "women share a common oppression and a common discrimination throughout the world ... this should not obscure the oppositions created by social class, education, ideology, and environment" (209).

Hester's class privilege is simultaneously devalued and revalued. Within the walls of the prison cell, her social class and education undergo devaluation. Even so, her education is put to practical use as she imparts to Tituba literary and historical knowledge,[19] thereby providing her with a formal "feminist education," to quote hooks (*Feminist Theory* xii). This education, which bears some similarities to Tituba's experiences, becomes a tool of integration and inclusion, establishing its transformative and transnational emphasis. Ironically, the prison walls serve as a space of reflection and rumination for both women and as a mirror-image of their differences (and their similarities). Hester confronts and reflects upon her class privilege, resulting not only in Tituba's diminished skepticism and criticism of feminism but also in the validation and centering of her "modern" brand of feminism into the larger feminist discourse. In essence, the women's incarceration symbolizes, while calling attention to, the need for gender-inclusive politics. Davis's celebration of Tituba's "active solidarity with women, black as well as white" (Foreword x) is instructive. Thus Condé has enlisted Hester in interrogating and dismantling the class, race, and socioeconomic barriers inherent in first-wave feminism that "contributed to the oppression of white women as well" (Hammonds 174).

One would be remiss to dismiss the apparent paradox in Hester's station in life and her lived experiences. A daughter of a Puritan minister, she is forcibly betrothed at the age of sixteen to a man of the cloth "who had laid to rest three wives and five children" (*Tituba* 97). While he is away on a religious mission, Hester commits the "unthinkable": adultery. In relating the sexual encounters with her secret lover to Tituba, Hester exacts simultaneous resistance and pleasure:

> There is something indecent about beauty in a man. Tituba, men shouldn't be beautiful! Two generations of visible saints stigmatizing carnal pleasure resulted in this man and the irresistible delights of the flesh. We started meeting under the pretext of discussing German pietism. Then we ended up in his bed making love and here I am. (98)

In the above pronouncement, Hester replicates Tituba's objectification of her lover, John Indian. This sexual objectification is anomalous for a woman of Hester's station, for Evelynn Hammonds reminds us: "White women were characterized as pure, passionless and de-sexed, while black women were the epitome of immorality, pathology, impurity, and sex itself" (173). Moreover, not only does Hester sully the image of the Puritans and their religious convictions, but she also contaminates the Cult of True Womanhood, of white respectability and chastity. The adulterous affair that culminated in pregnancy delivers the final rupture to the neat narrative of white respectability as Hester becomes an outcast of white femininity. We witness further disjunction in this narrative as Tituba exposes the Puritan women's sexual interest and fascination with John Indian: "Some of the ladies, however Puritan they might be, had not denied themselves the pleasure of flirting with [Indian]" (*Tituba* 101). This "contamination" of white femininity gains currency as Hester not only shares identifiable moments with black women, but she also partakes in forms of resistance engendered by slave women, that of abortion and/or infanticide. Along similar lines, Judah White practices witchcraft.

Resisting the puritanical beliefs or "fanaticism" (as she calls it) of her ancestors, Hester, sharing her secrets with Tituba, confesses to having killed four children that were conceived with her hated husband: "I would have found it impossible to love the offspring of a man I hated. The number of potions, concoctions, purges, and laxatives I took during my pregnancies helped me to arrive at this fortunate conclusion" (97). Hester's confession, particularly her underscoring of the "fortune" that resulted from her act, strongly echoes the act of will slave women enacted, taking their children's lives not only in order to save them but also registering their refusal to be complicit in the horrible institution of slavery. Yet again, this common practice which transcends borders and boundaries engenders transnational coalitions that result in the formation of female diasporas. Drawing a parallel with slave women who practiced abortions and infanticide to save their children from a life of hell and servitude, Dorothy Roberts tells a compelling story about a slave named Jane "who was charged with knowingly, willfully, feloniously and of her malice aforethought preparing a certain deadly poison and giving it to Angeline to drink (*Killing* 48). McCormick has leveled similar charges against Hester. Nonetheless, his indictment of Hester as "self-destructive" is not only narrow-sighted but also partial to the point where it denies her agency or free will. Clearly, Hester's action is motivated by selflessness as she attempts to protect her unborn children from the Puritans and their teachings. This protective maternal instinct resonates powerfully as she decidedly and unapologetically informs Tituba of her impending plans for her unborn "illegitimate" daughter: "She must simply die with me. I have already prepared her for that when we talk to each other at night" (98). By the same token, one would be wrong to dismiss the defiance in Hester's pronouncement.

Further, the decisive, premeditated language that Hester uses to recount the private conversations she has with her unborn child and to articulate her calculated action powerfully resonates with engaging an act of will, infanticide (this act also doubles as an abortion). Along these lines, Hester's act is undeniably carried out in the name of courage and not cowardice. This line of reasoning is reinforced by Hester's apparent refusal to be exploited as a martyr by the Puritans. Alternatively, Hester's adulterous affair functions as a reprieve from and resistance to her routinized prescribed existence as the wife of a Puritan minister. While Hester, without inhibition, indulges in sexual pleasures, she informs Tituba that "of the two of us," referring to her lover imprisoned by his puritanical beliefs, he is "the one to be most pitied" (97). Hence, free from puritanical reign, Hester, not surprisingly, in a strategic and symbolic gesture, labels her act of "saving her children" as sanctioned by God: "He [referring to her scorned husband] revolted me and yet he gave me four children that the good Lord called to him, thank God" (97).

In like manner, resistance manifests in the battle cry engendered by Sophie Caco and Xuela Richardson.[20] For example, Sophie engages in conversation with her mother, Martine, who is contemplating aborting her unborn child: "Are you going to *take it out?*" (Danticat, *Breath* 191; emphasis added). Martine's decision is implied in her equally caustic language: "It [the fetus] bites at the inside of my stomach like a leech" (191). Similarly, Kincaid's female protagonist, Xuela, who is forced to have sexual relations with her surrogate father, Monsieur LaBatte, by his wife, Madame LaBatte, to compensate for her inability to have children of her own, articulates the violence she experiences at the hand of her oppressors. Her resistance parallels the violent act: "[I]f there was child in me I could expel it through the sheer force of my will. I willed it out of me" (*Autobiography* 81). She later comes to the stark realization that Madame LaBatte's narrative of deliverance was fallacious: "it was not herself she wanted to save; it was me she wanted to consume" (*Autobiography* 94). In actuality, the (unwanted) pregnancy and attendant enforced motherhood signal her symbolic death. This revelation intensifies her resolve to resist as she (referring to Xuela, not the fetus) makes a concerted effort to survive her oppressive condition: "Exhausted from the agony of expelling from my body a child I could not love and so did not want, I dreamed of all the things that were mine" (*Autobiography* 89). Even when the act is not accompanied by words, resistance and revenge remain the motive: "Ma said nothing. No word of pity or of reproof, or of consolation, passed her lips, as she administered the potion. And Mary Gertrude Mathilda cried secretly and made a promise to herself" (Clarke 382).[21] Hence abortion becomes the language of female protest.

Hester and Tituba share a moment of female solidarity in that they both confess to having practiced abortion and/or infanticide. They also justify their acts as the only viable recourse. Consequently, Tituba is able to exercise freedom of choice by discontinuing her pregnancy. In the ensuing quote she recalls what prompted her decision: "It was shortly afterward [the execution by hanging of a witch] that I realized that I was pregnant and I decided to kill the child" (49). Later, at what one might call a confessional (here I am suggesting that Condé is parodying the religion of the Puritans), she confides in Hester: "I, too, killed my child" (98). Hester and Tituba's forthright pronouncements challenge and at the same time eliminate doubts about women's passive resistance. This removes the ambiguity that D. White and Dorothy Roberts have argued has prevented us from definitively determining whether slave women practiced selective abortion and infanticide (D. White 84; Dorothy Roberts, *Killing* 49). Tituba's pronouncement addresses this imprecision. In a similar vein, Tituba's choice of words as in "I, too, killed my child" with special emphasis on "killed," lends itself to a form of "doubling" in that the act committed could have easily qualified as either abortion or infanticide. This "doubling" unites the "twin act" as modes of resistance that slave women effectively employed to thwart the efforts of enslavers to control female reproduction. In the same breath, abortion and infanticide are simultaneous acts of resistance and (maternal) love, as many slave women confessed to being intensely concerned for their children's welfare (D. White 88).

Chronicling the inherent contradiction of being a mother and a slave, Tituba ruminates: "There is no happiness in motherhood for a slave. It is little more than the expulsion of an innocent baby, who will have no chance to change its fate, into a world of slavery and abjection" (50). In essence, motherhood for slave women is synonymous with loss and deprivation. Motherhood therefore is a symbolic "miscarriage" of justice as the term *expulsion* alludes. Significantly, *expulsion* does not refer to the acts of abortion or infanticide. Instead, it captures the brutal separation of the child from its mother at birth, attesting to the brutality of slavery that not only claims innocent babies from birth but also prevents mothers from adequately mothering and nurturing their offspring. The inhumane act that the mother-child separation incurs justifiably lends itself to the resultant protests that slave mothers engendered in an effort to spare their offspring from the horrors of slavery. Tituba calls attention to the violent but necessary act: "That night, my baby was carried out of my womb in a flow of black blood. I saw him wave his arms like a tadpole in distress and I burst into tears. . . . I had trouble getting over the murder of [my] child. I knew that I had acted for the best. Yet the image of that little face whose actual features I would never know haunted me" (52). Nevertheless, while these acts of protest are carried out as a means of exerting control and autonomy, albeit minimal, over female reproductive rights, slave women are reminded never to lose sight of their human side, not to engage mindlessly in reproducing colonial or patriarchal violence. Tituba is repeatedly cautioned by her mothers, Abena and Mama Yaya, not to "become like them knowing only how to kill and destroy." They further instructed her to put her energy and gift of witchcraft to good use: "Don't let yourself be eaten up by revenge. Use your powers to serve your own people and heal them" (29, 30).

Concurring that "infanticide was the most extreme form of slave mother's resistance," Dorothy Roberts declares that "some enslaved women killed their newborns to keep them from living as chattel" (*Killing* 48). She later substantiates that although there is no concrete evidence to support how often slave women practiced abortion or terminated pregnancies, what remains unquestionable is that slave mothers acted in desperation to protect, and not sacrifice, their children (*Killing* 49). Historicizing and authenticating infanticide and abortion as effective methods of female resistance, Tituba/Condé draws on documented annals of slave resistance, thereby locating Tituba's personal protest within a wider political framework of resistance:

> Throughout my childhood I had seen slaves kill their babies by sticking a long thorn into the still viscous-like egg of their heads, by cutting the umbilical cord with a poison blade, or else by abandoning them at night in a place frequented by angry spirits. Throughout my childhood I had heard slaves exchange formulas for potions, baths, and injections that sterilize the womb forever and turn it into a tomb lined with a scarlet shroud.
> (*Tituba* 50)

These shared, transatlantic methods of defiance demonstrate the effectiveness and potency of slave mothers' resistance as they address, if not erase, the ambiguous "record on self-imposed sterility and self-induced miscarriages" (D. White 85). Understandably concerned about the impending future of her unborn child as she identifies two untenable options for her life course: that of the life "of my brothers and sisters, the slaves, ruined by their conditions and their labors or a life like mine, which forced me to live in hiding as an outcast and a recluse on the edge of a secluded valley" (158), Tituba challenges the repressive system, stipulating that if "the world were going to receive my child, then it would have to change!" (159). This challenge resonates with Hester's resolute decision to spare her child the cruelty. The need for female alliance is rendered most potent as both women endure patriarchal oppression. Hence, refusing to "sustain slavery by producing human chattel," these acts of protest represent "one small step in bringing about slavery's demise" (Roberts, *Killing* 48). Additionally, as a midwife, Tituba played a pivotal role in female reproductive rights, for she wielded power both in the birthing of children and the terminating of pregnancies.

Barbara Bush ascertains that by relying on traditional midwifery and folkloric medicine, female slaves exerted more control over their bodies. She establishes that female agency and autonomy can be challenged by the "expropriation of the ancient art of midwifery by the new medical men of science and the development of what Foucault has termed 'Scientia

Sexualis' (the development of a 'scientific' explanation of sexuality), [resulting in the] reduc[tion] of control women had over their bodies" (134). However, Bush is quick to point out that this loss of control is more prevalent in middle- and upper-class women. Accordingly, Hester Prynne temporarily loses control of her body when she submits to the marriage to the minister and the subsequent unwanted pregnancies. However, she regains control through the engagement and embrace of folkloric medicine through her alliance with slave women.

Documenting the pivotal and omnipresent role of midwives, D. White articulates that "they were likely to attend all slave births and all slave deaths. Their knowledge delivered one into life, helped one survive it, and sometimes, hastened one to an early grave" (116). By designing motherhood to her own making, rejecting the nuclear family as the norm, and opting instead for the extended family, as she inhabits the role of "other" mother, Tituba was able to effect change, however small. While registering her resistance and despite grappling with the dehumanizing practices of enslavement, Tituba realizes the need to remain human, to remain maternal. As she experiences the joy of alternative mothering of Samantha, the daughter whom she delivered spiritually, Tituba proudly and self-assuredly verbalizes: "A child I didn't give birth to but whom I chose. What motherhood could be nobler!" (177). Furthermore, Tituba dismantles the framework of ideal motherhood and mothering. She intends to impart to Samantha this legacy of female resistance, admitting that "she had been singled out for a special destiny," as she reveals to "her the secrets . . . the hidden power of herbs" (177).

In rejecting the hypersexual and the hyposexual iconic images of black female subjects, Tituba rejects the attendant "tangle of pathology" that weighs on the definitions (Davis, "Reflections" 4).[22] Moreover, Tituba's rejecting John Indian's advice that she confess to the Puritans of wrongdoing signals her fervent desire to avoid engendering the "unspoken indictment" that lingers "beneath the notion of the black matriarch . . . of our female forebears as having actively assented to slavery" (4). Not only does Tituba refuse to assume the role of collaborator, relinquishing citizenship as defined by the nation-state, but she also adamantly maintains her innocence: "They want me to confess my faults. But I am not guilty" (*Tituba* 92). While Tituba refuses to become complicit with patriarchy, the same cannot be said for her and John Indian's owner, Susanna Endicott, whose mission arguably is to disarm and disempower Tituba by disavowing her (magical) powers. Furthermore, Endicott attempts to confine Tituba "bodily" by perpetuating her displacement and her non-citizenship status. Capturing the contentious nature of female complicity, Fabi explains: "The controversial issue of female complicity with patriarchy has often been dealt with in terms of the racism of white against black women" (230). Fabi's theorization provides an accurate analysis of the existing relationship between Susanna Endicott and Tituba. Even so, this turbulent relationship extends beyond race to include a complex gender (power) struggle. In reproducing patriarchy, Susanna Endicott enforces tyrannical rule and order upon her propertied possessions, but especially Tituba.[23] Consequently, Endicott perceives Tituba as a greater threat than John Indian. Davis's claim of how risky it was "for the slaveholding class to openly acknowledge symbols of authority—female symbols no less than male" is pertinent ("Reflections" 4). Fittingly, positioning Endicott's complicity within a classed and racialized framework while framing Tituba's narrative in tandem with female solidarity, Condé exposes white racist patriarchal structures and practices and reinforces transnationalism. Repeatedly Tituba refuses to impeach her fellow (indicted) women, all of whom are white, of practicing witchcraft, even at her own expense, her loss of freedom, her relinquishing of citizenship. Along these lines, her denunciation and subsequent rejection of John Indian's advice to falsely accuse the other women reinforces her commitment to female identity politics.

Tituba, like Abena, is a victim of rape, although her rape comes at the hands of the Puritans. This uncanny mother-daughter "body violation" parallel is not anomalous. Rather it is a factor in slavery, demonstrative of the common bond of oppression that women experience in slavery.[24] Recounting her dehumanization at the hands of her enslavers—the Puritan minister, Samuel Parris, and three other religious men—Tituba candidly reveals that she had been reduced to "nothing more than a heap of suffering" (*Tituba* 91). This "nothingness" finds expression in the graphic and public violation of her body. She recalls the horrific experience while being pinned to the ground with a sharpened stick thrust into her vagina: "Go on, take it, it's John Indian's prick" (91). Symbolically, Tituba is raped by the Puritans, but they also simulate her being raped by John Indian. Besides, Tituba's assumed promiscuity excuses, or most poignantly justifies, the rape. Additionally, as a slave and a woman, as a non-person, she is vulnerable to sexual domination that has been defined by "its openly terroristic character" (Davis, "Reflections" 13). Rape, in Davis's summation, is "the most elemental form of terrorism distinctively suited for the female" (13). This (female) gender-appropriated sexual domination is rendered potent in the ensuing scene.

After trying to solicit a confession from Tituba about her dealings in witchcraft, Samuel Parris summons John Indian. This summons finds a parallel moment in an earlier scene where Yao is forced not only to bear witness to Darnell's sexual advances to Abena but also to be present at her execution by hanging.[25] In the same way, having John Indian witness Tituba being raped reinforces his emasculation. It also symbolically manifests in his own sexual assault. Moreover, forcing John Indian to coerce Tituba to acknowledge guilt intimates that he performs a symbolic rape of sorts on her, on the black woman. In a similar vein, Darnell's attempted rape of Abena is "not exclusively an attack upon her. Indirectly, its target was also the slave community as a whole. In launching the sexual war on the woman, the master would not only assert his sovereignty over a critically important figure of the slave community, he would also be aiming a blow against the black man" (Davis, "Reflections" 13).[26] One can safely conclude that this "manifest inability" of John Indian "to rescue [Tituba] from sexual assaults of the master" places him in a vulnerable position where he experiences "deep-seated doubts about his ability to resist at all" (13). Notwithstanding, these doubts are further compromised by Samuel Parris requesting his complicity with white patriarchy through the coercion of Tituba.

John Indian is an eager accomplice. His act of coercion necessitates that he infantilize Tituba, "cradling [her] like an unruly baby," even as he attempts to persuade her to admit guilt so as to guarantee that she will survive and bear him children. John Indian employs manipulative tactics within which he paradoxically becomes ensnared, as he becomes the object of white patriarchal manipulation. This self-dehumanizing act in which he engages finds him relegated to non-citizen status. Just as he performs a symbolic rape of Tituba—as an enthusiastic co-conspirator of the Puritans, he denounces both Tituba and her craft and subsequently abandons her for Goodwife Sarah Porter. He is proverbially raped, emasculated by white patriarchy. Tituba appropriately intimates that John Indian's cohabitation with the wife of a Puritan minister, the very group that ridiculed and demonized her, is implicit of him signing a pact with "the devil," her tormentors (109). In his undertaking of the role of strange bedfellow, John Indian ascertains his sexual, political, and ideological affiliation with white patriarchy. It is therefore not surprising that in a dream in which Tituba was assaulted by three men, John Indian figured prominently as one of the victimizers, along with Samuel Parris and Christopher.

Deservedly, the ostensible link between white patriarchy and white supremacy merits some attention. Minutes prior to her rape, Tituba chronicles her attackers' descent on her in the following manner: "Like four great birds of prey the men surged into my room. They had slipped on *black hoods, with holes for their eyes*, and the steam from their mouths came through *the cloth*. Quickly they encircled the bed" (90; emphasis added). The hoods with peepholes allude to the conical hats, masks, and robes that members of the Ku Klux Klan don to attack their unsuspecting victims. Further, the link between white patriarchy and supremacy is reinforced by the fact that Tituba is not the only target of Puritan oppression and prejudice. Benjamin Cohen d'Azevedo, a Jewish merchant, is also the intended recipient of Puritan bigotry and religious intolerance. His home is burnt to the ground, killing his nine children. Additionally, two ships belonging to him and his friends go up in flames. The following utterance by a group of Puritan men and women who stood witnessing the burning of d'Azevedo's home decisively legitimizes the connection between white patriarchy and white supremacy: "Did we leave England for this? To see Jews and niggers multiply in our midst?" (133). Driving home the point even further, Condé confesses that her intent was to "show how petty the Puritans really were, how their minds were narrow, full of prejudice. The Puritans were opposed not only to the blacks, but also the Jews" (201).

Moreover, the violent "openly terroristic" rape committed against Tituba sheds light on the Ku Klux Klan's record on terrorism and violence. In a skillful discursive strategy, Condé employs the theory of inversion whereby *white* is substituted for the word *black* as in *black hoods*. This is Condé's attempt at illustrating that patriarchy, whether white or black, is one and the same, governed by similar masculinist principles. This conflation of blackness and whiteness, or more fittingly, the assumption of whiteness, represents an identity deficit that is indicative of black inferiority and subjugation. This line of reasoning is bolstered by the symbolic inversion of Frantz Fanon's seminal text *Black Skin, White Masks*, as Condé engenders a double inversion.[27] Here the black masks that the Puritans wear establish a connection with John Indian's black skin, which is accentuated by his donning a proverbial white mask. In keeping with

Fanon's theorization, John Indian, because of his characteristic inferiority complex, has lost his cultural moorings as he appropriates and imitates the cultural and religious codes of the enslavers, the Puritans. Although invoking Paul Laurence Dunbar's "We Wear the Mask" as a means to mask his resistance—he informs Tituba that his masking is strategic, for it will ultimately ensure his freedom—his verbal declaration is at great odds with his daily performances. Tituba is quick to point out that his performances are modeled on dependency, inadequacy, and minstrelsy rather than on resistance: "You're like a puppet in [the Puritans'] hands. I'll pull this string and you pull that one" (74). John Indian's "puppeteering" is rendered most effective when in a defeatist, self-pitying manner he acquiesces: "We're niggers, Tituba. The whole world's working against us" (74).

As evidenced, John Indian embodies what Fanon refers to as a "dependency complex" (83). His complete identification with the colonial patriarchal culture further magnifies his dependency and lack of autonomy, which Mama Yaya reveals as well as challenges from the onset of the novel. Unequivocally voicing her disapproval of Tituba's relationship with John Indian, she says: "He's a shallow nigger, full of hot air and bravado" (15). Hence John Indian's "unconscious desire" for "hallucinatory whitening" paradoxically results in him engaging in self-negation and self-denigration (Fanon 100). Relinquishing the pastoral for the colonial, ancestral history for colonial history, John Indian resolutely informs Tituba: "I'm not a bush nigger, a maroon! I'll never live in that rabbit hutch of yours. I belong to Susanna Endicott, but she's a good mistress" (17–18). John Indian's renouncement is illustrative of Fanon's theory that "the colonized is elevated above his jungle status in proportion to his adoption of the mother country's cultural standards. He becomes whiter as he renounces his blackness, his jungle" (18). Succumbing to the myth of black inferiority, John Indian is the consummate enslaved or colonized subject "in whose soul an inferiority complex has been created by the death and burial of its local cultural originality" (18).

Tituba, on the other hand, resists the oppressive colonial culture in favor of her African Caribbean cultural heritage, "'figuring' Africa as the mother" (Hall 235). Immersed in local cultural practices as a way to redefine and appropriate the existing restricted definition of citizenship, Tituba becomes the living embodiment of the localized folk figures, Ti-Noel, Nanny of the Maroons, and the witch-woman, locally identified as the ol'higue or the soucouyant.[28] Accordingly, she appropriates the methods of resistance and subversion of colonial rule and structures as espoused by these cultural icons. Moreover, Tituba's continued reliance on the Queen Mother, Nanny of the Maroons, the force and source of her resistance and resilience, corroborates Fanon's theory whereby she qualifies as the "local cultural originality." Karla Gottlieb ascertains that Nanny "developed Guerrilla warfare and the tactics she used were later studied by military strategists in the Vietnam War and others. Second, because she and her people established the first independent black polity in the New World, she led the way for freedom struggles in Haiti, Brazil, the U.S., Guadeloupe, Surinam . . . anywhere where there were enslaved Africans" (1). These diasporic moorings engender agency and autonomy or, paraphrasing Hall, give our cultural identity meaning (235). Illuminating women's involvement, Davis reinforces the invaluable contribution of women to freedom struggles:

> [W]ithout consciously rebellious black women, the theme of resistance could not have become so thoroughly intertwined in the fabric of daily existence. The status of black women within the community of slaves was definitely a barometer indicating the overall potential for resistance. (15)

Along similar lines, Judah White recounts to Tituba women's worth and value to society and their invaluable contribution to the nation-state in fulfilling their duty as good citizens: "What would the world be like without [women]. Eh? What would it be like? Men hate us and yet without us their lives would be sad and narrow. Thanks to us they can change the present and sometimes read the future. Thanks to us they can hope. Tituba, we are the salt of the earth" (52). Further showing female solidarity that is characterized by a politics of inclusion, Inderpal Grewal and Caren Kaplan ascertain that transnational feminism has a global, impartial agenda, whereby it "compare[s] multiple, overlapping, and discrete oppressions rather than construct a theory of hegemonic oppression under a unified category of gender" (17–18).

Resisting marginalization and obfuscation, relinquishing living "behind the shadowy realm of female passivity" (Davis, "Reflections" 14), resisting restricted state-sponsored citizenship, women are choosing instead to stand on the frontline as they not only resist patriarchal invasion but also stage their own preemptive strikes. In this regard, female agency facilitates the telling of women's stories (herstories) from their perspectives as they break the silences once deemed too horrific to tell, giving meaning to our cultural identity that was once lacking. Along these lines, Condé recuperates the rebel woman, Tituba, from obscurity, restores her dignity, and reinstates her through repatriation to her motherland, Barbados, as a desirable citizen. Consequently, the black woman is resurrected in "her true historical contours" (15). Having experienced a rite of passage, Tituba has emerged free and liberated, a citizen of the world. As "the salt of the earth," women have withstood male oppression, emerging renewed, redeemed, and recuperated.

4 Mothering the Nation

Women's Bodies as Nationalist Trope in Edwidge Danticat's *Breath, Eyes, Memory*

While the overriding concern in this chapter is to illustrate how women's bodies are used to promote and reinforce a nationalist cum masculinist agenda and how they resist, it would be remiss to dismiss the pervasive "othering" of the Haitian body as a whole. In its biological, social, and political context, the Haitian body is frequently framed within the national consciousness as a site of state conflict and (continued) violence. This positioning complicates both the construction and attainment of citizenship. As Danticat has repeatedly reminded us, the Haitian body has long been politicized or, more pointedly, demonized, deemed a site of both contestation and ridicule. In her debut novel, *Breath, Eyes, Memory*, her protagonist, Sophie Caco, serves as a conduit for disseminating and articulating the discrimination leveled against Haitians. Warned by her mother of the dire need to learn English quickly so as not to be identified as Haitian—fearing that she will become the subject of ridicule and be accused not only of possessing HBO (Haitian Body Odor) but also of being labeled a transmitter of AIDS—Sophie understandably expresses reservations about attending school in New York. The general consensus is that only "the 'Four Hs' got AIDS—Heroin addicts, Hemophiliacs, Homosexuals, and Haitians" (Danticat, *Breath* 51).[1]

Rendering a clear-cut, austere assessment of falsely consigning AIDS to Haitian citizens, Paul Farmer refers to this blame game as "the geography of blame" in which "the scapegoat role [was] assigned to Haiti" (Kidder, *Mountains* 106).[2] Explicitly detailing how the myth of the Four Hs was born and sustained, he provides some medical/historical background, squarely placing the blame where it belongs. In Tracy Kidder's words, the story goes as follows:

> He'd tell the story of how, early in the AIDS epidemic in the United States, sociologists and even medical people had hypothesized that HIV had come from Africa to Haiti, then to the United States. Some experts even hypothesized that the disease had originated in Haiti, where, it was said by some, Voodoo *hougans* ripped the heads off chickens and guzzled their blood, then had sex with little boys. He'd write about how the Centers for Disease Control, a federal U.S. agency, had gone so far as to identity Haitians as a 'risk group,' along with several other groups whose names began with homosexuals, hemophiliacs, and heroin users—and about the incalculable harm all this had done to Haiti's fragile economy and to Haitians wherever they lived. In his thesis, he'd marshal a host of epidemiological data to show that AIDS had almost certainly come from North America to Haiti, and might well have been carried there by American and Canadian and Haitian American sex tourists, who could buy assignations for pittances in Port-au-Prince. (106)

What is certain is that in the given situation one cannot accuse the United States of inconsistency in regard to its treatment of Haitians; this widespread mistreatment and disregard manifest in many palpable ways. A case in point is the United States' current immigration policy that routinely ostracizes Haitians. In contrast to Cubans who are granted citizenship upon landing on U.S. shores, Haitians, or "stowaways or boat people" as they are routinely labeled, are deported to their homeland.[3] Visiting Krome Detention Center in Florida, Farmer experienced firsthand this injustice that galvanized him to join protests "against what seemed to him the rank injustice of an American immigration policy that let in virtually every refugee from Cuba and sent nearly every fleeing Haitian back to hunger and disease and what had to be the Caribbean's cruelest, most self-serving dictatorship" (Kidder, *Mountains* 63). More recently, following the devastating 7.0 earthquake that took place on January 12, 2010, Haitians living in the United States have been granted Temporary Protected Status (TPS), allowing them to stay and work in the United States legally.[4] Paying much needed critical attention to the deplorable conditions in which Haitians find themselves at home and abroad, Farmer poignantly expresses that "Haitians [are] the underdogs of underdogs, 'the shafted of the shafted'" (63). More telling, Farmer draws a parallel with Haiti's history and *The Lord of the Rings*, "an ongoing story of a great and terrible struggle between the rich and the poor, between good and evil" (63).

Divulging firsthand information concerning the criminalization of Haitians, Danticat shares a personal anecdote.[5] While not by any stretch of the imagination a stowaway, Danticat's eighty-one-year-old-uncle, Joseph Dantica, was nonetheless treated like a common criminal by the U.S. Department of Homeland Security.[6] Escaping the violence that enveloped his homeland of Haiti, Dantica, a Baptist minister, attempted to seek asylum in the United States after his church and home were ravaged and his life was threatened by militant gang members. Upon declaring to U.S. immigration officials his desire to seek asylum, he was arrested and taken to Krome Detention Center in South Florida where he died on November 3, 2004, after being denied his blood pressure medication. Refusing to shoulder any responsibility for Dantica's sudden death, Homeland Security vindicates itself by claiming that the medical examiner's office established that his pancreatitis was a preexisting and fatal condition. Further employing racist tactics as a means to substantiate Dantica's assumed illegitimacy, the agency defensively argues that he was carrying "no legitimate prescribed medicine." Instead, "he had in his possession a folk remedy . . . some kind of 'poultice' or dressing."[7] This racial scapegoating is akin to Farmer's aforementioned declaration that priests were maligned for spreading AIDS.

Evidently, Dantica's possession of "illegitimate" (read nonwestern) medicine not only amplified his "illegality" but also served as fodder for his delegitimization, in spite of the fact that his passport contained a multiple-entry visa. Arguably, it was also a prescription for death. Completing the image of the criminalized body, Dantica was fittingly attired at the asylum hearing, as he appeared dressed in a blue detainee uniform. He suddenly became ill during the hearing and was hospitalized, where he was handcuffed to his bed. A special relief request was made by his family, asking that he not be handcuffed. The request was granted after review. However, he was warned that if he attempted to escape, he would be shot. He quickly succumbed to pancreatitis.[8] Danticat had to sue the federal government to learn how her uncle died five days after he was detained.

Hoping to escape the violence that had immersed his homeland, Dantica came to the stark and brutal realization that the precarious situation on home soil was rivaled by an equally hostile response in Florida. His distraught niece captured this irony, rendering a poignant assessment of the discrimination and inhumane treatment he received: "My uncle was a victim, not just of the violence in Haiti, but also of the prejudice of American immigration officials."[9] Caught at the crossroads, Joseph Dantica was a casualty of both "wars": the unspeakable violence in Haiti and the inhumane and prejudicial U.S. immigration policies. Danticat concluded that despite the tragedy of her uncle's case, the strained relationship between Haitians and Homeland Security was by no means an isolated incident. Rather, it was becoming increasingly routine.[10] Haitians are consistently targeted, placed under intense scrutiny and suspicion by Homeland Security, an act that denies them the privilege accorded Cubans, to embark on the path to acquiring and practicing citizenship.[11] This denial opposes the practice of transnationalism. Moreover, it denies the practice of flexible citizenship and the attendant freedom of movements in this global era in which identity, nationality, and citizenship are in constant flux.

Danticat reveals the contradictory if not illusory attainment of citizenship for the Haitian immigrant in a telling conversation she shared with renowned and distinguished Haitian journalist Jean Dominique, who was murdered, allegedly by the state, for his uninhibited criticisms of the Haitian regime.[12] This conversation is pivotal, for it offers an insight into the varied conceptualizations of citizenship, transnationalism, and the hybrid notions of home, homelands, and diaspora. Despite having lived in exile in the United States for a number of years during the Duvalier regime, Jean, as Danticat casually refers to him, still and without equivocation refers to Haiti as "my country" with confidence and certainty that Danticat admits she envied. She, on the other hand, underscores the ambiguity embedded in "my country," exacerbated by the fragile existence of the nation-state: "My country, Jean, is one of uncertainty. When I say 'my country' to some Haitians, they think I mean the United States. When I say 'my country' to some Americans, they think of Haiti" (*Create Dangerously* 49). Most likely, the "uncertainty" to which Danticat refers has geopolitical implications. On one hand, she sheds light on the complexity of the exilic existence of Haitian citizens, a forced exile that creates multiple and constantly shifting definitions of home and "country." In great part, the political upheavals and economic turmoil that have plagued Haiti for decades serve as a major contributing factor to the mass movements and migrations. (Haiti's demise is not of its own making. This issue will be discussed later. As a last resort, the United States has become a site of reterritorialization for many Haitian immigrants. Florida is home to the largest Haitian immigrant population, followed by New York and Boston.

Furthermore, the shifting definitions of home challenge the notion that the (home) state is the only or exclusive site for the conferral of citizenship. At the same time, multiple migrations reveal the need to implement a more adaptable route to attaining citizenship. This visible change in the migratory climate surely explains why many scholars have called for a reexamination and reconfiguration of the definition of citizen, one that reflects transnational movements and migrations. Among the scholars are Michel Laguerre and Aihwa Ong. Laguerre contends that the new definition must take into consideration the residual effects of globalization, the traveling diasporic experience, and the transnational activities of immigrants.[13] The term *diasporic citizenship*, in his estimation, "adds the transnational aspect to the classic definition of citizenship." This definition proportionately "presupposes some level of integration in the country of residence and some kind of attachment with the homeland" (10, 12–13). Referencing the multiple-passport holder as the symbol of a contemporary diasporic figure, Aihwa Ong's *flexible citizenship* is "flexibility in geographical and social positioning" (3). Ong's citizenship is predicated on "capitalist accumulation, travel, and displacement that induce subjects to respond fluidly and opportunistically to changing political-economic conditions" (6). Haitian immigrants arguably do not fit the bill for a fluid and opportunistic response to and acquisition of citizenship. Nevertheless, the models of citizenship that Laguerre and Ong propose are justified (if they are implemented), for they do not "privilege the geographical, political, cultural, and subjective spaces of the home-nation as an authentic space of belonging and civic participation, while devaluing and bastardizing the states of displacement or dislocation, rendering them inauthentic places of residence" (Braziel and LeBesco 6).

A "transplanted" individual, geographically (from Haiti to the United States), linguistically (from French and Haitian Creole to English), and socially/intellectually (immigrant daughter to Francophone author), Danticat, in essence, practices flexible or transnational citizenship. Not only has she integrated in the country of residence, albeit as a zealous critic of U.S. politics and policies, but she has also maintained close ties to her homeland, advocating for equal rights and justice for Haitian citizens. When questioned about her "refutable" flexible (Haitian) identity, Danticat rejects this monolithic, fixed definition of self, as she in turn questions the normalization or privileging of an (exclusive) American identity. Effecting in reverse what I refer to as the Haitianization of America, Danticat pontificates that her America is very Haitian.[14]

Moving beyond exclusive labor-determined migration or migrants, scholars have argued that both the politics and economics of migratory movements should be considered in analyzing migration patterns. In response to this call, there has been an increase in scholars examining migration resulting from political violence. Nevertheless, this area is still in need of further analysis, as Andrew R. Morrison and Rachel A. May remind us that "migration may be an even more significant response to violence" (113). This exclusion or marginal representation of violence as a determining factor of migration becomes the catalyst for Danticat's challenge to narrow, masculinist representations and appropriations of women's bodies and their predetermined roles in society. In reconfiguring the changing definition of (migratory) space, Danticat is fully aware that this process necessitates "demonstrat[ing], problematiz[ing], and transform[ing] women's social subordination to men" (Grosz viii).

In *Gender & Nation*, Nira Yuval-Davis argues that constructions of nationhood usually involve specific notions of womanhood and manhood and masculinity and femininity as a way of determining gender roles (1). Addressing the nationalist or masculinist bias in gendering the nation, wherein women and women's roles are seen as peripheral, she assertively evinces that it is "women who reproduce nations biologically, culturally and symbolically." Yet, she concludes, they remain excluded or "'hidden' in the various theorizations of nationalist phenomena" (2). These theorizations encompass a protracted list of dos and don'ts that limit women's public roles and also require them, as instructed by state mandates, to control their sexuality by espousing and practicing proper womanhood. Thus, excluded from "practicing citizenship" and relegated to operating behind the scene, the women embody the idiomatic phrase "children should be seen and not heard." As follows, Tamara Mayer's declaration is quite accurate. Nationalism functions as an approved language "through which sexual control and repression is justified and masculine prowess is expressed and exercised" (1). Edwidge Danticat, in *Breath, Eyes, Memory*, decodes this nationalist language that inscribes women in subservient and subjugated positions. This language within which women are scripted is, not surprisingly, articulated and dominated by men. The pervasive characteristic of male dominance remains incontestable as it is effected in state institutions and present in hegemonic masculinity and nationalism. As such, men are projected on the national scene as protectors/defenders of women and the state and enforcers of state-regulated laws. It comes as no surprise then, for feminist theories of nationalism have drawn attention to this conflation (of convenience), that nation or country is fundamentally constructed as feminine, implying that women deservedly require being saved and protected. In other words, the nationalist language establishes what Myriam Chancy refers to as "the illusion that men have rights, which they exercise on behalf of themselves and their families, and that women are cared for . . . covered by legal rights extended to them as minors or wives" (*Framing* 27). In keeping with this theory, women are burdened with the task of maintaining the nation's (read men's) honor and integrity. As a result, they are accorded the title "mothers of the nation," an assigned designation that surreptitiously further justifies controlling women's sexuality.

Despite making use of various state apparatuses, particularly conferral of the state title "mothers of the nation," women are perceived and accordingly treated as second-class citizens. The nationalist language, which serves to define women and womanhood, constructs them in the private, domestic sphere, while it designs the public, political arena to accommodate men, designated active agents, and their nationalist pursuits. Drawing from theoretical analyses of critics including Nira Yuval-Davis, Patricia Hill Collins, Deborah Gaitskell, and Elaine Unterhalter, I reiterate and expand the point of view that by serving as complement and supplement to men, women are used to promote ethnic mobilization. Furthermore, policies are put in place to regulate women's experiences (of motherhood) in defense of state interests. Reasonably concurring that some women are complicit in espousing the nationalist agenda, in Danticat's novel some women get pigeonholed into certain stereotypical roles. Nevertheless, in framing a counter discourse, these very women operate within the existing (patriarchal) structures of state violence, using their mutilated, abused bodies as weapons to resist and rebel against the nationalist agenda and state-mandated directives as a whole. Facilitating the rewriting of the script of their body narratives, the women are ever vigilant that this revised script refutes homogeneous categorizations of women and mothers. In registering rebellion and resistance, the women celebrate difference and otherness; at the same time, they engender the "othering" of the nation.

Offering an analytical close reading of Danticat's *Breath, Eyes, Memory*, I demonstrate how women's bodies undergo a form of militarization as they become subject to scrutiny by the nationalist regime over which men preside. Carolle Charles reminds us that "feminists in Latin America and the Caribbean have analyzed the direct impact of militarization and authoritarian regimes on the life of women" (138). She emphasizes that special attention was given to how the ideology of motherhood might impact women's (political) lives. Moreover, militaristic scrutiny can take the extreme form of rape. Addressing male hegemony under the Duvalier dictatorship and how it directly subjugated Haitian women, Charles, drawing on statistics provided by human rights groups in Haiti, confirms that women who were subjected to political violence, such as rape, were systematically attacked by "uniformed military personnel and their civilian allies" (135). Charles adds that not only were the assaults on women used as a "broad strategy to depoliticize society," but the greater political ramification of the assaults was calculated to destroy altogether "gender identity and to eliminate the women's movements that had emerged in the last two decades" (135). It is against this political backdrop of the emergence of various women's movements and feminist organizations that Danticat gives voice to women's concerns in her novel. Chancy's assertion that "literature produced by Haitian women over the last sixty years is rooted in a long tradition of feminist organizing and theorizing of women's condition in the Haitian context" adds validity to this line of reasoning (*Framing* 27). In essence, Danticat's recognition cum validation of Haitian feminists is itself a voiced protest against what Chancy calls elitism. Chancy unapologetically denounces western feminists for practicing elitism that served to undermine nonwestern feminists' achievements and that functioned as a road block that has prevented them "from recognizing the strides achieved by Haitian feminists along with other Third World women over several decades" (29). Thus operating within the continuum as a woman rights activist and advocate, Danticat politicizes women's role. More specifically, she gives voice to Haitian women's subjugation and their marginal positions under the repressive Duvalier regime. Effectively documenting various methods of real-life intimidation and terrorism employed by the regime as scare tactics to silence women,

Danticat addresses the relation of state and gender, appropriating state violence as a gendered construct.[15] Furthermore, Charles's claim that "the repressive policy of the military state" was rooted in "the gendering of state violence" lends credence to Danticat's appropriation (136).

The label "mothers of the nation" that purportedly functions as a qualifier for "good" citizenship has strong historical and cultural resonance for black women who have been socialized or pathologized as deviant, corrupt, and unfit. The label is an addition to the exhaustive list of derogatory icons of black women, adding to the politics of reductionism that discriminatorily portrays black women as "bearers of incurable immorality," to borrow Dorothy Roberts's phrase (*Killing* 8).[16] Accordingly, Roberts concludes that social policies have been established to "monitor and restrain this corrupting tendency of Black motherhood" (8). This pathological definition of black mothers as unfit is rooted in slavery and, to echo Roberts, "has left a lasting impression on the psyche" (8). Offering an unabashed assessment of this discriminatory practice of scapegoating black mothers, Roberts locates it within its historical context: "The degrading mythology about Black mothers is one aspect of a complex set of stereotypes that deny Black humanity in order to rationalize white supremacy. The white founding fathers justified their exclusion of Blacks from the new republic by imbuing them with a set of attributes that made them unfit for citizenship" (8).

Despite the delegitimization and dehumanization, black women and mothers, under the coinage "mothers of the nation," are conceptualized as both biological and social reproducers. Despite a seemingly transnational agenda embedded in the coinage, the rights to unconditional citizenship are denied to "mothers," as they experience subjugation within the nation-state. Caren Kaplan, Norma Alarcón, and Minoo Moallem are quick to point out that "From its very inception, as excentric subjects, women have had a problematic relationship to the modern nation-state and its construction of subjectivity" (1). They add: "[T]he nation-state sharpens the defining lines of citizenship for women, racialized ethnicities, and sexualities in the construction of a socially stratified society" (1).

Nevertheless, making a distinction between Haiti and other dictatorial regimes of Latin America, Charles calls our attention to the fact that unlike the image of "the suffering, self-sacrificing, patriotic mother who has no place in the political arena, the Duvalierist state focused on a 'patriotic woman' whose allegiance was first to Duvalier's nation and state" (139). It is this erroneous, mythic image or representation of female blind-sighted patriotism that Danticat sets out not only to debunk but also to challenge in her novel.

Set in Haiti and the United States, *Breath, Eyes, Memory*, records the lives of four generations of women and revolves primarily around a mother and daughter whose relationship is fraught with tension. This conflict is exacerbated by the flight of the mother-protagonist, Martine Caco, to America after she was raped by a Tonton Macoute, one of François Duvalier's militia men.[17] As follows, the novel is set during the Duvalier regime. Martine leaves behind her daughter, Sophie, the product of the rape, who at the age of twelve joins her mother in Brooklyn, New York, where this tumultuous relationship comes to a head: transcending borders, traditional beliefs migrate, patriarchal culture persists through practice, and family secrets are revealed and challenged.

Employing the trope "where the land meets the body,"[18] in other words, where woman's body metonymically parallels land and where the desire for land/woman's body is constructed as masculine desire, Martine's rape is referentially symbolic in that it is state-sanctioned, committed by a Tonton Macoute. Gaitskell and Unterhalter's theorization of Afrikaner mothers' suffering proves useful here. While giving full consideration to the racial and cultural differences and the attendant class dynamic between Afrikaner and Haitian women, Gaitskell and Unterhalter's theoretical interpretation is useful as it underscores the gendered relations of both groups of women and how they are/were subject to sexist oppression. In their analysis of the societal/national role of South African women and mothers, in which they reemphasize the land/woman's body dichotomous relation, Gaitskell and Unterhalter have argued that "the sufferings of Afrikaner mothers were central to the emotive portrayal of the nation's agony, since both were seen as blameless victims" (61). Pinpointing a parallel moment that denies Haitian women autonomy, Charles emphasizes how they "are barely recognized as equal citizens and political actors but are legally defined as dependent wives and daughters" (137). Reinforcing her point, she contends that "In Haiti, women, children, and old people were defined as political innocents" (139). These emotive portrayals of women are fueled by repressive state policies that are put in place to undermine women's worth. In Chancy's words, the purpose of the "neuterizing of nationalism" is to exclude women from the "nation's historical record" (*Framing* 39).[19] Patricia J. Williams takes this a step further by establishing that since black women are "the objects of a constitutional omission that has been incorporated into a theory of neutrality," their "racial omission" is orchestrated, "a literal part of original intent; it is fixed, reiterated prophesy of the Founding Fathers" (121). This strategic exclusion renders women faceless and voiceless. Furthering this dialogue, women's exclusion is political, but they are also subjected to physical abuse. Correspondingly, women's bodies are re-imagined as a metaphor for the land or state upon which state-sanctioned crimes are carried out. Conclusively, Martine's rape not only mirrors the atrocities (symbolic rape) Duvalier committed against the island, Haiti, and its people, but also the rape/invasion and occupation by the colonizers, old and new.[20] Further, the state functions as the agent of expulsion as Martine is driven out of her home, while the Tontons Macoutes operate under the directorship of the state as its surrogates (Van Hear 10). As becomes evident, Martine's homelessness is in great part constructed within the paradigm of her "motherlessness," her refusal to submit to state-sanctioned views or definitions of mothering and motherhood.

Indisputably, in Danticat's novel, female bodies are subject to the worst form of subjugation, colonization, and body theft. Nevertheless, body theft is carried out by Haitian men against Haitian women:

> Haitian men insist that their women are virgins and have their ten fingers. Each finger had a purpose. It was the way to prepare herself to become a woman. Mothering. Boiling. Loving. Baking. Nursing. Frying. Healing. Washing. Ironing. Scrubbing. (Danticat, *Breath* 151)

This quote serves as reinforcement of M. Jacqui Alexander's poignant observation that violence has "an original placement within heterosexual desires" (*Politics* 40). Furthermore, women are subordinates, valuable only in their relations with men and for their sexual and reproductive capacity and capability. We become witness to blatant subordination and body restriction in a particular scene in the novel where Martine and Sophie, making their way into a restaurant to which Marc had invited them, were made to "squeeze [themselves] between the wall and the table, [as their bodies wip[ed] the greasy wallpaper clean" (Danticat, *Breath* 52). Prior to this, they found themselves squashed between the motel and dry cleaner. Clearly, this is a strong indicator of the designed dualisms, domestic and sexual, that they are expected to embrace and put into practice. Nalini Natarajan puts it more poignantly in stating that "woman should fulfill the individual male psychic need for scopic/sexual gratification and yet be the figurehead for national culture" (401). Inevitably, this obligatory duality compromises and accounts for the contradiction in woman's position as sign and spectacle. Further, this national campaign waged for women's collective chastity reveals how they are painted as agents of homogenization. Haitian men's insistence on women's purity emphasizes "nobility, passivity, virtuous nurturing and protection of children." Likewise, men's desires are interwoven with women's "supposedly divinely ordained role as wife and mother." As critics Deborah Gaitskell and Elaine Unterhalter have pointed out, this image of women is "shaped by male cultural entrepreneurs, the women themselves as silent as in their stereotypical portrayal" (60, 63). Both Chancy and Charles have demonstrated how Haitian women are subjected to silencing by being relegated as dependent and infant-like. Martine Caco, whose body through rape is subjected to theft and colonization, embodies this silence both in body and presence. As a result, she experiences verbal and corporeal incapacitation. A paradox notwithstanding, Martine's rape has rendered her both visible and invisible.

The demand by Haitian men that Haitian women be paragons of virtue is the nation reaffirming "the boundaries of culturally acceptable feminine conduct" (Kandiyoti 380). Women, therefore, are expected to express their interests (read the nation's interest) "within the term of reference set by nationalist discourse" (380). This explains, although it does not justify, the "testing," the cultural practice where a mother inserts her finger into her daughter's vagina to ensure that she is virginal, that her hymen is intact, that Martine perpetuates and performs on Sophie, making her the third generation of Caco women subject to this brutality (Danticat, *Breath* 84–85, 152–57). Thus Martine, a victim of rape, in turn performs a (state-sanctioned) rape of sorts on her daughter as she re-appropriates and re-approximates torture. Furthermore, writes Vanessa Dickerson, the paradoxical practice of "testing," as a means to guarantee chastity, evidences "the black female body as anti-Victorian as it has not shared the 'impenetrable mystery,' the immutability, the immanence assigned to women in such nineteenth-century conventions as the Angel in the House or the Cult of True Womanhood" (196). Instead, Dickerson argues, the black female body is "linked to a knowable corporeality and to reproduction, the black female body has not been interiorized as ideal but localized as thing" (196). It is the demonization and vilification of the black female body that impels Martine to lecture Sophie on virtuous womanhood and on being proper. Mothers, in turn, are/were imaged nationalistically as protectors of their daughters' social status and, by default, their own. Grandmè Ifé relates to Sophie: "From the time a girl begins to menstruate to the time you turn her over to her husband, the mother is responsible for her purity. If I give a soiled daughter to her husband, he can shame my family, speak evil of me, even bring her back to me" (*Breath* 156). Perversely, they became enforcers, perpetuating violence and victimization, emulating the Tontons Macoutes as they police their daughters' bodies. Remarking on women's bodies as enduring sexual targets, Christine Obbo points to the fact that the control of women's sexuality is perpetuated in "both traditional and Christian ideologies" (80). Besides, the notion of proper is tied closely to a European (patriarchal) sense of womanhood, encapsulated in Sandra Gilbert and Susan Gubar's theory, where they demonstrate the transition of female purity from the heavenly mother goddess, the Virgin Mary, to an earthly "angel in the house" (20). Purity therefore functions as a blueprint for bridled female sexuality that should be preserved and protected at all costs. Chancy emphasizes that Martine's internalization of (black) female inferiority on one hand and her idealization of (white) female purity and chastity on the other become the propelling force of her abusing her daughter (*Framing* 121, 123). At the same time, properness is a visible marker on the female body. Martine reminds Sophie of the importance of being angelic, while choosing a loose-fitting, high-collared dress for her to wear as the symbol of virtuousness (Danticat, *Breath* 60). Christine Obbo convincingly argues that "attitudes towards childless women, family planning and women's dress are indicators of the ways in which women's sexuality is defined and controlled" (79). Offering a constructive and useful criticism of the 1973 Ugandan decree that regulated female attire and asserted that Ugandan women "should look dignified like 'our mothers,'" Obbo persuasively reasons that this decree was "premised on the often voiced belief that women who wear tight or short dresses are morally loose" (81).[21] Along these lines, the unclothed or improperly clad female (body) evokes images of vulnerability that subsequently provoke sexual exploitation. "Properly" attired, the black woman's deviant sexuality is clothed. Later, in a symbolic act of defiance, Sophie unclothes the deviant black female, whereby she adorns her mother in a seductive crimson two-piece suit for burial.

The land/body trope resonates further with Martine's pre-migration obsession with transplanted daffodils, which is linked to her rape. Martine's fascination with the flowers stems from their (unassuming) foreignness: "They grew in a place that they were not supposed to. They were really European flowers, French buds and stems, meant for colder climates" (Danticat, *Breath* 21). Inconspicuous, the transplanted daffodils, or more fittingly, French buds, represent one of the multifaceted notions of diaspora—in this case, an imperial diaspora. Daffodils are symbolic of the colonizers who not only impose their culture on their subjects but also exert political and economic control.[22] At the same time, the image of possession/penetration and conquest of Caribbean land/soil that the French buds and stems convey bears striking resemblance to Martine's rape, the forced body possession. Londa Schiebinger explains that Europe and its colonies were preoccupied with collecting rare and beautiful plants for "study and global exchange," and of utmost significance was an underlying mission, that of "cultivating those plants crucial for European colonizing efforts in tropical climates" (5). Cultural imposition and colonial indoctrination become quite evident as Martine's fixation on the European flowers can be interpreted as a longing for otherness, for foreignness. By the same token, Martine's obsession with the flower diminishes while it conveniently displaces state violence, the violence of colonial, namely, economic and political, expansion. Her obsession signals bodily repudiation and dislocation that prophetically precede Martine's actual migration, the physical expulsion of her body from the Haitian landscape to the United States, a new and equally suffocating space that further contributes to her body exile.[23] As she continues to suffer the aftereffects of body expulsion, Martine is rendered impotent by her inability to adopt or adapt to the new geographic landscape. Rape, a symbolic deflowering, becomes the culminating point of her total body dispossession.

The underlying colonial discourse comes to bear in Martine's daughter's downright rejection of daffodils that signals the fraught (impending) mother-daughter relationship. Furthermore, this relationship carries the imprint of a colonial mother affiliation. This fractured relationship is first evidenced by the lifeless daffodil that dangles and eventually falls out of the Mother's Day card that Sophie made for her aunt, Tante Atie, but upon Tante Atie's insistence she then gave to Martine. Second, the troubled relationship is exacerbated by Martine's continued attempt to link Sophie with the color of flowers. Not only does Sophie travel in a yellow dress adorned with daffodils to reunite with her mother in the United States, but Martine also decorates her room in yellow, with yellow sheets covering her bed and a yellow-haired doll to complete the picture (Danticat, *Breath* 45, 48).[24] Critically, in an earlier scene, before Sophie's migration, we witness a telling parallel or mirroring moment of colonial censorship and condemnation of foreign occupation. Whilst Sophie "*pressed* [her] palm over the flower and *squashed* it" into the card, she later "*plucked* out the flower, and dropped it under [her] shoes." In equal measure, a group of Haitian children engaged in child's play "crush[ed] dried yellow leaves into the ground" that will be burnt later at a potluck dinner (3, 9).

Nevertheless, Martine effects a "colonization in reverse," or decolonization, by partaking in freedom, albeit temporarily, in the form of growing hibiscus, a substitute for daffodils, in her backyard (Danticat, *Breath* 65).[25] A flowering shrub that bears large multicolored flowers, often used to make hedges, the hibiscus is indigenous to Haiti, originally grown in the mountainous area of the island (Allsopp 37). Representatively, Haiti now assumes the colonial enterprising role of the imperial state, France, by cultivating hibiscus not on French soil but on American soil. This enterprising ideology is validated, reinforced, and simultaneously nullified, twofold by the conspicuous fact that the once sought-after colonial venture is domesticated. The hibiscus is transformed exclusively into a domestic plant, cultivated in Martine's backyard. In a previous conversation, we learn that since her migration, Martine remains oblivious to whether daffodils grow in the United States. This diminished interest is a clear indication of her change of heart, observed by Sophie, who comments nonchalantly that her mother has grown tired of daffodils (Danticat, *Breath* 65). Danticat's/Martine's use of the indigenous hibiscus, therefore, becomes a space to explore an embodied identity that is not trapped in a mimetic relationship to colonialism and/or colonial enterprising. Effectively, Martine's cultivation of the indigenous flowers suggests a feminized code that provides a sustainable link between mother and daughter. At the same time, it stands in opposition to the daffodils' phallic bud and stems.

While the unification of body and soul (or land) appears to be a female preoccupation or necessity, men do not exhibit this interest or need. Contrastingly, discord or (bodily) scars are not visible on Marc, Martine's lover, who not only maintains relations with both the home country and the host country, but also retains his economic and political status as he enjoys the privileges of the masculine, mobile, and upper middle class. In conversation with Sophie, Martine emphasizes Marc's French colonial heritage as an indicator of his class privilege: "In Haiti, it would not be possible for someone like Marc to love someone like me. He is from a very upstanding family. His grandfather was a French man" (Danticat, *Breath* 59).[26] As the grandson of a white French man, Marc's identity is linked with the colonial state, France. His hybrid subjectivity manifests "continuity between white imperial heteropatriarchy . . . and black heteropatriarchy" (Alexander, *Pedagogies* 25). Subsequently, Martine establishes the distinction between the working class, the peasantry, to which she belongs, and the bourgeois, the Haitian elite. Furthermore, her statement serves as testimony to her being conscious of class discrimination and gender subordination; this awareness reinforces "Haitian barriers of class, race, and color," which Chancy claims that Martine attempts to transcend "by exiling herself to the United States" (*Framing* 123). Marc, in contrast, simultaneously identifies with and has allegiances to the home country, Haiti. This identity extends to include his current homeland, the United States, which shares a history of colonialism and conquest with France. Further, Marc's privileges extend to the diaspora as he is able to forge a relationship with both Martine and the diasporic community, serving as its legal representative. In contrast, Martine's membership status in the host country remains dubious at best, significantly conditioned by her immigration status: "She got her green card through an amnesty program. When she was going through her amnesty proceedings, she had to get a lawyer. She found [Marc] listed in a Haitian newspaper" (Danticat, *Breath* 59–60). Martine's soliciting legal representation from Marc to guarantee authorization of amnesty strongly resonates with the point raised by Syd Lindsley that women were not allowed unmitigated access to attaining amnesty. Rather, essential documentation "was much more likely to be held by men than women" (177). Martine's liminal status, or rather her homelessness, is punctuated vis-à-vis Marc, whose notion of home, which encompasses multiple sites of belonging, is "fixed"; in addition, his travels are documented as safe and legitimate. Martine's "integration" into American society follows a different trajectory from that of Marc. Her *legitimacy* results directly from pardon of the nation-state (America) and indirectly from the state representative, Marc, her lawyer.

In 1986, Congress passed and Ronald Reagan signed the Immigration Reform and Control Act. The signing of this act, at a time of intense anti-immigrant sentiment, perhaps was premeditated to create an image of liberal America. Thus this state intervention, the granting of amnesty or (temporary) legal status to undocumented immigrants, debatably was intended to be a "homogenizing agent which acts as a possible resource for more progressive gender politics" (Kandiyoti 376). Notwithstanding, many immigration scholars and critics argue that not only did the signing of this act exacerbate racial tensions, but it also created a more divisive gender and wage gap. Scholars Deborah Cobb-Clark and Sherrie Kossoudji argue that although amnesty "altered unauthorized workers' legal status for women, [it] does not appear to have dramatically altered labor market relations." Further, they surmise that "the change in legal status also did not change the structure of wage determinants for women, leaving human capital unrewarded and the penalties associated with traditional migrant employment unchanged" (8). These results for women significantly contrast with the results for men, who "have benefited from amnesty through a narrowing of the wage gap and structural changes in the returns to human capital which promoted additional wage growth" (10). Despite being granted permanent resident alien status, Martine is unable to practice citizenship within the nation-state or beyond its borders.[27] How then does one account for her lack of geographic flexibility and social positioning that Aihwa Ong writes comprises "*flexible* citizenship"?[28] Further, who are the beneficiaries or recipients of geographic flexibility? Although Ong does not indicate a gendered division in the above category, Martine continually experiences national unbelonging. The personal deficit she experiences in the host country is rivaled by her lack of desire to return to her home country. Although one can easily interpret Martine's denial of host and home countries as her disaffection with and renunciation of both nation-states, a more accurate explanation is that she faces a complex impasse. Regardless, the unlikelihood of Martine engaging fully in the practice of flexible citizenship resonates strongly with fellow immigrant women workers who are confronted with "westernization and disruption of traditional work structures" (Lindsley 178–79). Instead, she experiences what Laguerre calls "a disciplinary mechanism that places certain individuals in specific status sites . . . and creates a partitioning of membership categories" (11–12).[29] Amnesty labels Martine as an undocumented immigrant, underscoring her illegal entry into the United States, while simultaneously rendering her illegitimate.[30] Her inability to escape this label becomes evident in her lack of membership in any transnational community, which furthers her continued exilic existence. Her presence in the United States suggests that she is part of the "American nation, because [she resides here], yet [she is] not part of the state" (Laguerre 13).

In furthering her invisibility, Martine engages in self-induced amnesia.[31] Of Martine's amnesic experience, Donette Francis articulates that her "attempt to dissociate... induces a sense of fragmentation" (80). Ironically, Martine's amnesia is linked to her being granted amnesty. The word *amnesty* is derived from the Greek *amnēstía*, which means forgetting, not remembered. She becomes both the forgetful (self-induced amnesia) and the forgotten (illegal, undocumented immigrant). Conversely, Martine's inability (refusal) to practice citizenship can be linked, first and foremost, to her refusal to pledge allegiance to the document-granting state (a requirement of citizenship), due to a lack of trust. Second, she registers her disapproval with the state's interpretation of amnesty as a government pardon, granted to individuals who have committed political offenses. Revealing the lack of trust in the U.S. government, even as she vigorously and relentlessly advocates for the rights of Haitian immigrants, Danticat acknowledges that many Haitians loathe and are suspicious of the United States' asylum policy because it excludes Haitian refugees. Juxtaposing allegiance and lack of trust as counter and competing discourses, Danticat makes a point of revealing how one's allegiance can be tested. In fact, she admits the shakiness of her own allegiance, continually made vulnerable by U.S. foreign and domestic policies, but particularly after the death of her uncle: "I live in a country from which my uncle was catastrophically rejected, and come from one which he had to flee. I'm wrestling with the fact that both places let him down" (Jaggi 2004). Martine partakes of this double jeopardy. As the subject of state violation, Martine, as was the case with Danticat's violated uncle, is not the offender but rather the offended. Her skepticism therefore mimes Danticat's and is metonymic of the prolonged and turbulent relationship that the government of the United States has with the Haitian nation-state. By the same token, Martine's forgetting (staged or otherwise) is reminiscent of historical silence and (national and personal) amnesia.

While Martine's body meets the land in a shared history of turbulence, Marc, in stark contrast, navigates borders and identities with ease as he embodies both the assimilated immigrant and a diasporic (transnational) figure that has maintained allegiances and connections to his homeland and dispersed diasporic communities:

> He [took Martine] to restaurants, always Haitian restaurants, sometimes ones as far away as Philadelphia. They even went to Canada to eat at a Haitian restaurant in Montréal. Marc was *old fashioned* about a lot of things and had some of the *old ways*. He had never married and didn't have any children *back home*—that he knew of. (Danticat, Breath 60; emphasis mine)

Marc's uneventful assimilation resonates strongly with the gendering of privilege. Calling attention to the gender discrimination experienced by Haitian women of the Canadian-based feminist group Point de Ralliement (Rallying Force), Charles reiterates their complaint: "We were accused of lacking certain attributes. . . . It seemed that Haitian men did not face any difficulty in their assimilation into Canadian society" (151). Furthermore, Marc's strong nationalist interest extends to his culinary tastes that permit him to reestablish links not only with his mother/nation, Haiti, but also indirectly with his mother, from whose cooking, it is noted, he "will never recover from not eating" (Danticat, Breath 53). Correspondingly, Marc's old-fashioned ways arguably are rooted in nationalist desires and intent. Further, the casual dismissal of Marc's perceived fatherlessness reinforces Christine Obbo's claim that childless women were targets of the state as a means to control and define female sexuality. Not only is Marc's fatherlessness treated dismissively but also the presumption that he might have children, although he has no knowledge of them, is not subject to or deserving of scrutiny. Equally, the love affair he has with Martine is not rendered illegitimate, at least not from his end of the bargain.[32] Marc's manhood is asserted nevertheless; his heterosexuality is accorded primacy.

Marc's practice of dual/multiple citizenship is devoid of boundaries, an indicator of good statesmanship. Kandiyoti surmises that far from being gender-neutral, citizenship for women remains conditional, "predicated upon the transformation of institutions and customs that keep them bound to the particularistic traditions of their ethnic and religious communities" (376). As follows, citizenship constructs men and women differently. We are offered a glimpse of this variation in treatment of male and female citizens. The ongoing political/public debate about Haiti that takes place in the restaurant that Marc visits with Martine and Sophie is designed and dominated by men (Breath 54). Symbolically, the linguistic silencing of the women is prefaced by bodily silence. Martine and Sophie find themselves sandwiched "between the wall and the table" of the restaurant (*Breath* 53). Patricia Hill Collins offers a relevant analysis in her assessment of gender and class stratification in the United States: "In a nation-state like the United States where social class, race, gender and citizenship status operate as intersecting dimensions of social inequality, neither families nor the mothers within them experience the equal treatment associated with citizenship" ("Producing," 118). Despite her inability to engage in the nationalist discourse, Martine remains bound to the nation-state. She reproduces the Haitian/colonial culture—"testing," mode of dress, and deportment—and by doing so, she not only "transmits the culture [but also] reproduces the boundaries of ethnic/national groups" (Kandiyoti 377). Offering a relevant analysis of the different ways that women may be controlled by the state, Kandiyoti highlights women's relegation as "custodians of cultural particularisms, by virtue of being less assimilated, both culturally and linguistically, into the wider society" (382). Yuval-Davis and Anthias further explain that one of the complex links women have to the state is their social role in human reproduction (6). Gaitskell and Unterhalter take it a step further by claiming that when women appear, if they do, in nationalist discourses, they are figured overwhelmingly as mothers, "suffering mother[s] of the nation" (60, 61). The (presumed) unmediated link between women's bodies and reproduction and their analogous role as "mothers of the nation" strongly resonate in Marc's response. Confronted by Sophie for not preventing her mother's suicide (Martine stabbed herself several times in the stomach, also taking her unborn child's life), Marc says: "I tried to save her. Don't you know how *I wanted this child*?" Sophie challenges him, in turn: "Why *did you give her* a child? Didn't you know about the nightmares?" (Danticat, *Breath* 224, emphasis mine). Marc's response is rather telling as it uncovers his underlying reason for wanting to save Martine: to save his unborn child. Herein, Martine's social worth is defined by her biological role, her child-bearing ability, as her body is read and expected to function as a biological machine. Given that Martine does not assume or partake of citizenship, exemplary of her failure to embody national wholeness, Marc therefore imagines his unborn child as a "hypothetical citizen," to borrow Natarajan's coinage. At the same time, Martine's pregnancy symbolizes the "wholeness of [Marc and the nation] themselves" (Natarajan 403).

Nevertheless, Martine's identity is configured within the construct and confine of a suffering "mother of the nation." This designated status, as Gaitskell and Unterhalter argue, needs protection.[33]

Assessing how Afrikaner mothers are used by the state to promote ethnic mobilization, Gaitskell and Unterhalter argue convincingly that the conferral of the title "mothers of the nation" is a far cry from according women agency. Instead, they illuminate the hidden agenda of the title, one that shows partiality to women's subordination and victimization: "Afrikaner motherhood is exalted as saintly in suffering, admired for stoicism in victimization, its strength an inspiration to the rest of the defeated nation" (60). Emphasis, reinforced by Marc's response, is placed on the protection of children. Notwithstanding, equally potent is Martine's final (choice of) words to the paramedics before she draws her last breath: "I could not *carry* the baby" (224, emphasis mine). Earlier she confides in her daughter that she believes that Marc gave her the baby "that's going to take [her] life away" (190). On one hand, Martine's response calls attention to the fact that the label "mothers of the nation" is quite burdensome for women, connoting unrealistic expectations and demands. On the other hand, Martine, in dialogue with Sophie, establishes that her decision was a life-saving choice, a matter of life and death. This fact is crystallized further in the rhetorical declaration: "I will have it [the unborn child] at the expense of my sanity. They will take it out of me one day and put me away the next" (192). Therefore, Martine's choice to save herself that engenders the repositioning of the emphasis and the discourse as a whole from child to mother demands equal protection for mothers, for women, under the law. Expelled by the state, through her forced migration and exile, Martine in turn rejects the state's designation of women as "mothers of the nation" in her refusal to become a mother. This state-mandated designation undergoes additional nullification. Martine, although a mother biologically, did not partake in mothering or nurturing her own daughter when Sophie was a child. As surrogate mother, her sister, Tante Atie, satisfied this designation. As is obvious, Martine debunks another national myth that "conflat[es] mother with origin, land, family, Rule of Law," placing, yet again, the nation and nationalist teachings under intense scrutiny (Natarajan 405).

We then become witness to the further debunking of the nationalist agenda. While migration seemingly affords the legitimization of Martine's and Marc's love affair, Martine nonetheless remains unmarried. Notably,

Martine is not interested in marriage, admitting that she plans to stay with Marc "as long as he didn't make any demands that she couldn't fulfill" (Danticat, *Breath* 60). Martine's cautionary tale is a direct reaction to and negation of the Haitian patriarchal tradition where men make unscrupulous and unrealistic demands of women. Considering this fact, Martine's pronouncement registers her disaffection, her refutation of the state's use and definition of motherhood, of womanhood, in its effort to depoliticize women and women's roles. But more importantly, it attests to her independence of men and particularly Marc (read, the state), defying the statistic of immigrant women's dependency on their husbands or partners and, in their absence, on the state. Her independence of the state, and by default the state representative, manifests in limiting and altogether preventing state-regulated practices of defining her body (value) and her moral worth. Meanwhile, she refuses to lend legitimacy or accord special significance to the love affair she has with Marc and embraces her sexuality beyond the confines of marriage. This exercise of freedom is made more palpable by Sophie's choice of an all-enveloping red burial outfit that registers defiance and resistance.

In the final analysis, Martine and Marc's "illegitimate" affair serves to interrogate the tradition of "testing" that promotes and glorifies chastity. Sophie earlier criticizes this tradition by verbalizing her disgust and disagreement. Openly challenging the practice, she catalogs the invalidity of the practice of "testing" that was put into effect to guarantee men would have virgins as wives. Underscoring the ineffectiveness of the practice, she confronts Grandmè Ifé, who was once a practitioner of the tradition that she dutifully passed on to the next generation of women as it was previously passed down to her. The dialogue between grandmother and granddaughter is as follows:

> "When you tested my mother and Tante Atie, couldn't you tell that they hated it?"
> "I had to keep them clean until they had husbands."
> "But they don't have husbands."
> "The burden was not mine alone." (156)

The dialogue came to a close with Sophie articulating her own experience of testing, labeling it "the most horrible thing that ever happened to me" (156). Grandmè Ifé's response captures the nationalist framework within which mothers were constructed in the service of nationalist goals. As a result, the burden placed upon women becomes a generational practice. Nevertheless, Sophie sets herself an equally ambitious goal as she is determined to perform a postmortem on this violent practice. Moreover, not only does Martine arrive at a point in her life where she rejects the daffodils for which the Caribbean soil served as fertile ground for their germination, but she also rebuffs enforced maternity and imposed motherhood, which stands for rejection of the use of her body as fertile ground for reproduction. As Charles, in quoting Angela Davis, reminds us, "black slave women killed their children and performed abortions as a way to set the terms for control of their sexuality and reproduction" (146).

For this reason, Martine disrupts the link between black women's bodies and a knowable corporeality and reproduction by refusing (controlled and state-imposed) motherhood. She thereby refuses to facilitate or reproduce the nation and its nationalist discourse, its designation of her as a second-class and invisible citizen. In refusing to reproduce the nation, Martine uniformly refuses to reproduce the (initial) violence. Further, Martine's refusal to become a mother against her wishes is a denunciation of "female-biased and -restricted" state-sponsored citizenship. My reading runs antithetical to Yuval-Davis and Werbner's argument. The aforementioned critics contend that some women, who in an attempt to triumph over their identity as "'different' and non-rational, stress their superior 'maternal' qualities of caring, responsibility and compassion as key constituents of citizenship" (7). Martine, on the other hand, realizes the need to stay loyal to her conviction so as to effectuate real change. In denouncing the demonization and subjugation of women and emphasizing her demand for equal treatment of women and mothers under the law, she arrives at the conclusion that rejection of patriarchal laws and state-controlled motherhood entailed repudiation of state-mandated amnesty.[34] Even though a substantiated claim can be issued for Martine re-imagining citizenship "and the public sphere to encompass 'feminine' values," she falls victim to societal prejudices nonetheless (Yuval-Davis and Werbner 7).[35] Her increasingly displaced and distorted sense of self, warped by a European frame of reference, significantly contributed to her inability to practice citizenship. What follows is a clear indication that her thoughts are conditioned by the dictates of a racialized society, where blame is locatable within a larger context of the nation-state: "Of course he wants to marry me, but look at me. I am a fat woman trying to pass for thin. A dark woman trying to pass for light. And I have no breasts. . . . I am not an ideal mother" (Danticat, *Breath* 189). Conclusively, Martine categorizes motherhood and wifehood as mutually exclusive (and perhaps unattainable) categories. The very reason she gives for refuting motherhood, "bad mother syndrome," is the very reason she offers for not agreeing to marry Marc (189). Moreover, Martine's self-denigration is her questioning her suitability to be an ideal "mother of the nation." Chancy provides an appropriate answer/response to Martine's idealization of motherhood and mothering and her inability to embrace an alternative definition of mother and mothering: Martine "never comes to terms with the fact that the man who raped her in her late teens robbed her of her sexual autonomy; she perceives herself as 'damaged,' incapable, in fact, of being Erzulie, because she is no longer 'virginal,' or 'chaste,' a status the Caco women associate with social mobility" (*Framing* 123).

As Collins has pointed out, in the United States, definitions of American national identity are heavily influenced by notions of motherhood ("Producing" 118). In questioning her status, and falling short of becoming an "ideal mother," Martine perceives herself (black immigrant woman and mother) as ineligible for and unworthy of citizenship, as she embraces the "value placed on whiteness and its longstanding association with first-class American citizenship" ("Producing" 120). Martine's fixation with ideal (super) motherhood mirrors her obsession with ideal bodies, authenticated by her earlier comment. Heavily invested in maintaining this unattainable ideal that Roberts characterizes as "from the moment [black women] set foot in this country as slaves, they have fallen outside the American ideal of womanhood," Martine falls victim to herself, reinforcing her victimization (*Killing* 10). For Martine, the models of motherhood and ideal body are defined and reside within a European frame of reference. Her preoccupation with adopting and perpetuating standards of ideal womanhood bolsters Chancy's claim that she is "bound to self-negating mores of womanhood embedded in nineteenth-century ideals" (*Framing* 123). As a consequence, she puts her body at risk of self-abuse by conforming to a Victorian (western) ideal of true womanhood.[36]

Drawing attention to American population policies, Collins demonstrates how U.S. "social policies are designed to regulate experiences with motherhood of women from different racial, social class, and citizenship groups in defence of perceived nation-state interests" ("Producing" 118). Furthering Collins's line of reasoning, because whiteness is adopted as a barometer to gauge desirable (women) citizens, "white women's reproduction [is linked] to American national interests in profoundly important ways" (120).[37] In conversation with Sophie, Martine further intimates that citizenship is exclusionary and tailored for designated groups. When she states: "And repeat my great miracle of being a *super mother* with you? Some things one should not repeat" (Danticat, *Breath* 189), she substantiates Collins's claim that some "women emerge as more worthy 'mothers of the nation' than others" ("Producing" 119). While it might ring true that Martine is not an ideal mother, it is not for the reasons she underscores. The reality is that "cultural constructions of maternity idealize mothers who privilege the well-being of others over themselves" (Saywell 49).

Rather, Martine's "choice framed as sacrifice" is constructed beyond the parameters of "mothers of the nation," as it posits another dimension to her complex subjectivity. Chancy dubs this "doubling of identity [as] the revolutionary dimension of Haitian women's literature" (*Framing* 17). Defying easy categorization, Martine does not become "martyr to the idea of nation" (Natarajan 407). In accordance, Sophie does not employ rhetoric of sainthood or martyrdom to describe Martine or to analyze her final definitive choice. Rather, she demystifies the glory and honor embedded in martyrdom. We are presented with an assertive, funky, sexy, desirous, full-blooded woman attired in red and imaged in the likeness of the goddess Erzulie: "She look[s] like a Jezebel, hot-blooded Erzulie who feared no men, but rather made them her slaves, raped them, and killed them" (Danticat, *Breath* 227). Applying a politics of subversion, Danticat skillfully conjures up what Roberts claims to be one of the most prevalent images of slave women, Jezebel, embodying a full-blooded sexual being and relinquishing the image of the suffering and patriotic mother. Not only is Jezebel/Martine in control of her sexual desires and sexuality, but she also exercises dominion over men. By conjuring up the iconic Jezebel, Danticat simultaneously rejects her opposite, "the True Woman, who was chaste, pure, and white" (Roberts, *Killing* 11). Certainly, Martine's death disrupts the neat narrative of nationalism, revealing a disjunction that does not serve the nation's interest, but instead disrupts the image of "woman as spectacle of motherhood [that] evokes dreams of unity and wholeness" (Natarajan 403). Thus Martine rewrites the narrative in blood, demystifying and finally laying to rest the idealized image of mother/woman/wife. This, in turn, reflects women's reality. On a personal cum political level, Martine's demystification of the narrative of nationalism exposes the troubled history of the land, Haiti, and her body, her (continued) marginalization, and her peripheral existence in her adopted host country.

Despite Martine's ongoing battle with invisibility, illegitimacy, and self-worth, her death, at her own hands, is an act of courage. Once an agent of pain, whose captive body was "the source of an irresistible, destructive sensuality," Martine claims agency; she no longer relinquishes control of her body to men, specifically Marc (Spillers 67). To echo Dickerson, her body is no longer "shaped in the service of patriarchy" (203). Thus, by taking her body, literally speaking, into her own hands, Martine not only manipulates but also renders Marc powerless in the face of her self-inflicted act of violence. In her assessment and analysis of victims of torture, Elaine Scarry asserts that one of the most agonizing moments torture victims experience is being forced to stare at the weapon that will become the source of their pain and/or destruction (27). She later adds that the torturer usually appropriates the victim's pain into a perverted, "fraudulent assertion of power," whereby the "objectified pain is denied as pain and read as power" (45). I offer a subversive reading of Martine's role as tortured. Engaging in a role reversal of sorts, she does not deny or diminish her pain; rather, she transforms it into power and action. As such, Martine's weapon of choice is her body. Articulating his agony, Marc intimates that the performance was staged: "She had prepared this" (Danticat, *Breath* 224). Correspondingly, Marc is forced to experience and witness Martine's pain. Ultimately, he is forced not only to name the weapon of torture, a rusty knife, but also to speak the language of torture, reserved for female victims, as he repeats, "Seventeen times. It was seventeen times," referencing the numbers of stab wounds Martine inflicted upon her flesh (224). Martine subversively turns the punishment inflicted upon Haitian women, of remaining clean and virginal for undeserving men, into what Leila Neti regards as "a means of protest by seizing control" of the body (77). The bloodied, unchaste body afflicts Marc's "visual and sensory" sight/site and equally "serves as an utterance against the hegemonic structure" while it "graphically draw[s] attention to the physical conditions of [women's] existence" (77, 84).[38] Martine becomes the threatening and polluted outsider. On one hand, her bloodied and bleeding body is redolent of impurity. On the other hand, her illegal status, which the nation-state (the United States) seeks/attempts to contain within its regime by assigning labels to it, is a pollutant. As is obvious here, polluting is not used as a devalued category, that which Yuval-Davis, in quoting Henrietta Moore, mentions reinforces "women's symbolic devaluation . . . as women are often constructed as polluting when they are bleeding during menstruation or after child-birth" (6). Rather, and more importantly, pollution serves as a symbol of recuperative energy, force, and resistance.

Not only does Martine permeate or, more fittingly, penetrate the border by gaining entrance, but she also disturbs the regimental policing agenda of the nation-state, disallowing the state and its statesman, Marc, to exert control and power over her. Relatedly, we witness earlier attempts, albeit subtle, of Martine at revising the state-designed role of women as subservient and subjugated other. Whenever the opportunity presented itself, she wasted no time in reminding Sophie, oblivious to Marc's insistence that Sophie should exercise freedom of choice, that she will be the first generation of Caco women to "make something of [her]self, to serve within the medical profession" (Danticat, *Breath* 44, 56). Martine's unwavering pronouncement that Sophie is "going to be a doctor" underscores female access and mobility (*Breath* 56).[39] Chancy articulates this need, this quest for freedom: "In the United States, [Sophie] will be freed from the constraints of class that attend marriage in Haiti; she will gain an education and no man will be able to reject her as one Mr. Augustin rejected her Tante Atie because of her illiteracy" (*Framing* 124). Propositioning for women to rightfully and indiscriminately gain access to the medical profession (to education as a whole) that has been historically determined and defined by male privilege and access, Martine once again interrupts the neat narrative of nationalism that simultaneously witnesses the disruption of the status quo.

Meanwhile, the blood from the wounds that Marc is left to clean up mirrors the color of protest emblematized in Martine's crimson two-piece burial suit. She is the embodiment of the "seductress traditionally dressed in red, who manipulates men to her own ends" (Christian, "Contemporary Fables" 159). Marc is forced into a passive role as spectator; he is not a defender or protector, as pointed out by Sophie, who exposes his inability to protect her mother as he "eulogizes" Martine. His gaze is held, controlled, and contained by the bodily mutilation that Martine performs. As such, her pain is deflected unto him, his psyche, as he vicariously experiences it. Refusing to allow Marc to capitalize on or script her pain, Martine reclaims her flesh, which in Spillers's words comes before the body. Thus she prevents further body theft, putting an end to the "high crimes [committed] against the flesh" ("Mama's Baby" 67). No longer the script upon which men record pain or perform "hieroglyphics of the flesh," the (black female) body can no longer be rendered indecipherable. Martine's bodily assertion of power simultaneously allows her "to come clean" and points toward her denunciation of continued commodification and domestication of women's bodies ("Mama's Baby" 65). Martine may not fit the state's ideal of a model citizen, but nevertheless she is the embodiment of the self-sacrificing mother whose "sacrifice rather than her strength [becomes Sophie's] inspiration" (Gaitskell and Unterhalter 71). Dickerson's analysis of mothers who (are forced to) manipulate state apparatuses to ensure their children's security is indeed relevant: "the mother's very body can sometimes be the only insurance policy the black child has in this world" (204).

Martine's staged and timely death presents Sophie with the opportunity and responsibility of journeying to recuperate the mutilated, displaced black female body and reclaim her mother line. Renewing the contractual pact between mother and daughter, Sophie assertively declares: "My mother line was always with me. No matter what happens. Blood made us one" (Danticat, *Breath* 207). Blood, vital life force and source, is the (sexual) unifier of women's bodies and/in pain: "a signifier of violence [unavailable] to men" (Neti 77). At the same time, blood cements the undeniable kinship among these women. It possesses redemptive powers that engender renewal and change.[40] Freedom of the female captive body is omnipresent; it subsequently translates into freedom for all the Caco women, whose last name refers to both Haitian revolutionary heroes and a flamboyant scarlet bird. Fittingly described in picturesque language that captures the true essence of these heroines, the Caco bird is "so crimson, it makes the reddest hibiscus or the brightest flame trees seem white. When it dies, there is always a rush of blood that rises to its neck and the wings, they look so bright, you would think them on fire" (Danticat, *Breath* 150). The crimson two-piece suit, matching shoes and gloves "too loud a color for burial" are emblematic of the conferral of women's sexual autonomy (227). Danticat's message is not simply to bear witness. She underscores the necessity to document, to create a language, even if it consists of mimicked violence, that adequately captures and brings attention to women's pain or plight. As facilitators, women not only exercise agency but are also agents of their (body) narratives.

Taking a relevant cue from Martine, Sophie rejects patriarchal conventions placed on women and their sexuality by continuing the protest that becomes manifest in her own bodily/self-mutilation. Her body defacement therefore serves to reinforce and validate Arturo J. Aldama's claim that "sexual and discursive violence plays itself out on the bodies of those made subaltern by that violence" (14). In combating the violence enforced upon her, Sophie in turn reproduces violence that paradoxically resonates powerfully with the "testing" she experienced:

> I went down to the kitchen to search my mother's cabinet for the mortar and pestle we used to crush spices. *I took the pestle to bed with me and held it against my chest. My flesh ripped apart as I pressed the pestle into it.* I could see the blood slowly dripping onto the bed sheet. It was gone, the veil that always held my mother's finger back every time she tested me. [A few pages later, Sophie tells her husband that the act was] like *breaking manacles*, an act of freedom. (Danticat, *Breath* 87–88, 130, emphasis mine)

In reappropriating the language of violence located within a masculinist framework, Danticat effectively employs a system of (palpable) phallic imagery as counter hegemonic discourse; this imagery becomes, by extension, a means of reproducing the unspeakable violence to which women are subjected. The pestle, defined as a crusher or a rod, doubles as a domestic and sexual object; this correspondingly underscores the violence against women that is enacted within the private sphere. The analogous (vaginal) symbol, the mortar is evocative of female sex and sexuality. In the given scene, it serves as a synecdoche for Sophie's broken hymen. Furthermore, Danticat's use of erotic language is arresting: "*I took the pestle to bed with me and held it against my chest. My flesh ripped apart as I pressed the pestle into it.*" Danticat's engagement of the erotic fosters the refusal and removal of shame and blame from the female body, what Lorde otherwise terms the vilification, devaluation, and abuse of the erotic by western society ("Uses" 53). Moreover, Danticat's reappropriation of the supposed female "body shame" necessitates that she locate it within a sexualized, feminized framework.

Ritualized storytelling is employed as another form of narrative strategy. It serves as a rejoinder to the story of dispossession that Martine tells about the inseparable Marassas moments before she possessed her daughter's body via "testing." In response, Sophie articulates her own narrative of self-possession.[41] Just as she is about to shed her own blood by breaking her hymen to prevent further "testing," she narrates a salient tale about a woman who was tired of bleeding and so gave up her right to be human, transforming into a butterfly. On one level, Sophie's story reeks of the dehumanizing force of violence, that which in Scarry's summation "does not simply resist language but actively destroys it" (4). It, in effect, is symbolic of women who hemorrhage literally and figuratively as a result of physical and psychical acts committed against them. On another level, however, the tale charts the potential, the innate ability of women to effect change through defiance, resistance, and sacrifice, as emblematized in their bloodied and bleeding bodies. By spilling blood, breaking the "manacles," Sophie frees herself of the burden of "the virginity cult," as she rebelliously labels the demoralizing practice.

By having women appropriate the language of violence, the language of masculine prowess that is highly charged with an all-consuming phallic imagery, Danticat renders the state and its representatives impotent. The practice of "testing" itself, which women perform on their daughters, resides within the masculinist discourse of violence. Conversely, women are seemingly engaged in a complicit relationship with patriarchy as violence is adopted and now perpetuated by the women. Yuval-Davis and Anthias's point is quite effective here in addressing this act of complicity. Women, they observe, sometimes "actively participate in the process of reproducing and modifying their roles as well as being actively involved in controlling other women" (11). Offering another valuable dimension to women policing their own bodies, Margrit Shildrick and Janet Price remind us that "the efficacy of disciplinary practices may be greatest when they appear not as external demands on the individual but as self-generated and self-policed behaviours" (438). While some women are accessories to patriarchy, there is another side of the story that begs to be told. The systemic violence engendered by slavery, colonialism, and postcolonialism that pervades and seeps into the women's lives disputably leaves them no choice but to counter violence with violence, rendering effective the cliché "violence begets violence." Notwithstanding, to the women's credit, violence is employed tactically and subversively. They thus use their bodies, the only possession that they have minimal control of, as deadly weapons.[42] In traversing the sexist, masculinist discourse, the Caco women relinquish their previous roles as agents of pain, assuming instead roles as agents of their discourse. By literally and allegorically traversing borders and triumphantly negotiating terrains of torture and pain into a platform for action, the Caco women heed Lorde's cautionary words, "Your silence will not protect you," as they reclaim the women who were buried under silence (*Sister Outsider* 41). Hence unremitting negotiation and navigation of boundaries by Sophie (and the Caco women as a whole) serve as an invaluable instrument of protest that disrupts and challenges the masculinist, nationalist discourse as it disposes of the concept "mothers of the nation."

5   Performing the Body

Transgressive Doubles, Fatness and Blackness

When questioned at a poetry reading by a British audience of women about her representative female characters, Guyanese-born poet Grace Nichols refutes black female victimhood. This response not only draws attention to the prevailing assumption of blackness and womanness, but it also challenges the stereotypical representations of black female subjects. In refuting this predestined "victim mentality" or syndrome with which black women have been saddled as markers of their identity, Nichols posits language as the tool of resistance. Underscoring its importance, she specifically draws attention to the celebration and preservation of the language of our forefathers and foremothers. Consequently, Nichols posits a compelling line of reasoning for the validation and continued existence of Creole, which she argues was constantly interacting with standard English in her world, although Creole "was regarded, obviously, as the inferior by the colonial powers . . . and still has a social stigma attached to it in the Caribbean" (Nichols, "Battle" 284). On one hand, it signals our linguistic survival, our link to the past, being that it is a "language our foremothers and forefathers struggled to create and we're saying that it's a valid, vibrant language. We are no longer going to treat it with contempt or allow it to be misplaced" (284).

On the other hand, it provides spiritual sustenance that requires "the need to preserve something that's important to us" (Nichols, "Battle" 97–98). Creole therefore functions as a marker of identity and resistance; it legitimizes one's identity and citizenship. Furthermore, avoiding the entrapment that places women in a stranglehold of perpetual dependency and victimization, Nichols, in a symbolic gesture, rebutted in poetry:

> Of Course When They Ask for Poems
> About the 'realities' of Black Women
>
> they want a little black blood
> what they really want
> at times
> is a specimen
> whose heart is in the dust
>
> a mother-of-sufferer
> trampled/oppressed
> they want a little black blood
> undressed
> and validation
> for the abused stereotype
> already in their heads
>
> or else they want
> a perfect song
> ... maybe this poem is to say
> that I like to see
> we black women
> full-of we-selves walking
>
> crushing out
> with each dancing step
>
> the twisted self-negating
> history
> we've inherited
> crushing out
> with each dancing step.
>
> (285–87)

Bolstering Nichols's objection to black women being depicted as pathological, British-based sociologist Ife Amadiume, assessing the racist element in western women's movements, calls attention to the blatant misrepresentation of black women and their exclusion from the national discourse. Alleging that whereas a selective group of women (read middle-class white women) is chosen as representative of the movement, she ascertains that only "the downtrodden" are chosen "when it comes to African [women]" (*Male Daughters* 5). Further, she questions the routine portrayal of "Black women as universally deprived," arguing that this picture "only reinforces racism" (5). In this regard, Nichols is one of the many women who Amadiume recognizes has begun "to expose the racism in the women's movement and to accuse Western feminists of a new imperialism" (4). Nichols's verbal indictment—"they want a little black blood / whose heart is in the dust / a mother-of-sufferer / trampled/oppressed / for the abused stereotype / already in their heads"—substantiates the "fantasized measure of superiority" that Amadiume argues white feminists exert "over African and other Third World Women" (3).

Similar to the objectionable idea of a superior language, Nichols challenges the notion of a superimposed identity or, more poignantly, a monolithic European identity. Furthermore, the Fat Black Woman critiques monolithic construction of race, sexuality, and national identity; in other words, she fiercely interrogates the practice of exclusionary citizenship. *The Fat Black Woman's Poems* serves as testimony to this challenge even as it presents a formidable case for a broader, all-inclusive, and more realistic portrayal of black womanhood.[1] It is therefore not surprising that the first poem in this collection is titled "Beauty," exemplifying and validating varying interpretations of beauty and consequently rejecting a monolithic imposed definition. Fittingly, the final poem in this section is titled "Afterword," permitting self-affirmation and lending visibility to the "invisible" fat black woman and reinstating her as a worthy citizen. As such, Nichols renders her eponymous heroine, the Fat Black Woman, visible, making her the site/sight of public political debates as her fat black body functions as a platform, a discursive strategy, so to speak, that permits and validates alternative identity or subjectivity. This alternative identity challenges fixed identity and ideal citizenship. To this end, Nichols engages an interesting confluence of fatness and laziness in her poetry collections, *The Fat Black Woman's Poems* and *Lazy Thoughts of a Lazy Woman*, drawing on the age-old racist stereotypes of the Sambo and the Mammy archetypes assigned to black subjects. Just as these stereotypes stand in contradistinction to the nation's definition of the ideal body or citizen, in that they register blacks as non-persons and non-citizens, fatness and blackness are equally incompatible with the nation's agenda. Redefining the "vulgar," Nichols shows that "vulgarity" is innately present in the promotion of gender and body conformity. Along these lines, acceptance of the body in all its formations—deviance, outcast, othered, grotesque—signals rejection of Victorian ideals of normalcy, femininity, decency, and the ideal citizen. As Duany ascertains, the invalidation of decency, propriety, and heteronormativity has strong resonance with the traversing of legal and cultural borders and boundaries in that they disrupt established norms and interrupt the distinction between "us and them" (1). Consequently, the Fat Black Woman deconstructs the nation-state's definition of ideal citizenship, cross-examining the politics of identity and belonging and collapsing enforced boundaries and borders. Further in her promotion of transnational citizenship (and attendant diasporic communities), Nichols's *Fat Black Woman's Poems* spans borders and boundaries in its response to Saartjie Baartman's exploitation, which culminated in her orchestrated and staged performances across Europe. "Performing her excess flesh" by choice, in contradistinction to Baartman, the Fat Black Woman presents a formidable challenge to black women's denial of citizenship and their assumed hypervisibility and hypersexuality.

Analyzing the concept of the "vulgar" body in Jamaican popular culture, Carolyn Cooper reasons that "the 'vulgarity' of the vulgar must itself be contested" (*Noises* 8). Claiming that "this conception of the vulgar seems to originate in a fear of the coarse texture of the (feminised) body and the baseness of the flesh," Cooper shows that consequently the "vulgar" body is demonized and devalued. "In all domains, the 'vulgar' is that which can be traced to 'Africa'; the 'refined' is that which can be traced to 'Europe.' In the domain of language and verbal creativity, English is 'refined' and Jamaican is 'vulgar'; oral texts are 'vulgar'; written texts are 'refined.'" (8). This cultural/linguistic difference establishes a divide between highbrow and lowbrow, us versus them, and "euro/afrocentric [culture] that is encoded in the . . . body politic" (8). Decades earlier, Russian philosopher and literary theorist Mikhail Bakhtin employs the "grotesque" (which stands in opposition to the "classic") in his exploration of high/low symbolism.[2] Offering a concrete example of the high/low theorization of the body, Bakhtin summarizes that "one of the fundamental tendencies of the grotesque image of the body is to show two bodies in one: the one giving birth and dying, the other conceived, generated, and born. This is the pregnant and begetting body, or at least a body ready for conception and fertilization" (Bakhtin 26). In keeping with this analysis, the Fat Black Woman's body exemplifies the "unfinished and open body," the transgressive body that subverts and challenges the "classical" body (26). Furthermore, the Fat Black Woman's body in and of itself inhabits vulgarity owing to the fact that it does not fit the mold of the white, chaste, normalized body.[3] In other words, it does not fit into the framework of the "aesthetics of the beautiful" (29). Imagined beyond the domain of the "beautiful," the Fat Black Woman is not only socially displaced (for she is additionally excluded from the framework of respectability) but also politically displaced as a non-citizen.

Nichols's poem on beauty defiantly responds to fixity, to the "complete" body that models perfection. In this poem, beauty takes on another "unscripted" dimension, becoming synonymous with fatness, blackness, and womanness:

> Beauty
> is a fat black woman
> walking the fields
> pressing a breezed
> hibiscus
> to her cheek
> while the sun lights up
> her feet
>
> Beauty
> is a fat black woman
> riding the waves
> drifting in happy oblivion
> while the sea turns back
> to hug her shape
>
> (Nichols, *Fat Black Woman* 7)

Debunking conventional (colonial) paradigms of (white) female beauty, the Fat Black Woman redefines beauty, dismissing the material definition attributed to it as superficial. Extending the concept of beauty beyond the mere material/physical, the Fat Black Woman validates the natural and spiritual attributes of beauty that extend beyond a colonial geography to a tropical (Caribbean) landscape. In this decolonizing process, the Caribbean is reappropriated as the site of colonial occupation and conquest to a locale that fosters self-determination. The Fat Black Woman's acceptance in this tropical landscape can be accredited to a difference in cultural bodily requirements. Of this difference Andrea Shaw writes: "African Diaspora cultures have historically displayed a resistance to the idealization of slenderness evident in Westernized beauty contests" (6). Furthermore, the Fat Black Woman's autonomy is evident by the "sun [that] lights up her feet" as she navigates the hibiscus-filled fields at her leisure. Celebrating her (prized) difference and her freedom from the reins of societal (masculinist) conventions in this poem, the Fat Black Woman is at home (geographically and somatically) in her skin/body, poised for agency, action, and creative engagement with the world (Garland-Thomson, "Integrating Disability" 89). While the sea symbolizes a moment of turbulence that occasions the negation and obfuscation of the Fat Black Woman, she nevertheless, through perseverance and resistance, has withstood the test of time—an allusion to a symbiotic relationship with nature—"riding the waves / drifting in happy oblivion while the sea turns back / to hug her shape." Inclusion of the fat black body in the masculinist discourse as the normalized body challenges black female marginalization and refutes their non-citizen status. In this regard, citizenship is reimagined in its embrace of a more flexible, unscripted designation.

The existing symbiosis between the Fat Black Woman and nature is given further attention in the poem "Afterword," in which the Fat Black Woman articulates her wholesomeness. While alluding to the fact that she once shaped her own destiny (preslavery and precolonization), the Fat Black Woman promises a memorable homecoming: "[W]hen the wind pushes back the last curtain / of *male white blindness* / the fat black woman will emerge / and trembling fearlessly / stake her claim again" (Nichols, *Fat Black Woman* 24). This homecoming pays tribute to her once maligned past and her body. Mindful of the fact that some women are complicit with patriarchy in vilifying their bodies, the Fat Black Woman nevertheless calls attention to patriarchal interference that in great part accounts for women's self-betrayal. Despite the orchestrated oppression and subjugation entrenched in colonial paternalism, the Fat Black Woman remains hopeful as she prophesizes that with the collapse of white male supremacy the black female subject will make a triumphant resurgence. This disintegration of the seemingly impenetrable boundary of white male supremacy results in the collapse of the practice of exceptional citizenship.

Already we are witness to this self-reclamation as the Fat Black Woman has the last word.

The book's title, *The Fat Black Woman's Poems*, connotes voice and presence that are defined discursively, somatically, and racially. Furthermore, "unruliness and rebellion are implicit" in her physicality (Shaw 9). Despite the fact that rebellion and recalcitrance are clear markers of disqualification for citizenship, the Fat Black Woman performs the self, the body, whereby the articulated woman's body is imag(in)ed as a "performative instrument." Daphne Brooks asserts that the black woman's body as performative instrument is crucial to her sense of self and her identity as it provides a means to recuperate and recapture a narrative strategy where once marginalized black bodies are represented and made visible. Performance functions as a vehicle that enables the self to act both as performer and spectator (Brooks, "Deeds" 47–48). We witness the Fat Black Woman inhabiting this dual performer-spectator role that engenders the high/low, top/bottom, insider/outsider binary. This embodied/disembodied performance, which manifests in literal and figurative crisscrossing of borders and boundaries, finds expression in the poem "Looking at Miss World." Its title suggests the practice of exclusivity, of conditional citizenship, as Miss World is placed on a pedestal, raised above the Fat Black Woman's view even as her elevated status requires the Fat Black Woman's gaze (of passive admiration). Paradoxically, even as the title Miss World lends itself to all-inclusiveness, this intimation could not be further from the truth. In actuality, it advocates exceptionalism, promoting and validating a single, limited, and obviously racialized body.[4] In maintaining exceptional standards, the female aspirant is a paragon of chastity, virtue, and propriety, attributes that raise her stake as propertied possession, as trophy, and as potential wife and mother. In maintaining this aura of respectability, the contestant must demonstrate purity and virtuousness in her unmarried status. Susan Bordo reminds us that the "very first public act of second-wave feminist protest in the United States was the 'No More Miss America' demonstration in August 1986" that showcased an exceptional agenda that analyzed "the intersection of sexism, conformism, competition, ageism, racism, militarism, and consumer culture as they are constellated and crystallized in the pageant" ("Feminism" 249–50). In essence, the protest chronicled public (female) outrage and resistance to the preposterous physical requirements of the Miss America pageant.

These requirements strongly resonate with the compulsory demand that women wear a prosthesis after breast surgery. The prosthesis manifests artificiality as do the female apparel, including corsets that bodily and sexually restrain the normal white female body. At the same time, it exposed male chauvinism, commercialization of beauty, racism, and oppression of women symbolized by the pageant. Similarly, Shaw shares a few incidents of protests, one in which the spectators literally took matters into their own hands. A disenchanted Jamaican audience responded angrily when Lisa Mahfood, "a light-skinned, straight-haired Jamaican of Middle Eastern ancestry," won the 1986 Miss Jamaica beauty pageant, despite the country's predominant black population. The audience "erupted in shouts and jeers and hurled debris on the stage" (5).[5]

In like manner, the Fat Black Woman stages a verbal protest in "Looking at Miss World" as she fiercely interrogates the devaluation of blackness and the marginalization of the fat female subject. The first two stanzas of the poem read:

> The fat black woman
> is all agaze
> will some Miss (plump at least
> if not fat and black) uphold her name
> The fat black woman awaits in vain
> slim after slim aspirant appears
> baring her treasures in hopeful despair
> this the fat black woman can hardly bear.
>
> (Nichols, *Fat Black Woman* 20)

What the Fat Black Woman finds mystifying is not her assumed "unbearable weight," to borrow Bordo's coinage, but rather that she cannot bear to witness female complicity and the bodily assaults that the contestants inflict upon themselves.[6] This self-objectification renders them as nonpersons, as stateless. Furthermore, the homophonic use of the words *bear* and *bare* likens the intolerable disrobing of the contestants to a despicable act that exemplifies a lack of self-worth that compels the Fat Black Woman to read this body exposure as desperation as "slim after slim aspirant appears / baring her treasures in hopeful despair." The act of disrobing manifests itself clearly in the swimsuit competition of beauty pageants, a crucial and imperative component. Even so, the skin-tight, revealing gowns worn by the contestants give the allusion of disrobing. Amid this hopelessness, the Fat Black Woman is unable to reconcile that her body is deemed unacceptable (not light, not right, whereby light references both color and weight) by so-called European ideals that expose the supposed failure of the body "to meet some generalized aesthetic ideal, an ideal often molded from the matter of very specific bodies (in the given scenario, the contestants' slim, white bodies) that set the shifting standards for the whole" (McDowell 298). McDowell goes on to explain that coming to grips with this racial assault is one of the "most painful moments when our primordial desire to be desired is frustrated (or gratified) and our bodies take the credit or the blame" (298). Whereas the Fat Black Woman would welcome acceptance and appreciation, she nevertheless deflects the censure of the body onto the contestants, refuting this narrow, racialized description of female citizenship.

Craving societal (read male) acceptance, the female contestants exacerbate their own objectification and dehumanization as they become commodities ready for male consumption. Whereas they are the passive performers restricted within the male gaze and their man-made (pun intended) attire, the judges exercise unbridled freedom as they "mingl[e] with chiffons." In spite of this recreational pastime that requires suspension from judicial duties, they maintain their status quo, revered as judges and defined through official, judicial lenses. At the same time, they (white masculinity) stand outside the law. Although the *mingling* judges give the false sense of unrestricted movement, the female contestants under adjudication are paragons of femininity, discernible by their attire, chiffons, weight, and size. This regiment-like control of the body exercised by the contestant renders potent Cecilia Hartley's articulation that the female contestant is in obeisance with her sexual role of physical subordination to the man (62). The line "judges mingling with chiffons" reiterates male dominance even as it calls attention to the female contestants' material/peripheral existence, despite the western mainstream perception that these bodies portray "classic images of the finished, cleansed" (Bakhtin 25). By the same accord, it calls attention to the contestants' subordination as second-class citizens. While we bear witness to this all-pervasive male dominance, the pursuit of a "homogenizing, elusive ideal of femininity [requires that] female bodies become docile bodies—bodies whose forces and energies are habituated to external regulation, subjection, transformation, 'improvement'" (Bordo, *Unbearable Weight* 166). Laying bare the disabling factor within patriarchal conventions, Garland-Thomson points out that "Feminine cultural practices such as footbinding, clitorectomies, and corseting, as well as their less hyperbolic costuming rituals such as stiletto high heels, girdles, and chastity belts—impair women's bodies and restrict their physical agency, imposing disability on them" ("Integrating Disability" 89). Cynthia Wu expresses similar sentiments, revealing that these "compulsory forms of female disablement . . . ironically are socially enabling, increasing a woman's value and status" (250). Notwithstanding, the value remains conditional, as does her citizenship status.

By the same token, the chiffons signal sexual consumption: normally made of transparent material that frays easily, they connote easy access. Moreover, Nichols's use of chiffons is dualistic, referring to the lightweight fabric or to the attire made of chiffon. Either way, the persistent theme here is the composition of the textile that is of a very light, thin, sheer, plain-woven fabric. Margrit Shildrick and Janet Price contend that women subject themselves to the worst form of self-criticism as they often "police their own body, and report in intricate detail its failure to meet standards of normalcy; that [they] render [themselves] in effect transparent" (434). Likewise, the threadbare image of the chiffons captures the fragility of the contestants. Adversely, the body blame about which McDowell notes that some women take on because of the body's failure to attain the ideal could also affect the slim contestant, who if not crowned the beauty of beauties could perceive the slim white body as not meeting the established ideal or perception of beauty, leading to the onset of "body deficiency."[7] Even if not symptomatic of a deficient body, the chiffons worn by the female contestants in the Fat Black Woman's eyes mask an identity deficiency. Subsequently, being likened to chiffons made of plain-woven fabric, with emphasis on plain, the Fat Black Woman debunks the patriarchal (state) discourse that constructs the white contestant as the consummate beauty.

Marginalized racially, sexually, and physically, the Fat Black Woman is given no alternative but to adopt a subversive performative stance, performing her body into view and becoming the subject of her own discourse. In short, the Fat Black Woman is compelled to reconfigure citizenship on her own terms by "interven[ing] in the representation of her own body politics" (Brooks, "Deeds" 43). Furthermore, Daphne Brooks categorizes this moment as seizing "the potential of unruly performance to articulate heterogeneous identities," which in turn realize flexible citizenship (*Bodies* 4). Engaging a form of subversive theory, the Fat Black

Woman effectuates the dual imagery of excess and access. Whereas her assumed excess is diminished, devoid of spectatorship and articulated as nonexistent, the beauty contestants' public parading of their bodies calls attention to easy access. In other words, "white femininity [is] stripped of [its] arbitrary power" (Brooks, "Deeds" 63). Subsequently, normative femininity as manifested in the corseted bodies of the Miss World contestants is rejected by the Fat Black Woman. In equal manner, she refutes the current criteria for respectable female citizenship that involves the racialization and sexualization of the female body. In its (normative femininity) place, the Fat Black Woman proposes a divergent concept of beauty that not only contradicts European values and norms but also presents a threat to European perceptions of their own superiority.

Assuming the role of spectator, the Fat Black Woman disrupts the patriarchal order as she inducts herself into the judiciary chambers as the self-acclaimed adjudicator of both judges and contestants. In appointing herself the judge, the Fat Black Woman disrupts the neat narrative of white masculinity. However, this self-appointment witnesses the reconfiguration of the national discourse and the renegotiation of the criteria for citizenship. Furthermore, the Fat Black Woman draws an interesting parallel between female subordination and the requisite attire worn by the contestants: "o the night wears on / the night wears on / judges mingling with chiffons." Making a valid observation that the beauty contest has been reduced to a costume parade of sorts that witnesses the disembodiment of the female contestants, the Fat Black Woman intimates that the carnivalesque atmosphere equally *wears on* her patience: "And as the beauties yearn / the fat black woman wonders / when will the beauties ever really burn" (Nichols, *Fat Black Woman* 20). Demonstrating a lack of self-reliance exemplified by an innate need to be desired, the female contestant's performance nevertheless is impermanent; the Fat Black Woman is quick to accentuate this temporality, this suspension of reality, and their relinquishing of citizen rights. Capitalizing on this moment of inauthenticity and subordination, the Fat Black Woman crowns herself Miss World: "The fat black woman gets up / and pours some gin / toasting herself a likely win" (20). Herewith, we witness the debunking of lofty expectations of citizenship.

In the given scenario, the Fat Black Woman ruffles the patriarchal status quo, subverting law and order not simply by crowning herself Miss World but further by brazenly engaging in an "unladylike" or unworldly act, that of drinking gin. In so doing she de-sanitizes the pure and chaste image of the contestants. Moreover, the consumption of gin challenges the boundaries of respectability; in this manner, the Fat Black Woman's refusal to uphold a respectable femininity results in the displacement/disfigurement of the ideal white female (body). At the same time, toasting herself a likely win with gin, the Fat Black Woman invokes laughter, a form of grotesque realism that in Bakhtin's words "degrades and materializes" (20). Bakhtin goes on to explain that the "praise-mockery complex" is present in "toasts and festive speeches" (286). Within this theoretical framework, gin shares a common feature with wine in that it "liberates from fear and sanctimoniousness" (286).[8] Offering a similar but equally enlightening analogy, Bakhtin emphasizes that "in the act of eating the confines between the body and the world are overstepped by the body; it triumphs over the world, over its enemy, celebrates its victory at the world's expense" (282–83). Gin, in the given situation, engenders this analogous act of consumption. Furthermore, assuming the role of spectator, the Fat Black Woman subverts the male gaze as she now renders judgment against those who wrongfully judged and convicted her as a result of her physical and racial difference. The poem's title, "Looking at Miss World," is inverted as the gaze turned within is introspective, functioning as a celebration of the self that becomes manifest in the Fat Black Woman's self-coronation accompanied by the toast. Excluded from the diasporic community that only grants citizenship to white contestants, exemplified in the coronation of the white models, the Fat Black Woman has no choice but to forge an identity independent of the national identity.[9] By crowning herself Miss World, the Fat Black Woman carves a coveted (black) female space for herself within the racially biased white constructed space, declaring herself a desirable citizen (of the world).

The Fat Black Woman registers her verbal disagreement of regimented body management, and she voices bodily displeasure, clearly manifested in the poem "Invitation." To some degree, the title captures the inherent ambivalence inhabited by the Fat Black Woman/body. Sumi Colligan reiterates this ambivalence in her assertion that the Fat Black Woman's body "serve[s] as a cultural template for social order and disorder" (57). By virtue of its physical (nonconforming, deviant) appearance, the Fat Black Woman's body embodies resistance that finds additional articulation in the poem. Furthermore, "Invitation" is a misnomer on two counts. First, the "invitation" is articulated in a tongue-in-cheek gesture. Second, the

Fat Black Woman unequivocally articulates that her body is not public property and therefore is not open or available to public (male) access or consumption: "If my fat / was too much for me / I would have told you / I would have gone jogging / even when it was fogging" (Nichols, *Fat Black Woman* 12). Mindful of the benefits of diet and exercise, even as she explicitly challenges the normalizing role (of diet and exercise) and simultaneously resists the ideal of slenderness, the Fat Black Woman fiercely interrogates the politics of normalization that upholds the western white female body as the standard by which all other bodies are measured. Objectionably, her unruly and grotesque body is the subject of spontaneous assumptions, assumptions that characterize her as "ugly, monstrous, hideous from the point of view of 'classic' aesthetics, that is, the aesthetics of the ready-made and the completed" (Bakhtin 25). Offering a parallel analysis, Hartley illustrates the scathing characterization accorded fat women who are labeled "ugly, bad, and not valuable because they are in violation of so many of the rules" (66). Shedding light on this body craze, Bordo eloquently conveys that body management becomes an obsessive behavioral practice: "Through the exacting and normalizing disciplines of diet, makeup, and dress we are rendered less socially oriented and more centripetally focused on self-modification. Through these disciplines, we continue to memorize on our bodies the feel and conviction of lack, of insufficiency, of never being good enough" (*Unbearable Weight* 166). This ready-made and finished image posits the female body, envisioned through the lens of Victorian ideal and aesthetics, as a locus of control and desire, an image that is oppositional to the Fat Black Woman's identity formation. As Shaw reminds us, her fatness and blackness are already encoded, "understood as denoting bodily indiscipline and rebellion" (50). Along these lines, the unruly body does not constitute ideal citizenship.

While underscoring that chastity and sexual restraints are the hallmark of Victorian aesthetics of beauty and propriety, Bordo, expounding on Bakhtin's idea of existing classed distinctions between the grotesque and the "classic," draws attention to the fact that body management is suffused with issues of morality. As she succinctly puts it, when "associations of fat and lower-class status exist, they are usually mediated by moral qualities—fat being perceived as indicative of laziness, lack of discipline, unwillingness to conform" (*Unbearable Weight* 195). In a similar light, Bordo remarks that "excess body weight [is often] seen as reflecting moral or personal inadequacy" (192). In the ensuing discussion, this chapter examines how laziness is encoded and replicated within the parameters of blackness.

The unapologetic, defiant stance that the Fat Black Woman adopts against normalization, against disciplinary control of the body, lends itself to further hostility that the fat individual already inspires (Bordo, *Unbearable Weight* 203). Moira Gatens acquiesces that "women who step outside their allotted place in the body politic are frequently" the subjects of verbal abuse and are reduced to their "sex," resulting in the treatment of woman's "speech and behavior as hysterical" (84). This hysteria is regarded as a "physical disorder." In this fashion, the Fat Black Woman's monstrosity is concretized by her excess, the same way Baartman's is. Nevertheless, she resists being reduced to her sex; instead, she transcends established patriarchal norms and transgresses boundaries. Using her body as text, the Fat Black Woman demands that it be read on its own terms, all the while refuting its delegitimization based on the presumption of a controlled and contained white female sexuality and resultant white citizenship.

In an extremely symbolic gesture, the Fat Black Woman debunks the myth of a pure and chaste white femininity by invoking the highly suggestive question, "Why don't you come up sometime and see me?" turn declaration, "come up and see me sometime," of Brooklyn-born actress and author Mae West, known for her sexual debauchery and ribald humor.[10] The first section of the poem "Invitation" ends with the final line: "Come up and see me sometime." This same line opens the second section of the poem and serves as its final line. Repetition here has its discursive value, as the opening and closing lines serve as prelude and postlude to the Fat Black Woman's elusive sexuality that is upheld between these lines. She tantalizingly informs potential suitors that her breasts call to mind "huge exciting / amnions of watermelon" that are ungraspable; the "twin seals" that are representative of her thighs exemplify slipperiness indicative of inaccessibility (Nichols, *Fat Black Woman* 13). Laced with sexual overtones, the Fat Black Woman's embrace of her sexuality and sensuality symbolizes her resistance to female oppression, her refutation of the chaste, white, ideal body and citizen. Unsurprisingly, in "Invitation" sexuality and female power converge to create a potent self-affirming concoction. Promoting the idea that the Fat Black Woman flirts with stereotypical representations as a means to engage subversive politics, Cooper's insightful concept of "slackness" proves to be very instructive.

Employing the theory of *slackness* to interpret and analyze Jamaican dancehall culture, Cooper pays careful attention to the overt feminization and sexualization of the word that "has almost exclusively sexual overtones and is synonymous with licentiousness" (*Sound Clash* 2). Cooper nevertheless contends that although the "license in the English licentiousness is often repressed in its Jamaican equivalent... the censure remains" (2). Furthermore, extending the discourse on slackness beyond the sexual, Cooper argues that it "can be much more permissively theorized as a radical, underground confrontation with the patriarchal gender ideology and the duplicitous morality of fundamentalist Jamaican society" (3). She later adds: "Slackness is not mere sexual looseness, though it certainly is that. Slackness is a contestation of conventional definitions of law and order; an undermining of consensual standards of decency. At large, slackness is the antithesis of restrictive uppercase Culture. It thus challenges rigid status quo of social exclusivity and one-sided moral authority" (3–4).

As evidenced, slackness shares commonalities with the "grotesque." Both the "grotesque" and the "slack/loose" body are contested sites of disgust and desire, unworthy of citizenship. Thus engendering slackness challenges the arbitrarily imposed status quo, as it aids in the realization of self-autonomy. This collection of poems, and particularly the poem under discussion, becomes a discursive space that fosters free and uninhibited performance of female sexuality. More broadly, it accommodates an alternative identity that does not adhere to the highly repressive and authoritarian patriarchal ideology. Consequently, exerting control over her body, the Fat Black Woman breaks free from the oppressive gender ideology of female property and propriety.

Emulating Mae West's irreverence, her sexually charged language and persona, the Fat Black Woman effectively challenges societal assumptions about race, gender, and class. As Hartley has observed, the presence of the Fat Black Woman is evidence of her defiance and assumed power that "she has not submitted to the rules that society has established for feminine behavior. Overtly, her body shape may be a result of a conscious rejection of societal and cultural norms" (66). As discussed earlier, the Fat Black Woman rejects western beauty norms and constructions of race. In bolstering this line of reasoning, she therefore regards her body not simply as a hallmark of subordination but rather as a source of both pleasure and empowerment. Ever resistant, the Fat Black Woman does not fall prey to the bodily self-indictment that Hartley references. Offering an adverse reading of female (body) empowerment, Hartley explains that overt self-representation could be an act to mask reality, hidden compliance with the so-called standards. She writes: "More insidiously, that body may also be a result of years of dieting and refeeding in attempts to achieve the ideal form" (66–67).

Effectively, the Fat Black Woman refuses to succumb to societal pressure. She rejects the idea of dieting and jogging, an act that signals her noncompliance with patriarchal mandates that set the standards for, as well as polices, female bodily requirements. Her celebration of self-love equally serves as an invitation cum indictment to the critics to look beyond the (visceral) body, a baseless engagement that not only lends itself to unwarranted discrimination and marginalization of certain subjects but also debases the critics themselves (in stature, aspiration, and reasoning). The words *come up* in the line "come up and see me sometimes" fiercely challenge if not dismantle strict, seamless class boundaries, placing the former "highbrow" critics, now declassified, on a (subversive) quest for social standing and upward mobility. The words also allude to clandestine sexual escapades with which the lofty critics are engaged. Bakhtin's theory of hierarchy inversion is successfully at play here, as is the "crownings and uncrownings" motif (104).

As intimated earlier, Nichols engages the politics of satiety, an allusion to the Fat Black Woman's unquenchable hunger for both food and sex; symbolically, the two-part poem captures this duality. As Shaw readily reminds us, the image of the fat woman is one that is "eternally hungry, possessing a voracious appetite," which in turn is implicit in a ravenous sexual appetite (50). Angela Stukator reemphasizes this argument as she ascertains that "hunger has always been a cultural metaphor for female sexuality, desire, and power" (199). The celebration of excess, grossness, and the uncontainable is subject to intense public scrutiny and sustained ridicule, and Garland-Thomson reveals that society, with relative ease, overlooks the "ideal" body that performs "excessive femininity" ("Integrating Disability" 89).[11] Given the fact that Nichols's Fat Black Woman does not embellish or emphasize her fatness as bodily extravagance, her body nevertheless remains a site of conflict and contest, portrayed as freakish. One of the many loose and wide-ranging definitions assigned to the freakish body is "the embodiment of corporeal insufficiency and deviance" (Garland-Thomson, *Extraordinary Bodies* 6). Garland-Thomson points out that the freakish body is not necessarily afflicted with a physical disability. Rather, these bodies are often "interpret[ed] metaphorically and aesthetically" (9). As argued earlier, the Fat Black Woman's freakishness stems from her "excess flesh," which challenges and disrupts the neat narrative of white femininity. Furthering this disruption of normative standards, in a subversive play, the "ideal" body is de-normalized, its deficiency exposed. Performing her "excess flesh" in protest, the fat black woman engages in self-indulgence, the kind habitually equated not with compulsive eating but rather with excessive love for the self.

The Fat Black Woman's celebration of her sexuality evokes memories of a tumultuous past—slavery—defined by pervasive desexualization of her black female counterparts. We may recall that Sojourner Truth was forced to bare her breasts to an all-white, predominantly male crowd that had doubts about her gender, and so they challenged her to prove that she was female. Along similar lines, the Fat Black Woman's proverbial baring of her large breasts (emphasis on large here) stresses inaccessibility, a stark contrast to the easy (read forced) access to the black female body during slavery.[12] Concomitantly, she "transform[s] her corporeality into a contested terrain of social and cultural consumption," an act that Brooks defines as "restrategiz[ing] the public spectacle of [the] body through performance politics" ("Deeds" 49). Therefore, the image of the huge breasts is one that invokes and resists the Mammy image and repudiates the notion of the black woman as consummate nurturer and caretaker. Nichols eloquently articulates this refutation in the poem "The Fat Black Woman Remembers." Remembering her "Mama and them days of playing the Jovial Jemima," the Fat Black Woman, relying on personal and collective memory, recounts the oppression through domestication and asexualization to which she was subject (*Fat Black Woman* 9). Referencing the "happy hearty murderous blue laughter" of her mama as she "toss[es] pancakes to heaven," the Fat Black Woman calls attention to the required guile that the black slave woman had to assume as survival strategy. Furthering this line of reasoning, Deborah Gray White offers a lucid assessment of slave women's astuteness, suggesting that they not only "understood the value of silence and secrecy" but they also "deliberately dissemble their objective reality. Like all who are dependent upon the caprices of a master, they hide their real sentiments and turn toward him a changeless smile or enigmatic impassivity" (24). In like manner, the image of the "Jovial Jemima" draws on the historical representation of the happy, contented, and docile slave that in Diane Roberts's assessment exemplifies "the mythic Old South of benign slavery, grace, and abundance" (1).

Conclusively, White summarizes that masking was a necessary strategy adopted by slave women "in order to protect valued parts of their lives from white and male invasion" (24).

Even as she memorializes the quintessential Mammy figure, Aunt Jemima, the Fat Black Woman asserts that she is not a "stolen woman": "This fat black woman ain't no Jemima / Sure thing Honey / Yeah" (Nichols, *Fat Black Woman* 9).[13] As feminist critic Patricia Hill Collins cogently observes, "Created to justify the economic exploitation of house slaves and sustained to explain Black women's long-standing restriction to domestic service, the mammy image represents the normative yardstick used to evaluate all Black women's behavior" (*Black Feminist Thought* 72). Refusing to be held captive to the past, the Fat Black Woman avoids being pigeonholed as asexual or hypersexual, despite the fact that she "occupies personal territory in ways that violate the rules for the sexual politics of body movement" (Hartley 66). Rejecting codification and commodification of the black body, the Fat Black Woman invalidates the belief that her "desirability stems from . . . alleged sexual willingness and availability" (Wyatt 29–30). This invalidation manifests in the Fat Black Woman satirizing another stereotype, Jezebel, the sexually promiscuous and controlling woman.

Moreover, the term *honey*, which encapsulates the domestic and the celebratory (*honey* doubles as a term of endearment) pays belated tribute to Mammy, validating her invaluable domestic service. Asserting unequivocally that Mammy performed her role as domestic servant honorably and selflessly, the Fat Black Woman reminds us that whereas Mammy dutifully tended to "little white heads," she forcibly "[fed] her own children on Satanic bread" (Nichols, *Fat Black Woman* 9). Yet within Mammy radiates a doggedness of spirit that Gail Wyatt summarizes in the following manner:

> Mammy was . . . an obese, domesticated, asexual house slave with a world of wisdom, the patience of Job, a heart of gold, and the willingness to breastfeed the world. She was a good woman because she was self-sacrificing when it came to the well-being of white families, especially the children, whom she often raised. (31)

Nevertheless, White reminds us that contrary to widespread belief, slave women "were not submissive, subordinate, or prudish" (22).[14] Reinforcing Mammy's resolute character, Barbara Christian expounds upon this discourse: "Unlike the white southern image of mammy, she is cunning, prone to poisoning her master, and not at all content with her lot. Mammies kicked, fought, connived, plotted, most often covertly, to throw off the chains of bondage" (*Black Feminist Criticism* 5). Paying special tribute to Mammy's indomitable maternal quality, Christian is quick to remind us that "Mammy saw herself as a mother, but to her that role embodied a certain dignity and responsibility, rather than a physical debasement, doubtless a carry-over from the African view that every mother is a symbol of marvelous creativity of the earth" (5).

While not categorically denouncing the institution of motherhood, the Fat Black Woman expresses reservations about women being regarded as vessels of procreation. The following pronouncement sums it up: "Men who only see / a spring of children / in her thighs / when there are mountains / in her mites" (Nichols, *Fat Black Woman* 14). She also challenges the conventional belief that marriage and pregnancy/procreation go hand-in-hand, referring to the lure of marriage as entrapment, an idea proficiently exemplified in the title of the poem "Trap Evasions." The oxymoronic title foreshadows the subsequent cautionary message: "bride ties. grave lies." More specifically, the Fat Black Woman takes issue with the limitations placed on the domestic and the maternal, with the substitution of one for the other. Responding to this shortsightedness, she counters that women's worth transcends their domestic, procreative capability. Having "mountains in her mites" connotes an indomitable spirit and resiliency, invaluable character traits to which White and Christian earlier lend voice. True to her conviction, the Fat Black Woman disapproves of imposed domesticity of mothers and motherhood. By the same token, she rejects marriage and motherhood as the only redemptive paths to the black woman's self-realization. Furthermore, linking "bride ties" with (natural) disasters such as "bushswamps/quicksands/cesspits" illuminates the inhumane and devastating effect of male oppression. Even more telling is the inclusion of "treadmills" to the list as one of many traps to evade. The synthesis of these words further reinforces the catastrophic consequences of male tyranny.

The Fat Black Woman identifies politics as the site of tyranny, as politicians in pursuit of their political aspirations will go to extreme lengths to maintain their position of power. The snake oil tactic that they use to entice supporters resonates powerfully with their role as impostors. This predator/prey relationship is subverted, wherein the fat black woman who "could see through politicians like snake sees through rat" assumes the predatory role (Nichols, *Fat Black Woman* 22). The Fat Black Woman infuses the (elevated) political space with the language of the market place—engendering the dethroning of the politicians and the suspension of power—as she verbally indicts the politicians for not only engaging in corrupt practices but also for practicing nepotism. Stallybrass and White demonstrate that the marketplace is where the unsettling of fixed identities occurs, transformed by other non-local identities. Here is where we witness a "commingling of categories usually kept separate and apart." She regards this brand of politics—the practice of nepotism—as oppositional, resolutely deciding not to partake of this political discourse since it entails compromising her identity, her citizen status: "The fat black woman won't be their lover" (22). In other words, the Fat Black Woman refuses to have her body function metonymically as the site of political conflict and competition; she refuses to reproduce the nation. The poem's title communicates her uncompromising stance: "The Fat Black Woman versus Politics." Ensuring that she does not fall victim to the imposed silence (of corruption and tyranny), the fat black woman interrogates the patriarchal institutions that enforce and benefit from women's marginalization, threatening "to feed powercrazy politicians a manifesto of lard" (22). Countering patriarchal authority, this threat additionally elucidates the deficit, the proverbial hunger for trustworthy ideas.

In enforcing tyrannical ideals, patriarchy discursively imprisons women, relegating them to the margins of society. By centering her "excess flesh" as a part of the larger body politic, the Fat Black Woman exposes social and racial injustice. Unmistakably, this injustice is palpably and visibly inscribed on the body of the Fat Black Woman's namesake, Saartjie Baartman.[15] Since the first chapter offers an account of Baartman's history, here references will be made only in relation to her shared or parallel hypervisibility with the Fat Black Woman. Her "protruding" buttocks that go "beyond the body's confines" attest to her inhabiting a grotesque body (Bakhtin 316). In like manner, fat is a bodily protrusion. Along these lines, both Baartman and the Fat Black Woman inhabit the freakish body. Moreover, Baartman was labeled a freak of nature; her imprisonment in a cage completed this image. Further, the cage both amplified and contained her freakish body. Conversely, the Fat Black Woman retrieves this body part from the freakish domain, suggesting that it is anything but freakish; linking it instead to heritage: "There's a mole that gets a ride / each time I shift the heritage / of my behind" (*Fat Black Woman* 13). In this scene, the

Fat Black Woman posits her "behind" as unruly, resisting being silenced, contrasting the still, chiffon-clad, docile body of the earlier-referenced beauty contestants. This resistance manifests additionally through constant repetitions of the word *steatopygous,* which celebrates excess (and difference), and at the same time normalizes the term, substantiating its inclusion in the larger political discourse. The morphological insertion of the term *steatopygous* before the words *sky, sea,* and *waves* that precedes the Fat Black Woman's bodily insertion: "Steatopygous sky / Steatopygous sea / Steatopygous waves / Steatopygous me" validates and reinforces this process of normalization and expands the parameters of citizenship (15). By the same accord, this insertion symbolically reinstates Baartman into the nation and, by default, the national discourse as a reputable citizen.

Nichols's satirizing the British hierarchy is indisputable. Notably, the lengthy title of the poem "Thoughts drifting through the Fat Black Woman's head while having a full bubble bath" enacts "double" satire, so to speak. Describing how journalists capitalized on the opportunity to poke fun at "native English culture," Rachel Holmes narrates that William, the fourth Duke of Queensbury, also known as Old Q, was known for taking baths "daily in a silver bath filled with milk." Prior to his death, he invited Saartjie to his mansion where, in an imagined scene, she bathed in his tub, "slip[ping] into his tub in a posture of submission, to the duke's delight" (44–46). Contrastingly, Nichols's "double satire" positions the Fat Black Woman in a fulsome posture ("having a full bubble bath") of resistance and defiance. The word *full* also pays tribute to her fleshly body, while the bath in which she indulges challenges her presumed impurity. Addressing her historical silencing, the Fat Black Woman aims to commit a parallel evil of silencing the "makers" of history as she "long[s] to place [her] foot / on the head of anthropology / to swing [her] breasts / in the face of history / to scrub [her] back / with the dogma of theology" (Nichols, *Fat Black Woman* 15). Acquiescing with this line of reasoning, bell hooks ascertains that this act challenges "assumptions that the black body, its skin color and shape, is a mark of shame" (*Black Looks* 63). Additionally, hooks makes a poignant observation that buttocks are ignored because "they are associated with undesirable and unclean acts. [They] signif[y] animalistic sexuality" (64, 70). For Debra Walker King, "'Incarnation' of racial stereotypes and claims of 'animalistic humanity' [are] coded through skin color, or race" (11). Moreover, this poem, without equivocation, testifies to the continued fascination with black women's bodies, specifically their buttocks, or as Debra Singer puts it, the continued "fetishization of the black female body within the white imagination of Western culture" (94). Baartman serves as a classic example of the fetishized. Rachel Holmes attests to this continued fascination: "Britain was a nation obsessed by buttocks, bums, arses, posteriors, derrières, and every possible metaphor, joke, or pun that could be squeezed from this fundamental cultural obsession" (43).[16] Further acknowledging the existing ambivalent relationship, she remarks: "England both exuberantly celebrated and earnestly deplored excess, grossness, and the uncontainable" (43).

Stukator points out that one of the ways to contain the threat posed by the unruly fat woman is to construct her as a "comic spectacle" (198). This comic spectacle is akin to freak shows, a characterization reiterated by Garland-Thomson, who in underscoring the performative aspect of beauty pageants and freak shows categorizes them as "all related forms of representation grounded in the conventions of spectacle" (*Extraordinary Bodies* 12). This assessment holds true for Baartman, whose tragic theatrical display to European audience shares commonalities with beauty pageants. In both cases women are expendable, they are constructed as a commodity for male consumption, and their bodies function as the site upon which voyeuristic desires are mapped. Besides, it is public knowledge that the event "is dedicated and indebted to an ideology that constructs women through the discourses of sexual exploitation" (Banet-Weiser 146). So hooks sheds additional light on this topic whereby she contends that inscribing women as spectacle is disempowering; it symbolizes a deprivation of female agency. Offering a race-specific assessment of the threat that the unruly woman poses, she centers race as a looming menace that must be erased. Accordingly, this threat is neutralized by superimposing whiteness onto blackness, "whiteness dominates . . . obscuring and erasing the possibility of any assertion of black power" (*Black Looks* 71). This superimposition of whiteness onto blackness is a common practice in beauty pageants as articulated earlier.

In a similar gesture, addressing the race-based demonization of Baartman, Nicholas Hudson confirms that "the spectacle of the 'Hottentot Venus,' both on stage and on the dissecting table, provided an outlet for public scrutiny of female sexuality sanctioned by the fact that this female was black, not white, and could therefore be treated either as a freakshow or scientific specimen" (24). Along parallel lines, hooks asserts that when "flesh is exposed in attire that is meant to evoke sexual desirability it is worn by a non-white model" (*Black Looks* 72). Baartman, who was tightly clad in a skintight outfit that gave the appearance of nudity, clearly a reinforcement of her sexual victimization, serves as a classic example. As Hudson has suggested, Baartman's stage name, Venus, functioned as a tool of exploitation as a means to "exploit connections between Venus and female desirability in the popular imagination" (21). Baartman also evoked disgust. Her buttocks, which were a source of pleasure and entertainment, were equally regarded as a site of disgust, a lack of moral discipline exemplified by "the jiggling of her fleshly buttocks... [that] signaled her lack of control over the 'physical'" (Hudson 34). This blatant exposure of deviance opposes the mores of respectability, serving as a disqualifier for citizenship.

However, offering a subversive reading of Baartman's body, her exploitation, I would like to argue that her bodily exposure "accentuates the masquerade of femininity and exposes the contradictions in the ideology of 'true femininity'" (Stukator 197). Hudson validates this posturing as he remarks that "there was more in common between the Hottentot Venus and her Caucasian sisters than was suggested by the mockery of Saartje Baartman" (35). Essentially, Hudson unsettles the notion of the "ideal" female citizen and challenges the imposed borders and boundaries on the path to citizenship. As follows, this study extends this argument by reasoning that Baartman's "bodily" exposure serves as a counter narrative to the one within which her white counterparts were scripted. Existing within the confines of white femininity—constructed and mandated by patriarchal authority—these individuals reinforce the code of proper breeding and conduct, exemplary of the ideal citizen. Baartman's excess flesh on the other hand is undisciplined, resists being controlled, and as a result poses a threat to male power; it also imperils Victorian ideals of decency and order. It is quite interesting that while the female body is expected to adhere to high moral and aesthetic standards, the enforcers of this ridiculous ideal were themselves woefully lacking: "the male mind and body were themselves at odds, attracted and repelled at once by the flesh that men both love in its quivering undiscipline and sought to control" (35).

Furthermore, Baartman's explicit sexual fleshly exposure has a pornographic ring to it that calls to mind perversion. Nevertheless, it is not the kind of perversion mundanely mapped on to the black female body, but rather a perversion of male voyeurs feeding their perverted fantasies and repressed desires. Locating female "body exposure" within a larger framework, Singer dutifully reminds us that "images of naked women also served as a kind of substitute pornography" (93). Likewise, the continued exposure of Baartman's body parts posthumously has additional significance. Carole Boyce Davies reminds us that "[i]n pornography, one of the standard tropes is that women's bodies are dismembered, reduced to parts for easy consumption" ("Carnivalized" 334). Critic Sarah Banet-Weiser adds another critical piece to this analysis in revealing that historically "the black female body is almost always constructed as sexual, or as 'pornographic'—in relation to the chaste, respectable, white female body" (145). Moreover, Baartman's exposure foregrounds "historically powerful narratives about black women and sexuality . . . about insatiable and 'indefensible' black female sexuality" (150). By this accord, she is constructed as a sexually viable commodity that witnesses the silencing of other forms of self-representation. Pornography promotes systematic sexualization of the subordination of woman (Cornell 37). Predominantly men have fanned and fed the flames of pornography; it is therefore no mystery that these images are created in the name of male desire and consumption. Andrea Dworkin takes up this argument by remarking that the overarching goal of pornographers is to exact pleasure by any means necessary. Herewith she substantiates this claim: "Erotic pleasure for men is derived from and predicated on the savage destruction of women" (41).

Offering a viable distinction between pornography and the erotic, Lorde surmises that the erroneous coupling of the two concepts has shamed woman into suppressing their sexuality: "The erotic has often been misnamed by men and used against women. It has been made into the confused, the trivial, the psychotic, the plasticized sensation. For this reason, we have often turned away from the exploration and consideration of the erotic as a source of power and information, confusing it with its opposite, the pornographic" ("Uses" 54). Laying this blame directly at the foot of patriarchy, Lorde establishes that patriarchal authority has conditioned our minds (and bodies) to suffocate our feeling "in order to exercise it in the service of men. . . . So women are maintained at a distant/inferior position to be psychically milked, much the same way ants maintain colonies of aphids to provide a life-giving substance for their masters" (54). As a means to counter this misrepresentation and suppression of the erotic, Lorde offers an alternative course: "the erotic offers a well of replenishing and provocative force to the woman who does not fear its revelation" (54).

As evidenced, the overriding criticism leveled against pornography by many critics is that representation of female eroticism is often relegated to male-centered sex fantasy. Responding to this charge, Nichols eroticizes difference in her poetry collection, *Lazy Thoughts of a Lazy Woman*.[17] The erotic finds full expression in the disorderly behavior that the Fat Black Woman perpetuates, for Lorde reminds us that "our erotic knowledge empowers us, becomes a lens through which we scrutinize all aspects of our existence, forcing us to evaluate those aspects honestly in terms of their relative meaning within our lives. And this is a grave responsibility, projected from within each of us, not to settle for the convenient, the shoddy, the conventionally expected, nor the merely safe" ("Uses" 57). Accentuating the unruliness—undoubtedly a marker of female agency—that the Fat Black Woman embodies, Nichols creates her counterpart in the Lazy Woman, engaging an interesting confluence of fatness, blackness, and laziness. This racial troping of the black subject as lazy is historically entrenched in slavery, whereby slaves were regarded by their masters as lazy. Laziness was not necessarily applied to a biological condition, but was deeply ascribed to racial and class prejudices; laziness therefore was well established within the paradigm of the uncivilized and uncultured, a marker of inferior status. Ascribing a gendered definition to the concept of laziness, Davies reflects that for black women the notion "occupies an existence on the semiotic plain that challenges colonialist/racist critiques of blacks as lazy and redirects the political implications of laziness for both women and black people, on whose backs and with whose labor capitalist erections took place" ("Carnivalized" 344). Bordo earlier makes known that fat carries a presupposition of laziness. Concomitantly, Shaw points out that the Fat Black Woman's corpulence "codes her as a repository of latent energy" (9).

Nichols's painstaking engagement with the erotic leaves little doubt as the Lazy Woman exhibits immeasurable self-confidence. While many of the poems appear to have an impersonal, detached guise to them, this detachment is a discursive strategy that buttresses the theory of laziness. The first poem of the collection, "Dust," serves as a perfect example. Dust, most likely has accumulated as a result of a lack of cleaning. Rather than commit to maintaining a certain desirable standard of cleanliness (read purity), the lazy woman contends that "[d]ust has a right to settle / [m]ilk the right to curdle" (Nichols, *Lazy Thoughts* 3). Defiling the pure and chaste image of female decorum, "[s]cum and fungi are rich words" (3). Bakhtin reassures us that "grotesque satire consists in the exaggeration of the improper" (307). Measuring the obsession with normative standards as engaging in the act of defilement of the unruly body, the lazy woman articulates that "those who scrub and scrub . . . and dust and dust / incessantly / corrupt the body" (*Lazy Thoughts* 4–5).[18] This corruption of the body engenders self-effacement.

In the poem "Grease," the Lazy Woman plays out an eroticized role in which she celebrates female sexuality, removing the shame with which it is associated. Hence grease, despite its unclean (polluted) characteristic, becomes a liberating concept by means of which the Lazy Woman "assert[s] the freedom to play out eroticized roles that may not ordinarily be available to [her] in the rigid social conventions of the everyday" (Cooper, *Sound Clash* 17). In accordance with societal conventions, female sexuality is influenced by the notions of purity and pollution, a fact to which the Lazy Woman is quite responsive, prompting her to challenge this purity-pollution binary. Consequently, she performs her body beyond the locus of male control. In the (masculine) stead, grease "that steals in like a lover / over the body of [her] oven / [and] kisses the knobs of [her] stove" becomes her lover personified. Grease paradoxically is not the source of pollution, but it provides appreciated pleasure as it "caresse[s] the skin / and every crease," undeniably confirming that it is "having an affair with me" (Nichols, *Lazy Thoughts* 3). Additionally, the celebration cum eroticization of body excretions is symptomatic of a carnivalesque atmosphere. In tandem, "the grotesque carnival body . . . is articulated as social pleasure and celebration" (Stallybrass and White 183). For that reason, "the vulgar" does not symbolize degradation; instead, it engenders celebration. In essence, grease is a reassuring presence.

Envisioning her body through the lens of the polluted, the Lazy Woman performs an offensive, aberrant act whereby she contaminates the pure and chaste image of white femininity and womanhood. This contamination occasions chaos and disorder, as Mary Douglas points out: "Dirt is essentially disorder . . . it offends against order. . . . In chasing dirt, in papering, decorating, tidying, we are not governed by anxiety to escape disease, but are positively re-ordering our environment, making it conform to an idea" (3). Unmistakably, the Lazy Woman is not governed by conventions, and therefore not vying for the role of the ideal citizen. The personification/de-personification of grease and her body simultaneously challenges and blurs the lines between the sexual and the domestic. The conjunction of sex and/in the kitchen defies order in that it transforms the domestic space into a sexual one, attesting to the willful abandonment of culinary undertakings for sexual gratification. This conflation lends itself to flexible identities.

By a similar accord, the blurring of the domestic and the sexual elicits another but equally interesting interpretation. Even as it gives voice to bodily (sexual) freedom, the domestic (domestication) functions as a site of creative energy. In her exploration of female empowerment, Paule Marshall shares a personal anecdote where the "Mother Poets," a term she used to refer to her mother and female friends, who despite being situated in the assumed confines of the kitchen, give powerful voice to their poetic expressions (*Reena* 4). The kitchen therefore functions as a sanctuary, insulated from patriarchal impositions and censorship, and a site that promotes the practice of flexible female citizenship. This reconfiguration contradicts the masculinist definition of the woman-citizen as second class, as subordinate.

In an ironic twist, grease symptomatic of hard toil, whether physical or sexual, starkly contrasts with the picture of laziness. Theoretically, the lazy body epitomizes a docile body. Intimating that grease is a corollary to sweat (resulting from grueling labor), Bordo effectively recollects "representations of sweating, glistening bodies belonging to black slaves and prizefighters" (*Unbearable Weight* 195). Furthermore, the likening of slaves with sweat calls attention to their dehumanization, their denial of personhood and citizen rights. Besides, we witness once more the blurring of the lines—in this instance, between pain and pleasure.

The suspension of hierarchical rank, norms, and prohibitions is further depicted in the poem "Who Was It," which interrogates normative (body) standards and responds in kind to the threat meted out to transgressors. According special attention to the management and discipline of female bodies, the Lazy Woman wonders out loud who "introduced the hairless habit," vowing to "not defoliage [her] forests [and] let the hairline of the bikini / be fringed with indecency" (Nichols, *Lazy Thoughts* 6). Normalization of female conduct is imprinted onto a homogeneous femininity that requires self-erasure, exemplified by shaving the armpits and the genitalia. Many of the beauty products originally manufactured did not cater to or take into consideration black women's skin type, an oversight, whether deliberate or not, that promoted a normative (white) standard of beauty. This implied definition of beauty bears strong resonance with beauty pageants. Imam and other black models addressed this lapse in vision as their cosmetic products accommodated all black women's skin types. Further, this self-erasure manifests potently in the discursive presence of the cosmetic tycoons Mary Kay, Estée Lauder, and Helena Rubenstein, who are/were staunch advocates of female body discipline that requires women to routinely sanitize and/or to glamorize the unclean body. Notably, their presence attests to female complicity in enforcing rigorous bodily restrictions and management. In equal manner, self-erasure has a disabling, deformed effect that in the given scene is subversively deflected onto the body of the beauty moguls, resulting in the distortion, punning, and parodying of their names/bodies. "Cant" as in "O Mary Cant," the abbreviated "Laud" in Estée Lauder's last name, and the parodying of Helena Rubenstein's name as in "O Helena Frankinstein" are evocative of defiance, the refusal to conform, which in turn signals rejection of the code of normalcy (6). Moreover, this discursive protest, on one hand, substantiates women's acceptance of subordinate, conditional citizenship, and on the other, challenges women to fashion the discourse of citizenship, free of patriarchal compulsions. These distortions also have an uncanny resemblance to bodily transformations cum violations occasioned by cosmetic surgery that is discussed at length in chapter 2.

Additionally, the word *Frankinstein*, which carries a noticeable misspelling where the letter *e* is replaced with an *i*, demands further analysis. It alludes to deformity, bodily distortions, and violations, as previously suggested. Imagining Helena Rubenstein with the likes of Frankinstein brings attention to the self-acclaimed creator of female propriety, who provides women with a potent concoction that miraculously transforms them into presentable human beings, imaged in the likeness of white femininity. Ironically, one of Helena Rubenstein's numerous mantras was "There are no ugly women, only lazy ones." One can safely assume that black women were not viewed as viable participants in Rubenstein's beauty movement for privileged women. The burning question then is, are they the "lazy ones"? Nichols implies that they are in this "obligatory" duality. At the same time, the misidentification of the creator as the monster—many people have mistakenly referred to the monster as Frankenstein; I too am guilty of this act, albeit for the purpose of creative analysis—likens this colonial and patriarchal inspired decree to monstrosity. Similar to the "monster's power to inspire terror, awe, wonder, and divination" (Garland-Thomson, *Extraordinary Bodies* 57), the "monstrous" idea to adopt normative standards of beauty equally arouses curiosity: "I have an interest / though I will not shave the armpit" (Nichols, *Lazy Thoughts* 6). By the same token, the term conjures up an image of a "phantasmatic" unattainable identity, rivaled only by the gargantuan figure of the monster, a parody of the megalomaniac cosmetic industry. At the same time, the Frankenstein imagery is emblematic of the phantasmagoric attributes of patriarchy. Unattainability of the standard beauty, of the ideal citizen, remains insurmountable for the nonconforming black woman who constantly wrestles with proverbial borders and boundaries.

Caricatured, these "highbrow" female tycoons are brought down to the "bodily" stratum, relegated to the "fleshly" realm. This (body) degradation powerfully resonates with Baartman's exploitation and her monstrous treatment at the hands of European colonialists.[19] One wonders if this is a bizarre case of coincidence that Mary Shelley lived near 225 Piccadilly where Baartman was exhibited to the public. As we are informed, several of England's greatest writers, including Lord Bryon, Coleridge, and Keats, "lived in the immediate vicinity of Piccadilly" (Crais and Scully 93). Crais concludes that even if these writers did not attend the exhibit, it is highly unlikely that they would not have heard, read about, or discussed the controversy (93). Analytically, the employment of parody mocks the fantasy of the perfect body and the successive respectable citizen.

The politics of subversion is further deployed in the poem "With Apologies to Hamlet," in which punning is the tool of subversion. Analyzing the Bakhtinian concept of "*grammatica jocosa*," Stallybrass and White reflect on its meaning "whereby grammatical order is transgressed to reveal erotic and obscene or merely materially satisfying counter-meaning. Punning . . . that violates and unveils the structure of prevailing convention is one of the forms of *grammatica jocosa*" (10–11). Yet again the Lazy Woman is preoccupied with the "bodily lower stratum"—in this instance, pee. Parodying perhaps the most famous soliloquy of Shakespeare's Hamlet, Nichols/the Lazy Woman posits the life-altering question: "To pee or not to pee / That is the question" (*Lazy Thoughts* 6).

Nichols's "vulgarization" of this written "high" text challenges the aforementioned prevailing assumption that "English is 'refined'; written texts are 'refined' (Cooper 8). In a similar manner, her use of the term *pee*, instead of the more refined *urine*, engenders "abusive language" that is germane to the understanding of the discourse of the grotesque, an iteration that "the grotesque form of the body lived especially in the familiar and colloquial forms of the language" (Bakhtin 27, 341). By contrast, "'high' languages attempt to legitimate their authority by appealing to values inherent in the classical body" (Stallybrass and White 21). Further, as articulated by Bakhtin "urine . . . is gay matter, which degrades and relieves at the same time, transforming fear into laughter" (335). In accordance, the Lazy Woman transforms this aberrant (low) discourse (of disgust) into one of pleasure as she underscores the pleasure exacted from bodily relief. Engaging this process of degradation, otherwise known as "grotesque debasement" that features "the material bodily lower stratum, the zone of the genital organs" (Bakhtin 147), the bodily relief simultaneously occasions a regenerative force, epitomized by the word *apee-sing* (a visible pun on "appeasing" that captures the comfort and joy manifested in *sing*). Engaging this regenerative force, the Lazy Woman makes the sane decision not "[t]o suffer for sake of verse" but "to break poetic thought for loo" (Nichols, *Lazy Thoughts* 6). This double debasement gets additional reinforcement. The suffix *sing* also functions as a verb. *Sing* also alludes to the sound of pee. Furthermore, the choice of *pee* instead of *urine* lends itself to double debasement. The inverted phrase "as a course of matter," instead of the normative "as a matter of course" underscores the material, matter, normalizing this natural human act, while simultaneously challenging standard English as the norm. In like manner, her choice of "loo" is a pun on the word "low." Additionally, it encapsulates the lowly bodily function. Even this "verse" undergoes suspension when nature calls, relinquishing its high status to accommodate the low, as low bodily function converges with high intellectual thought. This royal collapse defies the attainment of citizenship as an exclusionary practice, reserved only for the intellectuals (read male) of the nation.

In all likelihood, Nichols satirizes one of the greatest British masterpoets of our time, corrupting not only the master tongue but also proverbially dethroning the master. This inversion of hierarchy, of "high culture," results in the "meeting" of the scripted English verse with the "unscripted" grotesque language of the body. This merging, exemplary of crisscrossing borders and boundaries, substantiates the need for transnational citizenship in the same way that it authenticates the members of the (British) diaspora as viable candidates for flexible citizenship.

In the poem "My Black Triangle" the Lazy Woman explores black female sexuality ad lib. The skillful engagement of grotesque realism becomes manifest in the swallowing, devouring, all-consuming image of the "black triangle," a clear allusion to the female genitals: "spreading and growing / trusting and flowing" (*Lazy Thoughts* 25). This image can also be likened to the perilous journey across the dark waters of the Middle Passage, bringing Gilroy's need for a "redemptive return to an African homeland" into focus, and reassigning Hall's missing term, Africa. In her careful analysis of the poem, Davies makes a valid point that "For Nichols, the triangular representations of the Middle Passage get re-presented in terms of female sexual space, pubic, vulvic, localized but also historicized in resistance to patriarchal, misogynistic, imperialistic and colonizing imperatives" ("Carnivalized" 345). Employing the female genitalia as the site of resistance to imperialistic expansion and enslavement, the Lazy Woman harks back to slavery and the forceful occupation cum penetration of the mother/land. Upholding this argument, the "black triangle" also functions as a point of access/entrance that resonates with colonial occupation and expansion. Equally, the devouring characteristic alludes to castration, substantiated by the dryness that patriarchy experiences: "my black triangle / has spread beyond his story / beyond the dry fears of parch-ri-archy" (25). Whereas the dryness epitomizes impotence, the loss of power, the "black triangle" is a picture-perfect image of fertility and fecundity, "so rich / that it flows over / on to the dry crotch / of the world" (25). This male-dominated world is consumed by the "black triangle" that is symbolically equated (conflated) with the Bermuda Triangle notoriously known for ships disappearing mysteriously beneath its waters. The disappearance of ships resonates with the weakening of patriarchal might and prowess, occasioning the lessening of the restrictions for female citizenship.

Relentlessly expressing disapproval of female commodification and subjugation, Nichols's heroines "[break] the slave stereotype of the dumb victim of circumstance" (Nichols, "Battle" 288). Illuminating black women's indomitable will to exist and resist, she creates them in the likeness of a mythic figure, establishing that "there ain't no / easy-belly category / for a black woman" (53). Offering a cautionary message, she warns against reductionism, reducing the black woman's condition to that of sufferer, embodied in the "long suffering black woman," or relegating her to the margins of society and rendering her a non-citizen (Nichols, "Battle"

284). Hence the black woman cannot be contained within patriarchal limits and limitations: "I can write / no poem big enough / to hold the essence / of a black woman" (52). Nichols's Fat Black Woman/Lazy Woman therefore celebrates her economic and sexual independence from patriarchal reign, performing her body as a site/sight of resistance and pleasure or, to echo Denise deCaires Narain, as a site of "multiple pleasures and [uninhibited] possibilities" (154). As Cooper so eloquently puts it, the Fat Black Woman "writes[s] and perform[s] a script of cultural resistance to the hegemony of anglocentrism" (*Noises* 9). As follows, Nichols's women create a new discourse of (black) womanhood that is included, albeit by force, in the national narrative and the larger body politic.

6   Bodies and DisEase

Finding AlterNative Cure, Assuming AlterNative Identity

Underscoring the importance of a multifaceted community-based model of health care, Ann Folwell Stanford acknowledges that the "institution of medicine is only a part, albeit an important part, of a more far-reaching health care enterprise. In this setting the body's health is inseparable from that body's relationship to the greater community (or world) and its health" (*Bodies* 4). While being mindful of severe physical illness, Stanford nevertheless feels that some diseased bodies are emblematic of social and racial injustices that reveal the disparity in the care and cure administered to certain (read blacks) individuals.[1] To reappropriate Jacqui Alexander's coinage, not just any body is eligible for care or cure. Certainly, this logic holds up in Dorothy Roberts's analysis of racial health disparities in the United States. Contending that "race matters," she reveals the stark and frightening reality that "[b]lacks are more likely to die prematurely (before the age of sixty-five) from most major illnesses: cancer, stroke, diabetes, kidney disease, AIDS, and coronary heart disease, to name a few" (*Fatal Invention* 81). Lindah Mhando notes: "The body . . . becomes the site of profound struggle in black communities; an indication that there are implicit and complex links between global power relations, local experiences in spatial location, and women's subjective experiences of health, illness, and disability" ("Under Ivory-Tower Eyes"). Stanford points out that "living human bodies pay the price for and carry within them the symptoms of a sick world" (*Bodies* 29). Often the cost is astronomical; in the given situation, the expense is self-erasure that bears the imprint of denial of personhood, and subsequently citizenship.

This multifaceted community-based model of health care that Stanford promotes is premised on the politics of inclusion and belonging. Furthermore, community support is complementary to one's survival. Along these lines, Stanford is calling for a transnational coalition between western and indigenous medicine and cultures, free of racial and geographic boundaries and borders.[2] She also brings attention to the black diasporic community that is disproportionately inflicted by diseases, rendering its inhabitants disabled and therefore unworthy of citizenship. Accordingly, she calls for the end to discrimination in western medical practices and the acknowledgment of race, gender, and biological differences. Promoting a comparable transnational agenda, Edwidge Danticat, Paule Marshall, Toni Morrison, Jamaica Kincaid, and Maryse Condé seek alternative cures as counter discourse to hegemonic, medical practices that become manifest in the embrace of indigeneity. This celebration of difference engenders an alternative identity and a more realistic route to becoming a viable patient cum citizen of the (medical) world.

Alvin Poussaint questions the devastating dismissal, "the rationales that legitimated the exclusion of blacks from the purview of universal rights and entitlements" (Hartman, *Scenes* 5). He reasons that "the persistent presence of racism despite the significant legal, social, and political progress made during the last half of the twentieth century, has created a physiological risk for black people that is virtually unknown to white Americans" (15). Dorothy Roberts bolsters this line of reasoning when she refers to the health disparity between whites and blacks as a "racial chasm in health" (*Fatal Invention* 82). This racial (body) divide provides a historical point of entry to the dehumanization of blacks even as it summons up images of exceptional (white) citizenship. In this regard, the unhealthy body carries traits of difference and deviance and therefore does not measure up to the nation's (read medical discourse) definition of ideal citizenship.[3] However, these bodies of difference and deviance were conjured up by the powers-that-be in a futile effort to justify their "sins." Roberts cogently observes that "white slaveholders explained race in biological terms to demarcate slaves from masters and to provide a moral excuse for slavery. Whites argued that the biological peculiarities of blacks made enslavement the only condition in which blacks could be productive and disciplined" (*Fatal Invention* 83). Quoting Lundy Braun, Roberts concludes, "It was precisely 'by locating disease in physiologic difference—be it susceptibility or resistance—that medicine served to mark blacks as deserving of their inferior social status in society'" (83). Whiteness and able-bodiedness therefore are imagined as the transcendental norm. Incidentally, black subjects undergo denationalization that resonates with disembodiment. Poussaint refers to this condition as "posttraumatic slave syndrome." Citing the predominance of black prison inmates despite the fact that only 12 percent of Americans are blacks, Poussaint effectively substantiates his findings as he reiterates that "a culture of oppression, a byproduct of this nation's development, has taken a tremendous toll on the minds and bodies of black people" (Hartman, *Scenes* 15). Lending to this discussion, Paul Farmer feels that oppression is a global phenomenon that specifically imperils the black diaspora, the underdogs of society, the "country within the country" (Create, 113).

While Farmer's analogy of the intricate link between illness and social ill specifically pertains to tuberculosis and AIDS, his findings are nonetheless pertinent to this discussion. Continued proliferation of tuberculosis and AIDS in certain diasporic communities gives voice to the previous rationalization that different diseases affect different people dissimilarly. All the same, the pervasive affliction of women from immigrant and black communities in the ensuing discussion is telling.[4] Compounded by their (untenable) immigrant status—just cause for the onset of illness—the "sick" body of the immigrant woman occupies a marginal position as it is imperiled by biological illness and invisibility. Existing discursively on the borderlands, outside and beyond the nation-state, the immigrant woman is rendered stateless and therefore lawless. As Yancy reminds us: "The 'outside world' functions as a trope that renders Black bodies . . . ostracized, different, and unwelcome. This outside world dialectically exists alongside a presumptive space of whiteness as unmarked, unraced, civilized, and normal" (xix). Disease, race, and social (immigrant) status all contribute to the immigrant woman's lawlessness and abnormality and to her being labeled an undesirable citizen. Undesirability also resides in the sick, deviant female body. To this end, the chapter draws upon Farmer's theorization of disease at length.

Writing that "countries with the steepest grades of inequality and the greatest poverty have the biggest AIDS problem," Farmer believes that to address this ill, "we need to erase social inequalities" (Kidder 199). Revealing that women are the casualties of this proverbial battle, Farmer habitually cites a Haitian peasant woman who responded to the increase in AIDS in women in the following manner: "You want to stop HIV in women? Give them jobs" (199). Yet in light of the disparities, Farmer reveals that "medicine addresses only the symptoms of poverty" (100). In upholding this decision, professionals do not even attempt to cure the ills. In other words, no one is "sincerely trying to change the 'political economies' of countries like Haiti" (100). Farmer reveals that the United States and France are key players in the orchestrated demise of Haiti. He notes that "political correction [was] a very well-crafted tool to distract" from the real concerns at hand; consequently, it functioned as a deterrent to providing proper medical care to patients. He intimates that many health workers, including academics, conveniently invoke "cultural barriers" to underscore the futility in administering free medicine. Confessing that in administering western medicine to Haitian patients, he was expecting to come away with the preconceived idea that "what's in people's minds affects their behavior and the outcomes," Farmer was rudely awakened by an elderly peasant woman that he was treating for tuberculosis who took offense to him questioning her about sorcery (Kidder 34–35). Despite her belief in sorcery, she poignantly informed Farmer: "I'm not stupid. I know that tuberculosis comes from people coughing germs" (35). Having taken all her medicines, the patient had been cured. This "contradiction" (despite widespread assumptions) is not exclusive to Haitians, as Farmer was duly reminded: "[I]t dawned on him that he knew plenty of Americans—he was one himself—who held apparently contradictory beliefs, such as faith in both medicine and prayer. He felt as though he hung in the air before his patient, 'suspended by her sympathy and bemusement'" (35). Ultimately, Farmer concluded that "[w]hether a patient believed that TB came from germs or sorcery didn't seem to have made any difference at all" (34). Consequently, Farmer's theorization on disease reveals the intricate transnational connection between modern and homeopathic (nontraditional) medicine, shedding light on the error in judgment in dismissing the latter.

Hence the adverse employment of cultural beliefs resonates powerfully with "the geography of blame." These forms of stigmatization or pathologization have left an indelible mark both on the landscape and on the bodies of the diseased. In turn, medicine lends itself to distrust among blacks who, not surprisingly, have a strained relationship with western medicine. Even so, this tension is discernibly exacerbated by the disqualification of cultural beliefs (read barriers) as a disincentive to proper care. A perfect example manifests not only in U.S. Homeland Security's mistreatment of Joseph Dantica but also in its dismissal and ultimate destruction of his medicine, rendering it "illegal" because it was not a "legitimate prescribed medicine."[5] The "illegitimate" nonwestern medicine becomes a marker of his illegality, his immigrant (non-citizen) status. Accordingly, his body is marked as undesirable. This practice of racial discrimination by the nation-state is designed to both reinforce normative (read western) standards that result in the dismissal of folk or homeopathic (nonwestern) remedy, and to delegitimize Dantica. Revealing the inherent biases to differences, namely, to beliefs that do not conform to western ideals, Farmer interrogates even as he challenges western hypocrisy. He reveals that "in trying to control TB and AIDS . . . he had ended up wrangling, not much with third world myths, like beliefs in sorcery, but usually with first world ones, like expert theories that exaggerated the power poor women had to protect themselves" (Kidder 199). Thus Farmer feels that danger lies not in one's cultural belief but in the gross misrepresentations of facts and the superimposition of western beliefs on indigenous cultures. In other words, medicine should be in the business of dismantling systems of oppression and not reproducing them. Likewise, decontextualizing illness—disconnecting social issues from personal turmoil—has dangerous consequences. Campaigning for tolerance of difference, Farmer suggests that grassroots involvement would go a long way in bridging the gap between the Third World and the First, between "us" and "them."

Appalled by the vilification of Haitian religious and cultural practices, specifically the dismissal and demonization of vodou, Danticat is dumbfounded by the disdain for this extraordinary religion of memory. Farmer equally expresses disbelief in the demonization of indigeneity as he gestures toward the ingenuity of the Haitian people who had "created their own complex religion, Voodoo—with a rather distant supreme deity and a host of other gods, a pantheon including Catholic saints." He further points out that because vodou was "so widely misunderstood and ridiculed, it was a system of belief that seemed all the more worth studying" (Kidder 63–64). Farmer practiced what he preached. Undoubtedly, the aforementioned call for a politics of inclusion would destabilize the monopoly of western medicine.

It should come as no surprise that Farmer was heavily influenced by the German polymath Rudolf Virchow. Commissioned by the German government to conduct a study on the epidemic of famine fever or relapsing fever, Virchow provided the following analysis:

He wrote that abysmal social conditions, which the government had fostered and done nothing to relieve, had caused the epidemic. Epidemics of the illness usually occur after social upheavals, in the ensuing overcrowding, poor hygiene, and malnutrition. Furthermore, he concludes that if disease is an expression of individual life under unfavorable conditions, then epidemics must be indicative of mass disturbances of mass life. (Kidder 60–61)

Obviously Virchow's finding did not sit well with the government, a fact that resulted in him being terminated. But he also remained relatively unknown, in spite of the groundbreaking research about inequities that he conducted, especially when compared to "Pasteur, Schweitzer, or Florence Nightingale" (Kidder 60). Significantly, Virchow prescribed "full and unlimited democracy" to cure the fever which in his research findings was brought on by social and political inequities such as religious interference and racial and economic oppression of the poor (61). Virchow further exposed the government's hidden agenda as he responded to his termination in the following manner: "My politics were those of prophylaxis, my opponents preferred those of palliation" (61).

In like manner, one can reasonably conclude that Edwidge Danticat, Paule Marshall, Jamaica Kincaid, and Maryse Condé are staunch advocates of prophylaxis, as their theoretical and transnational platforms advance the philosophy that bodily experiences are sociosomatic and therefore closely tied to one's social or socioeconomic position in society. Centering bodily experiences as pivotal in determining women's disease, these women writers are quick to point out the social and political inequities—a sample of the real world and the lived experiences of their female characters—in their fictional work, emphasizing how women are disproportionately affected. For instance, Garland-Thomson aptly reminds us that "the fundamental aim of African American women's writing is to construct a black female subject that displaces the negative cultural images generated by America's aggregate history of racism and sexism" (*Extraordinary Bodies* 103).

In a similar vein, the skepticism toward western medicine expressed in the narratives is evocative of the historical relationship between blacks and medicine. This troubled past has arguably resulted in some individuals seeking homeopathic remedies. A perfect example manifests in Lorde availing her body to various nonwestern medicines. More specifically, she sought homeopathic alternatives to surgery in Berlin and then in Switzerland to treat her liver cancer, which had metastasized from breast cancer. Lorde's obligatory migrations crystallize the benefits of transnationalism and simultaneously interrogate (medical) borders and boundaries. In like manner, the aforementioned women writers are united in their validation of indigeneity, of indigenous, homeopathic remedies, promoted and practiced by various black diasporic communities. This reliance on indigeneity registers a divergence from western ideology as it resists "infestations" by the dominant ideology. Although Lorde ultimately lost her battle with the disease, she unequivocally insisted that not only had her decision to seek an alternative cure permitted her to maintain some control over her life, but it also prolonged her life (*Burst of Light* 49). Lorde's realization of her humanity and individuality lent legitimacy to her flexible identity, her suitability as a transnational citizen (of the world). Further establishing that "western medicine doesn't have a very impressive track record with cancer metastasized to the liver," she accentuated medicine's limits (54). She provided the following justification for seeking alternative treatment: "[T]here is absolutely nothing they can do for me at Sloane Kettering except cut me open and then sew me back up with their condemnations inside me" (75–76). In this scenario, Lorde chronicled her impending doom that she poignantly attributed to "race" politics and not to her medical condition. Consequently, Lorde consulted an anthroposophic doctor, Dr. Rosenberg, who believed in surgery only as a last resort (58). Honoring her request and her alternative belief, he administered Iscador treatments.

In battling the disease, Lorde exposed the destructive attributes of racism and sexism, revealing that they are symptomatic of alienation and annihilation. She shared the following sentiments: "As an African-American woman, I feel the tragedy of being an oppressed hyphenated person in America, of having no land to be our primary teacher" (*Burst* 66). Here, Lorde revealed the tenuous nature of citizenship for the black woman whose "borderland existence" was problematic. She wrote that her existence as a black woman was fortuitous because the source of female oppression was white patriarchy: "I wasn't supposed to exist anyway, not in any meaningful way in this fucked-up whiteboys' world" (61). Further addressing black women's invisibility, she wrote that "to survive in the mouth of this dragon we call america, we have had to learn this first and most vital lesson—that we were never meant to survive. Not as human beings" (*Sister Outsider* 42).

Capturing the historical dehumanization of blacks, Roberts recounts Thomas Jefferson's denial of equal citizenship to black subjects: "[The] unfortunate difference in colour, and perhaps of faculty, is a powerful obstacle to the emancipation of these people" (*Fatal Invention* 83). Lorde called attention to the surplus, the dispensable black bodies to which Deborah White and Roberts refer in chapter 3. Drawing on the experiences of their forebears who practiced infanticide and abortion to resist being taken as chattel, the women healers in the novels to be analyzed administer (another form of) care and cure through homeopathy. In contrast to western medicine, homeopathic remedies do not discipline the so-called unruly, undesirable black body, but instead aim to provide alternative cures. In other words, the female practitioners are heavily invested in the survival of the black female subject. Moreover, this care-cure dyad punctuates their humanity (both the practitioners and their characters) and establishes their rights as citizens. Evidently, one's survival is inextricably linked to resistance. Consequently, homeopathy that is rooted in oral (nonwestern) tradition and cultures registers resistance from its inception. Along these lines, the female practitioners as well as their clients, or "participants," to borrow Morrison's term, embody resistance.[6]

Lorde likens her experiences as an "outsider" to the dehumanization of enslaved Africans who were robbed of their basic human rights. This parallel that facilitates the un-silencing of the brutal past engenders resistance. As a result, Lorde's survival is intricately interwoven with the struggle of her forebears. This fact becomes manifest in her emphasizing her privilege, most palpably exemplified in her access to and treatment at the Lukas Klinik in Switzerland. She expresses concern for the many black women who do not have proper health care: "I have been very blessed in my life. Accidents of privilege allowed me to gain information about holistic/biological medicine and their approach to cancers, and that information has helped keep me alive, along with my original gut feeling that said, *Stay out of my body*" (*Burst of Light* 130). Reinforcing Virchow's philosophy that disease is intricately linked to social and political inequities, Lorde contends that the commercial benefit of cancer lies in treatment and not in prevention. Subsequently, she arrives at the stark realization that the medical practitioners were primarily interested in her health benefits and method of payment, which in turn determined the kind of plastic ID card she received in order to gain access to a specialist. "The uniformed, pistoled guards at all the stairwells" served as reinforcement of the hospital's policy that only ID card holders are allowed access" (113).[7] Attentive to her privileged status, Lorde nevertheless is wary of the practice of exceptional citizenship.

Despite the geographic distance from home/America occasioned by her treatment in Arlesheim, Switzerland, Lorde confesses that "yet it is the only place that offers any hope . . . that will treat [her] and [her] liver seriously" (*Burst of Light* 88). More importantly, Lorde identifies with the practitioners that embrace a holistic approach in dealing with disease. The holistic approach lends itself to transnational female alliances. Lorde accentuates the "native/indigenous" in Old World cultural practices and tradition and in alternative medicinal remedies as she highlights the parallel between herself and Dilnawaz, an East Indian woman who administers curative eurhythmy, their shared reverence for spirituality. In revealing their veneration for spiritual well-being, Lorde exposes the reluctance of "most Northern Europeans to give themselves to eurhythmy." She writes: "Deep respect for the spiritual aspect of our lives and its power over us is something most of the rationalists here do not have, despite their adherence to Steiner's anthroposophy" (83). She identifies Steiner's rigid rules as a major shortcoming, arguing that "his insistence upon the basic rule of a Christian god . . . is limiting" (83).

These instituted limits and limitations—palpably exemplified in the blanketed refutation of Dantica's alternative medicine and the denouncement of nonwestern cultures and beliefs—that abound in the national consciousness are the very principles that the aforementioned women writers fiercely resist. In other words, in promoting and administering homeopathic alternatives to treat disease, these writers challenge "provincialism," a term used to categorize (what is perceived as) Americans' unyielding belief in and relation to western medicine. Along these lines, Lorde articulates that her presence—not simply as an American, but more importantly as a black American—at the Lukas Klinik is regarded as anomalous in light of the fact that "Americans are known for being quite provincial" (*Burst of Light* 85). This alternative care administered primarily by traditional (herbal) practitioners is complementary to Old World culture. For the same reason, it does not advocate dissonance with western medicine. Rather, it often operates in congruence with western medicine, a fact that Farmer underscored earlier by remarking that medicine and beliefs converge. Farmer nevertheless interprets this convergence as a contradiction, which opposes my reading of this relationship. Proposing an alternative interpretation of this relationship, this study illuminates the complementary attributes of this blending that is a recurring phenomenon in black culture. Toni Morrison credits this effortless and natural convergence to the "practicality" of black folks, who spontaneously and unequivocally authenticate their belief in "superstition and magic," whilst simultaneously maintaining a "profound rootedness in the real world ... with neither taking precedence over the other" ("Rootedness" 342). Morrison is quick to point out that blending the supernatural world and the real world "together at the same time was enhancing, not limiting" (342).

For the same reason, the extent to which one engages or relies on homeopathic alternatives is determined by the following variables: generational and gender difference, physical location, and spiritual connectedness and continuity. For example, whereas Ma Chess, the grandmother in Kincaid's *Annie John*, is immersed in Old World cultural practices and beliefs, her daughter, Annie John, finds herself at the crossroads of Old World values and New World religion, epitomized by the juxtaposition of western medicine with local remedies in her medicine chest. Ma Chess's daughter and granddaughter are both named Annie John, doubling as the eponymous heroines of the novel. The creation of Annie Senior and Junior destabilizes state laws and boundaries of male inheritance and privilege. I interpret this "doubling" as the union of Old and New Worlds, of western medicine and traditional beliefs. Moreover, placing modern medicine and home remedies side by side expresses mutual interdependence, registering a balance that is necessary in ensuring proper care and cure.

Western medicine is put to the test when young Annie inexplicably falls ill and her health deteriorates, despite the administering of various western medications.[8] Only Ma Chess's application of folk remedy seems effective, a clear indication of medicine's limits. Moreover, Ma Chess's presence validates that Annie's illness is sociosomatic. We later find out that Annie's breakdown resulted from imminent separation and alienation from her mother.

Likewise, Toni Morrison narrates that M'Dear, a quiet woman and a "competent midwife and decisive diagnostician" was summoned to attend to Aunt Jimmy when her body refused to respond to "Miss Alice's Bible reading" (*Bluest Eye* 136). We are informed: "Finally it was decided to fetch M'Dear. Few could remember when M'Dear was not around. In any illness that could not be handled by ordinary means—known cures, intuition, or endurance—the word was always, 'Fetch M'Dear'" (136). We sense M'Dear's presence—a subversion of female marginalization—even before she appears on the scene: "M'Dear loomed taller than the preacher that accompanied her. Four big white knots of hair gave power and authority to her soft black face" (136). Even as Morrison describes M'Dear's female attributes, she focuses attention on her commanding presence. Significantly, it is not the preacher who sermonizes Aunt Jimmy, but rather M'Dear. Instead, the preacher plays a secondary role as he "put her in his buggy to take her home" (137). M'Dear's infallibility is irrefutable; her exemplary citizenship cannot be denied. We are presented with another midwife cum ancestral figure, Circe, in Morrison's *Song of Solomon*, who has delivered everybody in Danville, Pennsylvania, hometown of the Dead family. Morrison assesses Circe's gift of healing: "Healer, deliverer, in another world she would have been the head nurse" (*Song* 246).[9] In this other world, Circe would have been revered as a desirable citizen that safeguards rather than threatens the nation-state. Analogously, Baby Suggs performs a masterful sermon at "the clearing" (*Beloved* 87–89). These women reside in a female-centered diaspora as exemplified by "the clearing"; accordingly, these theorizations of bodily experiences challenge mainstream discourse and ideology. Female alliance is certainly seen in the administering of an alternative approach to reading black women bodies, thus manifesting in "a blurring . . . , a reordering of the binary cultural, social, and epistemological distinctions" (quoted in Duany 1). This reordering of the predetermined masculine world fosters female inclusion in the decision-making process of the nation's agenda.

Medicine's limit is once again placed under the microscope in Condé's *I, Tituba, Black Witch of Salem*. Unable to administer a proper cure for Tituba's assumed mental illness, the Harvard College–bound aspiring Doctor Zerobabel resorts to local remedies, applying "one of his potions" that resulted in Tituba's immediate recovery (111–12). In the given scenario, Condé enacts a skillful act of subversion (and co-optation) whereby the western-educated doctor adopts homeopathic remedies as his own. This adoption/adaptation substantiates nonwestern medicine as a valid alternative to healing.[10] To say the least, Condé exposes the double condemnation and co-optation of homeopathic remedies by having the Harvard-bound doctor assume the role of a local witch doctor whereby he administers local potions as cures. Furthermore, likening him to a witch doctor neutralizes the dominance of western medicine; this indigenization is rendered most palpable by the pervasive use of local remedies. A healer herself, Tituba diagnosed Elizabeth Parris, the wife of Samuel Parris, as suffering from a nonmedicalized illness, "the soul dragging down the body, as in so many cases of mortal sickness" (39). Significantly, Tituba renders her diagnosis after Elizabeth complains that "over twenty physicians have come to my bedside and none has found the cause of my illness" (38). Tituba's gift of magic and healing was bequeathed to her by her biological mother, Abena, and her ancestral mother, Mama Yaya. This convergence of female power engenders the discursive crisscrossing of borders and the merging of two seemingly disparate worlds. Remarkably, these worlds are peopled by women who practice flexible citizenship and traverse the real and the ancestral worlds with ease.

Women's desire for legitimacy gains potency in an oppressive masculine world, a yearning that men do not crave due to their privileged citizen status as guardians of the state and women. Validating this line of reasoning, the male members of the John family are staunch proponents of institutionalized western medicine, indicative of their adoption and perpetuation of patriarchal values. Despite the presence of the physician, Mrs. John relies heavily on Ma Jolie, the local obeah woman who was highly recommended by Ma Chess and who, like Ma Chess, hailed from Dominica. Whereas the men promote western patriarchal medicine, the women rely on the local diaspora of women and female healers to combat their marginalization. On those occasions that Mrs. John sought the advice and support of the obeah woman, Mr. John requested that his wife consult with her in his absence (Kincaid, *Annie John* 109–10). Along similar lines, Pa Chess was adamant about Ma Chess administering traditional medicine to their sick son, John. Announcing that "a doctor was the last thing he needed," Ma Chess contradicts Pa Chess, who was convinced that "a doctor was the one thing he needed" (125). Pa Chess triumphed. However, John succumbed to his illness despite showing signs of perfect health: "On the day that he died, he had never looked better" (125). This image of perfection is deceptive, exemplified by the large worm that inexplicably "bore its way out of [John's] leg and rested on his shinbone. Then it, too, died" (125). This deceptiveness bears the imprint of elusiveness as John's illness/death is anomalous if not mysterious, undiagnosed, or more poignantly misdiagnosed, by western medicine. John's death in turn gives rise to a symbolic death, the estrangement of Ma and Pa Chess. Holding

Pa Chess accountable for his blind obsession and absolute reliance on western medicine, which resulted in her son's untimely death, Ma Chess, apart from not attending John's funeral, "never spoke to Pa Chess again, [wearing only black] from that day on" (125).

We encounter a similar scene in which pervasive medical authority is challenged. Annie's reemergence into society necessitated a rebirth, an exclusive female undertaking that destabilizes male power and the male-dominated medical profession.[11] Annie recounts that Ma Chess occupied a permanent position at the foot of her bed where she ate and slept; she left her side only to join her in bed where she remained until she was "herself" (124). Mr. John, on the other hand, kept out of Ma Chess's way "because they didn't see the world in the same way" (126). Unable to identify the cause of Annie's illness, Dr. Stephens is usurped by Ma Chess as the female tradition of midwifery is reinstituted; this practice occasioned the reinstating of female healers as legitimate and desirable citizens of the world. Consequently, in recent times, many pregnant women are reverting to "choosing midwives—with their empowering and attentive approach—to deliver their babies."[12] Thus women's clairvoyant abilities are unsurpassed. Grounded in African cultures and traditions, these (oral) cultural practices and beliefs have withstood migrations and displacements.

The fact that Annie's parents' words "f[e]ll to the floor, suddenly dead just as they reached [her] ears," is indicative of the need for nonverbal, spiritual communication that is realized by Ma Chess (109). This strong spiritual wholeness necessitates and accounts for Ma Chess's miraculous appearance on the island, which profoundly resonates with Annie's inexplicable onset of illness and an equally analogous mysterious healing of her disease. In the given situation, Ma Chess's statelessness is empowering as she traverses real and imagined borders efficiently. This navigation of borders reconfigures female citizenship beyond patriarchal dictates. Given that Ma Chess arrived on the island on a day when the steamer was not scheduled to run, it is reasonable to argue that she embodies the legendary witch-woman or the ol'higue (old higue) or soucouyant, or lougarou, as she is interchangeably referred to in the Caribbean.[13] The ever-elusive persona of the ol'higue blurs boundaries and identities. Thus the ol'higue's migration, exemplified by her "transgressive" body and her engagement with folk tradition, manifestly challenges homogeneity and female immobility in the same way that it challenges the masculinist medical discourse. Not only is the witch-woman empowered by her ability to fly, but she also possesses transformative powers as she is able to shed her skin. Along these lines, the witch-woman is the figure that most palpably resists institutionalized (western) medicine and conditional citizenship in that she doubles as healer and midwife. Tituba underscores this embrace of an alternative belief when she remarks that "In the West Indies our science is nobler and relies more on unseen forces than on things" (54). Thus a vibrant female diaspora resides within the real and imagined worlds.

Having the power of flight, Ma Chess's "out of body" experience registers transgression. Consequently, her transgressive female body resists male control and resists being scripted in the masculinist, hegemonic discourse. More poignantly, the witch-woman is in the business of subverting male power and hegemony. The shedding of her skin (i.e., her ability to transform) substantiates this argument.

This powerful symbol of female empowerment embodied by the witch-woman is a common recurrence in black women's writing. In addition to the aforementioned authors, Karen King-Aribisala and Nalo Hopkinson actively engage this theme in their writing.[14] Calling attention to this "superior gift of nature" bestowed upon the female subject, Tituba expresses puzzlement over the demonization of the witch-woman: "Isn't the ability to communicate with the invisible world, to keep constant links with the dead, to care for others and heal, a superior gift of nature that inspires respect, admiration, and gratitude? Consequently, shouldn't the witch (if that's what the person who has this gift is to be called) be cherished and revered rather than feared?" (*Tituba* 17). This bewilderment extends to her being labeled an undesirable citizen and a threat to the nation. It is therefore not surprising that Tituba's embrace and acceptance of her role as a witch is deemed pathological as she is characterized as suffering from mental illness. Notwithstanding, feminist critic Xavière Gauthier offers a formidable response to Tituba's question, defining the witch-woman "as a historical anchor, an immense political revolt from the past" (200–203). She further ascertains that women's direct connection with their bodies and with nature affords them the ability to cure or to poison, to live as midwives, and to liberate other women from patriarchal dictates. Advancing her argument, Gauthier makes a clear-cut case for the term *witch* to be used as a departure from masculinist representations and definitions, and phallocratism, upholding that it should be claimed as a space not only for women coming into being and power but also for those struggling and seeking. She assertively insists that the marginalization of women and the repression of female strength are primarily because women pose a danger for this society (203). In the same vein, Tituba's rhetorical question manifests her resistance to the patriarchal structure that limits or constricts female mobility and autonomy.

Female mobility and autonomy find expression in the trope of flight, the ability to fly or soar. Flight engenders freedom and transnational yearnings. This fervent desire for freedom is deeply embedded in the slave past that inspired us with stories about Africans who fiercely resisted enslavement by flying back home to Africa.[15] The loss of flight for African people translates into loss of freedom; flight therefore becomes a site of resistance. Even as captive subjects, enslaved Africans were a force with which to reckon. Engendering another form of resistance, Virginia Hamilton recounts that "the [Africans] that could fly shed their wings. They couldn't take their wings across the water on the slave ships. Too crowded. So they forgot about flying when they could no longer breathe the sweet scent of Africa" (166). Recounting a parallel story, Earl Lovelace in his inspirational novel, *Salt*, narrates that New World Africans were deprived of the power of flight, were denied a return home because they "had eaten salt and made themselves too heavy to fly" (3). Along these lines, the shedding of wings is likened to the witch-woman's shedding of her skin, which curtails infestations of dominant western ideology.

Operating within this historic-cultural, transnational continuum, Danticat reenacts the story of female oppression wherein a witch/wife is deprived of flying by her husband. Known to fly "without her skin at night . . . she came back home [and] found her skin peppered and could not put it back on. Her husband had done it to teach her a lesson. He ended up killing her" (*Breath* 150).[16] The demonization and eventual death of the witch-woman signals the suppression of female power and the desecration of the body. Analyzing the inherent power of the witch-woman, scholar Giselle Anatol argues that the "soucouyant figure has been used to condemn female power and socialize women according to patriarchal dictates" (33). Drawing on Margarite Fernández Olmos and Lizabeth Paravisini-Gebert's discussion on the censorship of African religions and cultural practices in the Caribbean region, Anatol establishes that they conclusively point to the fact that "African-derived religions and systems of belief have been vilified by mainstream culture, often in response to a real or perceived threat to European cultural and political dominance" (34). In the given situation, the witch-woman poses a threat to patriarchal dominance. Olmos and Paravisini-Gebert concur as they share Gauthier's view that the "figure of the witch appears wicked because she poses a real danger to phallocratic society" (302). Furthering this analysis, Anatol summarizes that the "demonized female folk figure indicates society's negative attitudes toward women who appear to be threats to patriarchal structures" (34). This threat becomes quite apparent, exemplified by the men in Danticat's novel who keep the legend of the witch-woman's demise alive in songs. In like manner, Tituba poses a threat to the patriarchal structure, first to the Puritan society with Samuel Parris at its helm, and later to her husband, John Indian, and lover, Christopher, who both condemned and vilified her for being a witch and for unapologetically practicing witchcraft. This free will is what becomes most threatening because according to Gauthier it "left [her] too much room for happiness, for freedom, for power over [her] own bod[y] (201) and for reconfiguring citizenship to suit her personal (not state) needs.

Danticat's skillful insertion of this marginalized, devalued tale of the witch-woman into the master narrative serves as positive reinforcement of Anatol's "woman-centered, woman-positive reinterpretation of the tales" (34). This reinsertion necessitates revision of this once-marginal tale, resulting in a shift from the periphery to the center. As a result, the witch is re-imagined as a positive symbol of resistance and resilience. The shedding of her skin, the ability to assume an alternative identity, attests to the witch-woman's resiliency; at the same time, it symbolizes female power and agency.

This ability to transform the self powerfully resonates in the trope of "doubling," that is, assuming another form or self. Sophie engages this act during sexual intercourse. Doubling, a form of masking, functions as a skillful strategy for survival that permits one to deal with brutality and harsh realities of life. Further, locating the act of doubling within a historical context, Danticat remarks: "There were many cases in our history where our ancestors had doubled" (*Breath* 155–56). Danticat exposes how doubling can be employed as a tool of oppression for political gains: "Following the *vaudou* tradition, most of our presidents were actually one body split in two: part flesh and part shadow. That was the only way they could murder and rape so many people and still go home to play with their children and make love to their wives" (156). In this instance, they doubled to conceal their tyrannical undertakings.

In the case of the wife who doubled as a witch-woman, doubling permits temporary relief from one's skin, from womanly, wifely, and motherly responsibilities. It also validates the practice of transnationalism and allows the discursive crossing of borders. Similarly, doubling during sexual intercourse allows Sophie temporary relief from her "skin," whereby she transforms the raped body as the site of oppression to a site of resistance. The body once dubbed as state possession is now one of self-possession. Similar to the witch-woman, Sophie being able to assume an alternative identity can be likened to possessing supernatural powers, what Anzaldúa calls an "inborn extraordinary gift" (19). Further stressing the benefits of assuming alternative identities, Anzaldúa articulates that it is "compelling having an entry into both worlds," dismissing the preconceived notion that female (body) transformation points toward a gender or identity crisis (19). Rather, she counters, "what we are suffering from is an absolute despot duality that says we are able to be only one or the other" (19).[17]

In response to female limitations, Danticat permits her female characters to assume multiple identities that engender flexible citizenship. For example, the tale of shedding skin parallels another tale in the novel that offers a similar portrayal of women's transformative, supernatural power. Tired of bleeding literally and figuratively, this female heroine opted for an alternative identity that required her metamorphosing from human to butterfly. In a similar way, we witness the mother-heroine, Martine, adopting the form of a butterfly. Equally, we behold women's resistance to victimization as Sophie recalls that her mother was one "who could never bleed and then could never stop bleeding" (*Breath* 234). Unequivocally, this "double" narrative of self-possession and self-transformation exemplifies women exercising agency. The woman's ability to relinquish her old, former identity for a new one symbolizes a disjunction in the neat narrative of patriarchal domination, and it is also emblematizes subversion of female subjugation.

This tale of the demonized witch-woman serves as a prelude to the narrative of repressed female sexuality that chronicles male obsession with women's purity and chastity. The cultural practice of keeping women pure is diabolical, to say the least—a claim substantiated by the "testing" to which women are subjected.[18] As the powers dictate, mothers habitually tested their daughters by inserting their pinky into their private parts to ensure that they were virgins (*Breath* 60, 154). This study argues that the witch-wife transgresses this virginal (pure) space, or "virginity cult," as the main protagonist, Sophie, refers to the practice. As established earlier, the witch-woman's ability to transform herself, to shed her skin of her own free will, is indicative of subversion of male control. Transforming, or more pointedly performing the body to one's own likeness, renders the female subject autonomous. Notably, this autonomy resides beyond patriarchal dictates. At the same time, this body "makeover" disallows abuse, and refutes the commodification and configuration of the body as sexualized object. Reasoning that witches "are the most deliberate violators of societal tradition," Davies readily points out that this act of subversion is "a political revolt by women against 'category maintenance'" and that the witch is a "source of transgressive female power" (*Black Women* 74). Bolstering this line of reasoning, Gauthier ascertains that witches "submit to no law least of all that of gravity" (199). As trangressive subjects or calculated "violators of societal" norms, witches do not allow their bodies to be violated, primarily because they operate outside the framework of patriarchal governance. Rejection of purity and chastity as markers of female propriety and respectability corroborates that the witch-woman does not fit the description of the ideal, obedient woman/wife and citizen.

Danticat's preoccupation with female (body) transgression finds representation in another tale that strongly resonates with the narrative of "testing." Offered a marriage proposal by an extremely rich man based solely on her virginal status and not on her beauty, a black girl's resistant body challenges the "virginity cult." The transgressive act manifests in her unyielding body that refuses to bleed or "shed skin" on her wedding night.[19] Terribly disappointed that his new wife did not bleed on their wedding night, especially since this "impurity" will tarnish his honor, the husband decides that he will not face the town humiliated, and so he sets out to defend his honor by any means necessary.[20] This involves cutting "between her legs to get some blood to show" (*Breath* 154). The bride then hemorrhages to death.

On one hand, the steady flow of blood calls attention to female oppression, the profusion of women's pain and suffering. On the other hand, the bleeding body that resists and defies in turn signals the bleeding cum depletion of patriarchal control. The continually bleeding body is uncontrollable, contaminated, and deviant in the eyes of patriarchy, and therefore it is something to be feared. Anzaldúa writes that the body's uncontrollability that indicates loss, not of blood but of patriarchal control, is intricately linked to the supernatural:

> Humans fear the supernatural, both the undivine (the animal impulses such as sexuality, the unconscious, the unknown, the alien) and the divine (the superhuman, the god in us). Culture and religion seek to protect us from these two forces. The female, by virtue of creating entities of flesh and blood in her stomach (she bleeds every month but does not die), by virtue of being in tune with nature's cycle, is feared. Because, according to Christianity and most other major religions, woman is carnal, animal, close to the undivine, she must be protected. Protected from herself. Woman is the stranger, the other. She is man's recognized nightmarish pieces, his Shadow-Beast. The sight of her sends him into a frenzy of anger and fear. (17)

By Anzaldúa's account, a woman by her mere nature qualifies as a witch, a deviant. Since she poses a threat to patriarchal dominance, the most logical course of action is to "try to get rid of their deviants," their undesirable citizens (18). As we have seen, women repeatedly fall victim to this form of male censorship.

Although Gautier and Anzaldúa agree that fear of female strength occasions women's exclusion and repression, it is safe to say that there are instances when female power remains incontestable and unrivalled. A case in point is the affluent husband who, despite his financial wealth and standing in society, needed a "pure" woman to define and embolden his social status and respectability. Joan Dayan's assessment that "differences were sometimes collapsed in a reciprocity that made those supposedly inferior absolutely necessary to those who imagined themselves superior" is most useful here ("Erzulie" 10). After the young bride's death, the husband's assumed superiority diminishes as he is infantilized, equated to a child in need of maternal love and nurturance: "At the grave site, [he] drank his blood-spotted goat milk and cried like a child" (Danticat, *Breath* 155). The original purpose of drinking the blood-spotted milk was to celebrate the wife's virginal state after the consummation of their marriage. He still follows through with the ritual, sprinkling a drop of blood that he obtained from his dying wife in his milk. The consumption of milk reinforces the husband's childlike status. Furthermore, the husband's infantilization casts light on women's assertion of power, of women reclaiming the body once maligned as polluted and sexualized (object). Consuming the blood-spotted milk disproves the body as mere commodity, as the object of male sexual gratification.

Leila Neti establishes that "menstrual blood was perceived as taboo not only because it was dirty but also because it was explicitly sexualized" (80). No longer seen as a contaminant, the female body is absolved of all impurities, substantiated by the consumption of the blood-spotted milk. Hence the ingestion of blood implies alliance with the bleeding or menstruating body that is reappropriated as a site of protest. Furthering this line of reasoning, the grieving husband symbolically voices his disapproval of patriarchal dominance by decidedly refusing to partake in the silencing of women.

The language of female protest manifests further in the family name Caco, which translates as a scarlet bird. The flaming bird emblematizes freedom through flight, or to reiterate Gauthier's brilliant analysis, flight is suggestive of refusing to submit to the law of gravity, which in turn leads to the empowerment of the Caco women. Grandmè Ifé's rhetorical question to her granddaughter, Sophie, which further underscores female autonomy, encapsulates this authoritative position: "Ou libéré? Are you free, my daughter?" (*Breath* 234).[21] The description of the bird in flame—"there is always a rush of blood that rises to its neck and the wings, you would think them on fire"—bears a strong resemblance to the old higue, who transforms into a ball of fire in preparation for flight (150).[22]

Freedom is further linked with being well, with being wholesome. Wholesomeness is rendered most palpable in presenting a parallel analogy of Grandmè Ifé's rhetorical question "Are you free, my daughter?" with fellow ancestress Minnie Ransom's question to the protagonist, Velma Henry: "Are you sure, sweetheart, that you want to be well?" (Bambara 3). The uncanny similarity here is unmistakable, signaling an unspoken diasporic kinship and transnational female coalition. In her careful analysis of Bambara's *The Salt Eaters*, bell hooks ascertains that "wellness is synonymous with radical [black female] subjectivity," as she argues that Velma "has grounded her struggle for meaning within activist work for black liberation" (*Black Looks* 49). Hooks goes on to say that Velma's temporary loss of self results from her quest to "assimilate, to follow alien maps, that leads to the loss of perspective" (49). While Sophie, in her own rights, commits a radical act in reenacting the "testing" by breaking her hymen, this study locates Martine's "radical activism" within the framework of women liberation.[23] A victim of state abuse, Martine rejects reproducing the nation and takes her unborn child's life by killing herself; this radical act frees not only her but all women silenced by state violence.[24] Hence, like Velma, whose activist work exemplifies her quest for black liberation, Martine's struggle is grounded within a historical context in that it mirrors slave women who employed abortion and infanticide as potent symbols of female resistance.[25]

Martine's journey to wholesomeness finally culminates with her spiritual return to the motherland: "She is going to Guinea, or she is going to be a star. She's going to be a butterfly or a lark in a tree. She's going to be free" (Danticat, *Breath* 228). Noticeably, Martine embodies the omnipotent old higue, the all-powerful witch-woman, as she soars the ancestral realm, imitative of heaven, which exists beyond the reach of patriarchy. Her crimson two-piece burial suit and matching gloves and shoes complete the image.

Martine shares a history with Bambara's Velma in that she also suffered from momentary loss of perspective. In some respect, Martine's loss of self manifests in her quest to assimilate by whitening her skin. Further, this skin bleaching epitomizes the estrangement between Martine and Sophie, who is the first to articulate her mother's noticeable "racial" difference: "It had been almost two years since the last time we saw each other. My mother's skin was unusually light, a pale mocha, three or four shades lighter than any of ours" (Danticat, *Breath* 159). Sophie's observation precedes Grandmè Ifé's: "Your skin looks lighter. Is it prodwi? You use something?" (160). Martine's response, which was meant to deflect attention from her disembodiment, instead reinforces it: "It is very cold in America. The cold turns us into ghosts" (160). At the same time, this circumvention focuses on social disease brought on by alienation that results in the neutralization of the fixed western definition of disease as biological. Accordingly, the postcolonial ghosts that occasion Martine's haunting need to be exorcised, a fact underscored by Grandmè Ifé, who calls on the ancestor to redirect Martine's cultural unmooring: "Papa Shango, the sun here, will change that" (160).[26] There is a noticeable dichotomous distinction between "here" as in Haiti and "there," the United States; between warmth and cold; between homeliness and alienation.

Along similar lines, Martine's reference to a collective "us," as in "the cold turns us into ghosts," suggests a gendered or racialized/ethnic separation, whereby the diseased or alienated individual identifies either as female or Haitian or both. However, Martine's assertion of collective (female) disembodiment is nullified by Sophie's articulation of Martine's difference as she creates another distinct collective, "ours," remarking on the unusual lightness of Martine's skin: "three or four shades lighter than any of ours." Markedly, Martine's body estrangement sets her apart as "other," as undesirable. Whereas she is aligned with the West, with her adopted home, the United States—she is quick to remind Grandmè Ifé that she is visiting Haiti "for only three days"—the other women clearly identify with the landscape, the motherland, Haiti (160).[27] Martine's otherness is magnified threefold when a neighborhood teenage boy, Eliab, announces her return to Haiti, presenting her to her own mother in the following manner: "That lady, she says she belongs to you" (158). Later, Eliab poses the same question to Sophie, inquiring if "the new lady . . . belong[s] to [her]" (166). Thus Martine's skin lightening belies her claim of belonging. This claim is simultaneously a disclaimer as Martine's difference is both somatic and geographic.

Martine's ambivalence starkly contrasts with Grandmè Ifé's resoluteness, her permanence. This fact is punctuated in a conversation they share in which Martine remarks that Grandmè Ifé is "still wear[ing] the deuil," to which Grandmè Ifé responds, "The black is easier; it does not get dirty" (*Breath* 160).[28] One can reasonably analogize that the color "black" has racial connotations, in that it stands in opposition to Martine's whitened skin. Grandmè Ifé's declaration about Martine's skin reinforces this line of reasoning. Furthermore, the durability of the deuil debatably reveals Martine's presumed instability. As Donna Hope reminds us about those who engage in the process of skin whitening: "Bleachers [are seen] as mentally unstable, traitors to their race and colour, and social deviants and outcasts" (132).[29] Despite the fact that Hope analyzes skin bleaching within dancehall culture in Jamaica, her analysis is pertinent to this discourse. Winnifred Brown-Glaude upholds this view that bleachers "violate racial norms and are viewed, in many ways, as 'race traitors'" (35). As we have seen time and time again, deviance is encoded onto the female body; it is constructed as female disease. In her analysis of dancehall culture, Hope ascertains that skin bleaching "has historically been coded as feminine" (131). Analyzing bleaching within dancehall culture, Hope reveals that the reception to bleaching is ambivalent whereby it is "simultaneously derogated and uplifted" (132). Martine's bleached body undeniably sets her apart from the other Caco women and from the Haitian landscape. Perhaps this difference is most tangible because Martine constructs herself within the white gaze, emblematized by her adopted homeland, the United States.

Martine's bleached body lends itself equally to her visibility/invisibility. It invalidates the more serious affliction of breast cancer, from which she suffers. This practice of bleaching debatably entails a body- or self-betrayal that consequently manifests in Martine's denial or silencing of breast cancer as she casually informs Grandmè Ifé that the prosthetics she intermittently wears "are not really part of me" (*Breath* 163). In essence, the cosmetic practice of bleaching eclipsed this serious female affliction.

The loss of perspective and citizen rights is a recurring theme in black women's writing. Paule Marshall's *Praisesong for the Widow* is one example. On a cruise aboard the *Bianca Pride*, the middle-aged protagonist, Avatara (Avey) Johnson, suffers a temporary loss of self after consuming a Peach Parfait à la Versailles (49). This loss of self, which bears the imprint of excess and extravagance, manifests in body discomfort that culminates in the eventual termination of Avey's European vacation:

> She might have gorged herself only to have her system break down under the overload, leaving the mass of undigested food stalled not only in her stomach but across the entire middle of her body. Oddly enough there was no nausea or pain, nothing to suggest seasickness or—the terrifying thought had instantly crossed her mind—the first signs of a heart attack. She felt perfectly all right otherwise. There was only the mysterious clogged and swollen feeling which differed in intensity and came and went at will.
> (*Praisesong* 51–52)

The parfait connotes strangeness or alienation, and the European language reinforces the estrangement Avey experiences. Significantly, Avey's European cruise is abruptly terminated by her great-aunt Cuney, who redirects her wanderings, compelling her to visit the island of Carriacou, where she not only regains her cultural mooring but also regains contact with the ancestors. Moreover, this estrangement occasions the disease that leads to Avey's disembodiment, which "Felt like a huge tumor had suddenly ballooned up at her center" (*Praisesong* 52). Avey's consumption of the foreign food, therefore, is detrimental to her sense of self, as it destabilizes her connection with her culture and her community at large. Furthermore, her disease is brought on by the relentless pursuit of material acquisition. In this regard, disease is linked with capitalism cum Europeanization and obsessive consumerism. Being well necessitates that Avey perform a literal purging and cleansing of her body. It is not surprising that Avey is displaced on the cruise ship; she experiences chronic body discomfort. While her body undergoes turbulence, "this ship's steady as a rock":

> Her head would start to ache again, and then there would be the mysterious welling up in her stomach. Moreover, each time she rose to leave, a tremor would sweep the deck under her feet for an instant as the liner gave the troubled heave and roll only she seemed to be aware of. (*Praisesong* 53, 54)

Astoundingly, Avey's body regains its balance; it achieves spiritual equanimity and wholeness as she finds herself among her kinfolks on the island of Carriacou, despite never having met or set eyes on them.

Along similar lines, Valérie Loichot directs our attention to "food consumption" as a form of detachment. Eating disorders are a known consequence of sexual violence (Flores-Ortiz 352). We witness how Sophie's experiences manifest somatically. In analyzing Sophie Caco's displacement into the "foreign urban space of Brooklyn," Loichot remarks: "Sophie's body, like the serialized food products she consumes, becomes detached from any coherent system of reference. The body turned thing does not fit the predetermined Western mold" (93). Consequently, Loichot concludes that Sophie's rejection of the food she ingests leads to the onset of bulimia: "Furthermore, this disease, which her Haitian grandmother does not understand, makes her body untranslatable to the Haitian language and system of communication" (93). Sophie's body is no more or less translatable on American soil than it is on the Haitian landscape. Regardless, her affliction with the "foreign" disease on foreign soil signals alienation and dislocation. Logically, this affliction can be interpreted as the making of a subsumed identity in keeping with the American principle of unreserved assimilation and conditional citizenship. As we have witnessed, this process of assimilation comes at an exorbitant price: loss of perspective and loss of self.

In her theorization of bulimia as a female disease, Bordo addresses how disorders such as anorexia and bulimia have "historically been class- and race-biased, largely (although not exclusively) occurring among white middle- and upper-middle-class women" (*Unbearable Weight* 167–68). In light of this fact, Grandmè Ifé's proclamation about bulimia being inherently an American disease has currency in that it points to access and accessibility as it constructs the disease as a social rather than a biological malaise. Punctuating this classed distinction, Martine's interpretation of her "undiagnosed" eating disorder is constructed within a socioeconomic framework: "When I first came, I used to eat the way we ate at home. I ate for tomorrow and the next day and the day after that, just in case I had nothing to eat for the next couple of days. I ate reserves" (Danticat, *Breath* 179–80). Along these lines, Martine's eating disorder is brought on by lack of resources, monetarily and material, epitomized by the term *reserves*. Thus her body functions as a reserve, the stockpile for excess. However, once located in the "land of excess," once the body meets the (foreign) land, it is constructed as diseased, functioning palpably as a site of isolation, exile, discrimination, and racism. Consequently, Sophie and Martine experience alienation and body estrangement from both home and host country; their bodies become the site upon which estrangement is encoded. This discomfiture registers on Martine's body through the practice of bleaching and on Sophie's by way of bulimia. Notwithstanding, the "bodily inflictions" are different and therefore experienced differently. Whereas Martine's illness is self-inflicted, resulting from an identity crisis, that is, her desire for whiteness (a strong signifier of her estrangement), Sophie's is a medical disorder. This malaise disproportionately infects migrating subjects, despite different body experiences in the host and home countries. Furthermore, both women are victims of rape.

Although not a victim of rape or diagnosed with bulimia or anorexia, Marie-Noëlle Titane, the protagonist of Condé's novel *Desirada*, suffers from another form of body disorder, tuberculosis, which manifests in weight loss and rejection of food. During her quarantine at the sanatorium for TB patients, Marie-Noëlle makes the stark discovery that her disease is symptomatic of a world composed of selfish adults. Accordingly, those inflicted with disease are the helpless, dependent offspring:

> The boarders all suffered from the illness she had been exposed to, an illness more widespread than tuberculosis—the absence of love. These poor children had been exiled to the boarding school to humor a stepfather or stepmother who could not put up with them . . . so as not to encumber the life of parents busy earning more and more money or treating themselves to the good life in far-off places. (*Desirada* 69)

Paradoxically, consumption, a colloquial term for tuberculosis, is subverted by the parents' compulsive overindulgence. A greater paradox is Marie-Noëlle's rejection of food, which parallels her mother's rejection of her. The potential loss of her right lung—"A routine medical check-up at school showed that Marie-Noëlle had tuberculosis in her right lung"—is illustrative of both dependence and independence (59). On one hand, her dependence is rendered palpable because she has lost her life support, her mother, her right hand, so to speak. Marie-Noëlle is repeatedly abandoned. Left in the care of her adopted mother, Ranélise, by her biological mother, Reynalda, her idyllic life comes to a halt when Reynalda sends for her. Having left Guadeloupe for Paris, Marie-Noëlle is completely ignored yet again by her mother and left in the care of her stepfather, Ludovic. She later migrates to the United States where she becomes romantically involved with Stanley and Terri, who subsequently abandon her. Her independence becomes manifest for the reason that she now has to fend for herself; the remaining left lung reinforces this line of argument. .

Alternatively, as Bordo eloquently puts it, "the symptomatology of these disorders reveals itself as textuality. Loss of mobility, loss of voice, inability to leave the home, feeding others while starving oneself . . . all have symbolic meaning" (*Unbearable Weight* 168). Given these circumstances, configuring bulimia as an American disease underscores privilege, excess, and access, which contrast with the lived experiences of the Caco women. Martine is quick to point this out after expressing dismay that a Haitian woman, let alone her daughter, had contracted bulimia: "I have never heard of a Haitian woman getting anything like that. Food, it was so rare when we were growing up. We could not waste it. . . . I couldn't believe all the different kinds of apples and ice cream. All the things that only the rich eat in Haiti, everyone could eat them here, dirt cheap" (Danticat, *Breath* 179). Whereas "waste" here connotes extravagance of consumer culture, Martine's account implies that the United States is a classless society that permits unrestricted movement and migrations. This purported view is almost immediately invalidated. All the while articulating that Sophie contracting the disease induces her Americanization, Martine nevertheless accentuates both her and Sophie's difference as cause for celebration.

Sophie's bulimia resonates with the gorging and eventual purging that Avey also accomplishes in ridding herself of consumer culture. Addressing the structural contradiction of this disease that leaves its imprint on the female body, Bordo articulates:

Bulimia precisely and explicitly expresses the extreme development of the hunger for unrestrained consumption (exhibited in the bulimic's uncontrollable food binges) existing in unstable tension alongside the requirement that we sober up, "clean up our act," get back in firm control on Monday morning (the necessity for purge—exhibited in the bulimic's vomiting, compulsive exercising, and laxative purges). (*Unbearable Weight* 201)

Binging can be seen as exacting control over the body. Loichot points out that "controlling food intake appears to be the only way to master the body," but it also calls attention to one's lack of control, manifested in obsessive and uncontrollable consumption (101). Situating the act of purging within a political framework, the study contends that the action denotes expulsion of the processed, genetically engineered, and modified food that engenders contamination of the body through congestion. Likewise, the ingestion of foreign foods engenders de-familiarization of the self, of the body. This is manifestly exemplified in the frozen foods that Sophie and Martine habitually consume. Sophie recounts: "I usually ate random concoctions: frozen dinner, samples from global cookbooks, food that was easy to put together. . . . Fried chicken, glazed potatoes, and broiled vegetables. Everything came frozen out of a box" (Danticat, *Breath* 151, 198). Consequently, Sophie is unable to digest the alien products. In the same vein, "good food" is contrasted with foreign, processed food; it is decisively local and specifically Haitian. While vacationing in Haiti, Martine proposes to treat Sophie's bulimia: "We'll have no more of that bulimia. I'll cure it with some good food" (182). Purging therefore is a decontaminant. Keeping with this line of reasoning, purging enables eradication of the European or western value system. We only need to recall how ingestion of foreign products or European values lends to the disfiguration of the body. Martine's use of a bleaching agent to whiten her skin serves as a prime example. Moreover, the act of purging shares a common feature with the shedding of skin in that they both engender the politics of resistance.

In her analysis of Tsitsi Dangarembga's novel *Nervous Conditions*, Andrea Shaw reveals that the black anorexic female body is configured as the "destabilizing result of colonialization" (7). Scholar Lily Mabura concurs, establishing that Nyasha Sigauke "experiences a nervous breakdown when faced with the dual oppressions of her father's patriarchal ways and colonial racism" (91). Like Sophie, Nyasha is afflicted by anorexia, a disease not normally associated with black women. Like Martine, who mistakenly diagnoses Sophie's bulimia as a sign that she is becoming very American (*Breath* 179), Nyasha's mother cautions her about becoming "too Anglicised" (Dangarembga 74). Along these lines, many scholars read black female affliction with bulimia and anorexia as adopting white values. I, however, choose an alternative discursive path that illustrates that the body resists and appropriates western values. As follows, Nyasha's emaciated body, which is anomalous to the African notion of wellness and the landscape, not only embodies the devastating effects of colonization but also exemplifies the demise of the African nation-state at the hands of the colonizers.[30] By the same accord, Nyasha's body functions as a site of resistance to colonial and indigenous patriarchal oppression. Grandmè Ifé engages a destabilizing act of her own by skillfully blurring the lines between the biological and the social, thereby bolstering the inherent contradiction of disease. Sophie explains how she configures or, more pointedly, reappropriates her disorder: "To my grandmother, chagrin was a genuine physical disease. Like a hurt leg or a broken arm. To treat chagrin, you drank tea from leaves that only my grandmother and other old wise women could recognize" (*Breath* 24). Tante Atie then explains to Sophie that chagrin "was not a sudden illness, but something that could kill you slowly, taking a small piece of you every day until one day it finally takes all of you away" (25). Giving social disease and biological disease equal attention underscores the dire need to address socioeconomic and racial inequities and consequently the necessity of a transnational understanding of and approach to illness. It also demands that society acknowledge that social disorder is a corollary to biological disorder.

While Sophie's bulimia is undoubtedly conditioned by male hegemony, it exhibits traits of obscurity, which begs the question: is Sophie's bulimia misappropriated or, more pointedly, reappropriated, since it sets forth a challenge by having more in common with anorexia? Bordo's response is most effective. She says that the anorectic "is quite aware of the social and sexual vulnerability involved in having a female body; many, in fact, were sexually abused as children" (*Unbearable Weight* 179). She adds: "Anorexia . . . is seen as an extreme development of the capacity for self-denial and repression of desire" (201). Operating within the framework of Bordo's theorization, in "doubling" during sex acts, Sophie engenders self-mastery as she arguably "transcends the flesh" (202). In other words, Sophie engenders the "process of dissociation" that Yvette Flores-Ortiz labels "a psychological strategy [that causes] the mind and body to separate" (350). "Doubling" places Sophie in a zone where she is unreachable, untouchable, "out of reach of hurt," to echo Bordo (178). Recounting her pain during sexual intercourse, she tells Grandmè Ifé: "It is very painful for me ... I have no desire. I feel like it is an evil thing to do.... I hate my body. I am ashamed to show it to anybody, including my husband. Sometimes I feel like I should be off somewhere by myself" (Danticat, *Breath* 123). Nevertheless, this illusory power that Sophie exacts through "doubling" is interrupted by her timely return to the site of the abuse—the cane fields, where the once violated female body is recuperated, made well and whole again, and rendered desirable.

It is interesting that although Sophie admits that she is bulimic, she paradoxically seeks a therapeutic remedy from a Santería priestess and not from a physician. Even so, naming her disease simultaneously bears the imprint of a disclaimer, as she remains aloof to the diagnosis by not lending it specificity. As a result, we sense some level of indeterminacy, which arguably accounts for her subtle denouncement of modern medicine as she seeks help from a female spiritual leader. This spiritual leader doubles as Sophie's therapist. By the same accord, Sophie's midwife, notably an Indian woman who delivered her daughter, Brigitte, later doubles as Brigitte's pediatrician (*Breath* 197). Here again we witness a female-centered diaspora at work. The reasoning behind this pervasive choice of female practitioners finds articulation in Susan Wendell's analysis. She observes that philosophers of medical ethics engage in perpetuating the idea that the main goal of medicine is to control the body ("Toward" 73). By referring to Santería, the Caribbean African-derived religion, Sophie resists complete absorption into western medicine. Arguably, Martine's circumvention of western practitioners registers her fear of self-absorption into western medicine. She refuses to visit a psychiatrist, citing hypnosis as a deterrent; later she rejects the idea of seeing a doctor, predicting that the diagnosis will result in her being committed to a mental institution. Additionally, through Sophie's questioning, we find out that Martine does not take birth control (*Breath* 190–91). Yet the administering of local medicine, in lieu of modern medicine, to prevent pregnancy is a persistent theme.

Highlighting the need for medicine to move "further into the community as one agent of social change among many," Stanford cautions that medicine should "adopt a realistic view of its limits. It is not and cannot be the cure for all ills" (*Bodies* 31). Further, offering a plausible assessment of Sophie's refusal to name the illness, Stanford underscores the strategic implication of this act: "Refusing to *name* the illness . . . render[s] the concept of disease problematic and resist[s] the naming definitions that would serve as access points for institutionalized, technological medicine" ("Mechanisms" 31). Hence, by resisting the "naming definitions," Sophie circumvents easy and unlimited access to her body, therefore forestalling possible misdiagnosis. In this same vein, her reluctance to name the illness lends itself to subconscious fear of being overmedicalized. In this climate of overdiagnosis and misdiagnosis, that has seemingly become the trademark of western medicine.

Santería, with its rejection of individualization, further provides Sophie with the power to resist institutionalized medicine. As Miguel Barnet observes, the importance of family lies at the core of this religion: "The orisha relation is linked to the idea of family. The extended family originates from a common ancestor and includes both the living and the dead" (22). This family-centered religion is diasporic and transnational in scope. Moreover, this reverence to a common ancestor finds representation in the weekly healing sessions that Sophie and fellow victims of male oppression attend to address their "sexual phobia" (Danticat, *Breath* 201). Buki, an Ethiopian college student, was a victim of clitoridectomy; Davina, a middle-aged Chicana woman, was raped by her grandfather for ten years. During their sessions, the women dress in white and have their keepsakes with them at all times; Sophie takes the statue of Erzulie. In this safe female space, the women are unrestrained by social and patriarchal boundaries and borders.

Even so, global female oppression is alive and well, as these immigrant women have ironically exchanged one site of oppression for another. Their bodies then become the text upon which disease is inscribed. This inscription is most visible on the bodies of the Caco woman, who all suffer from a disfigured body or body parts: Grandmè Ifé has a "curved spine and a pineapple size hump," Martine has "grown egg-sized mounds in both her breasts," Tante Atie has "a lump on her calf," and Sophie is bulimic (*Breath* 113, 148).[31] Similarly, Kincaid's immigrant women are afflicted bodily, while their American counterparts live in luxury.[32] In the given context, colonization functions as the primary disabling factor for the underprivileged female protagonists. While these physical scars are emblematic of the women's lived experiences, they are equally symptomatic of societal ills.

By shedding additional light on the racialized migrating bodies of women, the goal here is to underscore that by virtue of their immigrant status, these female migrants' bodies are marked, rendered disabled by their migrant (non-citizen) status. Anzaldúa poignantly categorizes this "disability" as "*una herida abierta* where the Third World grates against the first and bleeds" (3). Consequently, the women who belong to this "border culture" are inhabitants of the "borderland" (3). Marginalization, therefore, occurs in the form of race, class, and gender. Stanford's position reverberates loud and clear as she unequivocally champions the idea that social context is of utmost importance in accessing women's illnesses. She writes: "Without biomedical diagnostic labels, these illnesses are out of medicine's reach and remain in the domain of those people and communities best equipped to understand, those who have the wisdom and skill to facilitate a healing that is not and cannot be separate from social context" (Stanford, "Mechanisms" 31). Stanford's reasoning holds true. We witness repeatedly that the treatment of the protagonists (Annie, Avey, Marie-Noëlle, and Sophie) is spearheaded by women healers, who unequivocally inhabit the ancestral realm, where they operate beyond the reach of the nation-state.[33]

Modern medicine's inability to render a diagnosis or cure undergirds the line of argument that the women's illnesses are sociosomatic and deeply embedded in a sexist and racist society. Tante Atie's requiring "leeches [to suck] the blood out of her lump" as a form of therapeutic remedy (*Breath* 148) substantiates the assertion that "in some cases, medicine's tools are simply inappropriate or that the cure may be actually worse than the illness" (Stanford, "Mechanisms" 31). Moreover, a perfect example of the cure being worse than the illness is exemplified in the earlier scene where Ma Chess's son, John, dies after being treated with western medicine.

In the above analyses, class is pivotal, as the women are marked not only by their immigrant status but also by their destitution and impoverished state. Farmer's proclamation about "a comprehensive theory of poverty, of a world designed by the elites of all nations to serve their own ends" is most valuable here (Kidder 73). As discussed earlier, the women who are identified as diseased are disadvantaged politically, socially, and economically. Nevertheless, Farmer readily reminds us that these individuals are disenfranchised not by choice but by design, as he repeatedly cites colonizing spaces, "Western powers, those of France and the United States," for the strategic demise of Haiti and other countries (73). State censorship in turn lends itself to individual (bodily) restrictions; unsuspecting women are used as mouthpieces for state propaganda, or they are erroneously constructed as mothers of the nation-state. Despite this classed difference, and regardless of the limitations ascribed to the black immigrant woman, Lorde calls for a construction of a language of our own, one that repudiates the existing hegemonic language and captures and accommodates the full essence of the black woman. She shares with us this language of female empowerment by means of a personal account of her mother's strength and resilience:

> My mother was a powerful woman. This was so in a time when that word-combination of woman and powerful was almost unexpressable in the white American common tongue, except or unless it was accompanied by some aberrant explaining adjective like blind, or hunchback, or crazy, or black. Therefore when I was growing up, powerful woman equaled something else quite different from ordinary woman, from simply "woman." It certainly did not, on the other hand, equal "man." (*Zami* 15)

Empowered women were once regarded as deviant and anomalous, constructed within a pathological framework. Lorde cautions that this language of difference penned by the male hegemony is divisive, convenient, and concocted to appease racist and sexist ideology and age-old fantasies of white male patriarchy. Furthermore, Lorde's adoption/adaptation of a third space, what Garland-Thomson calls the "third designation" that repudiates strict Western medical standards through its definition of bodies in strict biological terms, serves as counter narrative to white racist ideology and to the masculinist discourse. This alternative space not only confronts and challenges gender and race prejudices, but it also provides an alternative politic of bodies and wellness. Moreover, in feminizing the highly charged masculinist medical discourse that was once an exclusive tool of patriarchy, Lorde neutralizes, or, more poignantly, normalizes it. Conclusively, Lorde's analysis of her mother's power serves as a blueprint for female empowerment and autonomy.

Danticat, Marshall, Condé, and Kincaid chronicle "bodily experiences" as they re-member the dismembered and displaced bodies of black women. Giving voice to women's migratory experiences, they reinstate them as desirable citizens. As a result, the disfigured and diseased female body is claimed and celebrated, resulting in the un-silencing of the severed flesh. Subversively, the flesh cum body becomes a space of narration and female empowerment. This space chronicles bodily ruptures and dispersals, and it also promotes knowledge and acceptance of the body, even while underscoring female agency. This space, which permits healing through administering alternative cures, becomes a site of reconciliation and recuperation, where the body once deemed unfit, disabled, diseased, deviant, obscene, and unseen is rendered well and whole(some) again.

3. Alongside Côte d'Ivoire, other countries included in this grouping are Democratic Republic of Congo, Zimbabwe, Mauritania, and Uganda.

4. Baartman's theft is substantiated by the fact that a "new law barred colonists from taking native-born Khoekhoe outside the colony." See Frith, "Searching for Sara Baartman."

5. See http://dictionary.reference.com/.

6. Baartman's status as enslaved or free in the household of her colonist, Pieter Cesars, continues to be the subject of ongoing debate. Nevertheless, Cesars transferred ownership of Baartman to Dunlop, who convinced Baartman she would make a fortune if she traveled with him to London. She accompanied him in 1810; this migratory journey signaled the beginning of her descent, her loss of self. In 1814 she was traded yet again to London theater impresario Henry Taylor, who took her to Paris, where she continued to be on public display, before Taylor traded her to the animal trainer Reaux. Baartman died in 1815.

7. I borrowed the subtitle of Davies's book, *Black Women, Writing, and Identity: Migrations of the Subject*.

8. In 1817 the French zoologist Baron Georges Cuvier dissected her, casting her body in a plaster and preserving her brain and genitalia in a jar that remained on display at the Musée de L'Homme in Paris until 1974, at which time her remains were removed from public view.

9. I use the word *excess* to focus on the constricting binaries within which Baartman and Lorde, and by default all black women, are framed. While Baartman's hypervisibility, her excess flesh, results in public humiliation and derision, Lorde's hypovisibility, her lack, is also the subject of debate.

10. Allegedly Baartman was also a prostitute. Even so, her provocative display for profit echoed and simulated the figure of the prostitute. Furthermore, the touching and prodding of Baartman's buttocks becomes reminiscent of black slave women on the auction block.

11. Claiming his autonomy, his manhood, the value of his body by talking/fighting back, Sixo challenges white supremacy by refusing to have his self-worth defined by those terms.

12. "Letter from the President: Saartjie's Return Restores Our Common Dignity," http://web.mit.edu/racescience/in_media/baartman/baartman_mbekiletter.htm.

13. Other probable causes of Baartman's death include syphilis, smallpox, pneumonia, and poor diet. Harriet Washington explains that although Baartman's death is widely ascribed to syphilis, there is no proof. However, she ascertains that Baartman took to drinking heavily in the final year of her life. Other critics such as Stephen Gould ascribe the cause of death to "an inflammatory ailment," and Crais and Scully suggest that the cause of death was pneumonia resulting from a "poor diet and terrible cold." For further details, see Stephen J. Gould, *The Flamingo's Smile: Reflections in Natural History*.

14. Magubane is critical of Sander Gilman's (racial) assessment of Baartman, arguing that Baartman and the KhoiKhoi people in general are seen as representatives of all Africans.

15. Rachel Holmes takes issue with Mbeki's reference to Baartman as "a simple African

woman," arguing that even though he meant well, it "struck an odd patronizing note." I arrive at a very different conclusion from Holmes. In choosing to underscore Baartman's "simplicity," Mbeki intimates that race and class are pivotal in her definition—specifically, her denunciation at the hands of white supremacists. Additionally, her "simplicity" bridged the gap between rich and poor as South African women of all class, race, and creed took to the streets to denounce the passbook laws and to demand their lawful rights.

16. See Biseswar's "A New Discourse on 'Gender' in Ethiopia."

17. Ndinda and Adar cite the Pan Africanist Congress (PAC), the South African Communist Party (SACP), and the Inkatha Freedom Party (IFP) as other groups that represented African nationalism.

18. My intention is not to make light of the many women and girls who continue to face routinized physical and verbal abuse. Ndinda and Adar remind us that "South Africa currently has one of the highest rape incidences in the world. The incidences of rape are recorded in terms of the number of women raped per minute." See Ndinda and Adar, "The Interaction of Nationalist and Feminist Goals with Reference to the South African Liberation Movement."

19. "The Long Walk of Nelson Mandela: An Intimate Portrait of One of the Twentieth Century's Greatest Leaders," *Frontline,* PBS, WGBH, Boston, May 25, 1999, transcript, http://www.pbs.org/wgbh/pages/frontline/shows/mandela/etc/script.html.

20. Dr. Frene Ginwala is a journalist, politician, and former speaker of the National Assembly of South Africa (1994–2004). On September 30, 2007, President Thabo Mbeki appointed her to investigate the national director of public prosecutions, Vusi Pikoli.

21. It can be reasonably argued that Baartman's return/rebirth coincides with the birth of the post-apartheid South African nation. Crais and Scully document that discussions about Baartman's return to South Africa were initiated by the Khoekhoe people, who invoked the book of Ezekiel in which the Spirit serves as a guiding light to the path of "reconciliation and rebirth." Further, Crais and Scully explain that the Griqua National Conference leader and chief A.A.S. Le Fleur brought to President Nelson Mandela's attention the plight of Saartjie Baartman, suggesting her repatriation. It is somewhat surprising that Mandela was not (made) aware of Baartman's plight prior to this scheduled meeting with the chief. However, the meeting's success became the catalyst for further success, as Mandela was able to initiate meaningful dialogue with President François Mitterrand, resulting in Baartman's repatriation. What remains indisputable, nevertheless, is that Mandela's international influence facilitated, and perhaps even expedited, Baartman's eventual return.

22. On December 10, 1996, Mandela signed South Africa's new constitution, which included sweeping human rights and antidiscrimination guarantees. In a highly symbolic gesture, Mandela chose Sharpeville, the locale where the conflict (massacre) climaxed between the black opposition and the apartheid promoters, leaving 69 blacks dead and over 180 injured, as the site for signing the constitution into law. Debatably the most revered man in the country, Mandela initiated the country's transition from tyranny to democracy.

23. Similar to Mandela and following in his father's (Govan Mbeki, a stalwart of ANC) footsteps, Thabo Mbeki was an active member of the African National Congress. He

took part in underground activities and was involved in mobilizing students in support of the ANC. Exiled in several countries, including the United Kingdom, Botswana, Swaziland, and Namibia—his primary base, for his participation in anti-apartheid engagements, he returned to South Africa after Mandela was released from prison.

24. Contributing to Baartman's stature as national symbol, filmmaker Zola Mazeko has directed two documentaries, *The Life and Times of Sara Baartman* and *The Return of Sarah Bartman*.

25. "Black History Spotlight: Saartjie Baartman," http://concreteloop.com/2008/03/black-history-spotlight-saartjie-baartman.

26. Baartman was also a biological mother. However, her experience of mothering/motherhood was short-lived, having given birth to three children who all died shortly after they were born. Baartman served as a surrogate mother, specifically a wet nurse, to the daughter of Henrik Cesars, brother of Pieter Cesars.

27. "Black History Spotlight: Saartjie Baartman," http://concreteloop.com/2008/03/black-history-spotlight-saartjie-baartman.

28. Ibid.

29. Instituted in 1994, National Women's Day Celebrations now takes place annually in South Africa.

30. Crais and Scully explain that the reference group that was created by the Department of Arts and Culture to oversee the return, burial, and memorialization of Baartman is now commonly referred to as "Mama Saartjie, the maternal figure of the new South Africa" (155).

Chapter 2. "Crimes against the Flesh"

1. Although Alexander is writing specifically about homosexuality, her argument is germane to this discussion.

2. For Lorde, medical "intrusion" manifests in the pervasive and relentless promotion of cosmetic surgery, often at the expense of real health concerns.

For more on policing or profiling of the body, see Silliman and Bhattacharjee, eds., *Policing the National Body*; Yancy, *Black Bodies, White Gazes*; and Van Thompson, *Eating the Black Body*.

3. In the postscript to *A Burst of Light*, Lorde chronicles her declining health, detailing how her breast cancer has metastasized into liver cancer.

4. Other black writers who discursively link biological ills with social/societal ills include Jamaica Kincaid, Paule Marshall, Toni Cade Bambara, Edwidge Danticat, and Erna Brodber.

5. Tricked into believing that they were being treated for syphilis, 399 black men became victim to what has been regarded as the worst medical breach of trust in the history of the United States. Actually, the men were used as experiments. Originally projected to last six months, the study, which began in 1932, continued for forty years.

6. De Veaux examines how through these diasporic affiliations and exchanges, Lorde fostered a relationship with the "South African writer-activist Ellen Kuzwayo, and a link with a black women's movement in South Africa [which] signified a powerful, contemporary example of the international links between the quest for black liberation in American and in Africa" (280).

7. Reporting on black women and breast cancer for the *CBS Evening News*, James M. Klatell confirmed that "black women under the age of 50 are 77 percent more likely to die from the disease than white women of all ages." He was referring to one of the most aggressive and deadly forms of breast cancer, which has become known as "triple negative": estrogen receptor-negative, progesterone receptor-negative, and HER2-negative. See James M. Klatell, "Black Women and Breast Cancer: At Higher Risks, According to Statistics, for One Form of the Disease," *CBS Evening News*, August 26, 2007. http://www.cbsnews.com/stories/2007/08/26/eveningnews/main3204747.shtml. Suspicion among some blacks prevails, specifically in regard to labeling disease "black disease." An immediate example is found in the comments posted in response to Klatell's article. While race consideration to effect diagnosis and cure is sometimes necessary or required, one need not throw caution to the wind because race could be used (and has been) subversively as a bait to engender (medical) discrimination.

8. Thatcher Carter cites Susan Sontag's *Illness as Metaphor* as another seminal autobiographical work that was published as a result of this public awareness campaign.

9. "Dahomey Amazons," http://www.athleticwomen.com/blog/archives/28-Dahomey-Amazons.html.

10. The Amazonian women are known to practice celibacy and to reject the tradition of marriage. In an interesting parallel, Lorde's belief is at odds with conventional marriages, even though she had been married.

11. In this article Hammonds makes specific reference to another disease, AIDS, that has afflicted black women in large numbers. She cites their presumed "uncontrolled sexuality" as one of the key features in their representation in the AIDS epidemic.

12. I envision Lorde's mastectomy surgically and symbolically.

13. One may recall the much publicized coverage of Laci Peterson of Modesto, California, who was murdered by her husband, Scott Peterson, when she was seven and a half months pregnant with her first child. King calls attention to the fact that although Laci Peterson is presented to the public as "a white, Anglo-American woman, [she] was white racially, but of Hispanic identity."

14. James Byrd Jr., a black man of Jasper, Texas, was brutally murdered by three white supremacists. Stripped naked and chained by the ankles to their pickup truck, he was dragged for three miles, resulting in his decapitation and loss of his arm.

15. Accused of being a man at one of her lectures on the abolition of slavery, Sojourner Truth was challenged by a man to prove that she wasn't male. She, in turn, bared her breasts in public to disprove this vicious allegation. See Deborah Gray White, *Ar'n't I a Woman*.

In a closely related matter, genitals as a marker of gender difference are now up for debate, according to Sumi Colligan, who documents that the Intersex Society of North America (ISNA) questions the medical assertion that genitals are natural signifiers of gender.

16. Some of the cultural extremities which Creed cites that have become attached to the lesbian body include pseudo-male, animalistic, and narcissistic.

17. Placing under intense scrutiny the reduction of women to objects and the veneration of men as warriors, Lorde points out that the society, the world at large, has unquestionably accepted Israeli prime minister Moshe Dayan's "abnormality," his missing eye.

Yet women with breast cancer are commanded, or at least expected, to be conspiratorial as they trivialize their scars by concealing or disguising them.

18. Since the late 1990s we have also witnessed a rapid increase in lip augmentation surgery, which aims to improve the appearance of the lips by increasing their fullness.

19. As radio personality Don Imus's outburst substantiates, this practice gets reappropriated and reimagined in the dominant culture. On his April 2, 2007, edition of MSNBC's *Imus in the Morning,* Imus referred to the eight black and two white players on the Rutgers women's basketball team as "nappy-headed hos." In one of his previously featured shows, his sports announcer, Sid Rosenberg, not only referred to the renowned sister duo Venus and Serena Williams as "animals," but he also said that they stood a better chance of being featured in *National Geographic* than in *Playboy.*

20. I argue that Lorde's frequent reference to America with the lowercase *a* is symbolic of grammatical (surgical) amputation that engenders the de-normalization of the standard, the imperial power.

Chapter 3. Framing Violence

1. Abena ultimately attempts to regain her citizen rights. Refusing the sexual overtures of her master, Darnell Davis, she attempts to kill him, an act for which she is murdered by hanging.

2. Although Yao is Tituba's stepfather, he effectively "mothers" her, standing in for her own mother whose relationship with Tituba is momentarily strained as a result of her rape. Furthermore, Yao's ability to effectively mother alludes to the weakening of the nation defined by masculine power and prowess.

3. Tituba's radicalism resonates with Lorde's militarization.

4. The full title of Cathy Caruth's book reads *Unclaimed Experience: Trauma, Narrative, and History.*

5. The inclusion of Angela Davis to write the foreword to this book crystallizes Morrison's concept of the global neighborhood as we witness the female diaspora in dialogue, transcending space, time, and geography.

6. Yao, an Ashanti, was bought by Darnell Davis in the same batch as Abena. When he found out that Abena was with child as a result of the rape she suffered by the English sailor, he took her away from the service of his wife, Jennifer, and gave her to Yao as punishment.

7. My use of the word *murder* is deliberate. It punctuates the modes of resistance employed by slave women that range from murder to poisoning, abortion, and infanticide.

8. Darnell viewed Abena's pregnancy as a burden, likening it to ill health. In other words, she becomes an unprofitable investment, especially since he had already lost one male slave to death. By offering Abena to Yao, he hoped that it would renew Yao's desire to live; thereby, his investment would prove valuable.

9. White argues that black men were able to escape the label of Negro by identifying or being identified with things masculine, aggressive, and dominant. Similarly, white women, as part of the dominant group, could break free from the label of woman. Unjustly, the black woman was entrapped and could not escape either myth as she is ensnared in one or the other.

10. White remarks that these debates take place not only in parlor and dinner conversations but also in articles in major periodicals.

11. I place *shortcomings* in quotes because obviously Mosher did not interpret Indian's action or character as flawed.

12. Upon Tituba's insistence that she did not know her, and therefore she should not pursue her, Judah White simply blurted out: "Come on, don't be silly. I'm a friend of Mama Yaya. My name is Judah White" (51). This sole, persuasive pronouncement intimates unquestionable kinship.

13. I am suggesting here that Tituba's unrestricted migrations engender the practice of flexible citizenship.

14. White documents that slave women were able to skillfully delay childbearing after attaining reproductive capacity. See *Ar'n't I a Woman*, 104.

15. Benjamin d'Azevedo eventually granted Tituba her freedom.

16. Condé explicitly distinguishes the oppositional role of invisible forces in any given community. On one hand, the individual embodies good. On the other hand, s/he represents evil. As a witch, Tituba's resolute goal was to improve the lives of the inhabitants of her community.

17. Jamaican dub poet Louise Bennett was one of the first critics to bring it to our attention that whereas Nanny was relegated to the margins of history, Cudjoe, her brother, was revered as the most valiant maroon leader. See Bennett's *Aunty Roachy Seh*.

18. Hester is Condé's appropriation of Nathaniel Hawthorne's Hester Prynne of the *Scarlet Letter*. Here again, Condé transcends borders; in the given situation, she engenders a discursive border crossing that removes Hester from beneath the cloak of victimhood and secrecy as her adulterous affair is shrouded in perpetual sin, shame, and guilt. Furthermore, Condé transforms Hester into a speaking subject.

19. Hester shares with Tituba her ancestral history, documenting the journey her ancestors made on the Mayflower. In addition to sharing her Puritan upbringing with Tituba, Hester also introduces her to Milton's *Paradise Lost*.

20. I am referring here to Danticat's debut novel, *Breath, Eyes, Memory* and Kincaid's *Autobiography of My Mother*. Although these novels are not set during slavery, the novelists draw on African women's practice of abortion and infanticide as means of resistance. I offer a detailed analysis of *Breath, Eyes, Memory* in chapter 4.

21. Mary later gets her revenge by murdering her oppressor/rapist, Mr. Bellfeels, with the same hoe she used in the cane fields.

22. The hypersexual is represented in the Jezebel figure and the hyposexual is imbued in the Mammy or matriarchal figure.

23. In many documented instances, it is the wives of the slave enforcers who have contentious relationships with slave women as a result of these wives having to compete for their husbands' attention. However, this is not the case in the given situation; rather, we witness the reverse whereby Susanna Endicott is seemingly competing for Indian's attention and is therefore more civil and amiable to him than she is to Tituba, a fact that does not go unnoticed by Tituba.

24. Condé underscores some underlying voyeuristic fascination of the rapists with their female subjects. She reveals that Abena was raped aboard the slave ship *Christ the*

King, "surrounded by a circle of obscene voyeurs" (*Tituba* 1992: 6). In a similar fashion, Tituba was gang-raped. Both women were hanged/lynched by their enslavers.

25. This act of witnessing the staged execution of slaves was a general tactic employed by slave masters as a way to drive fear in other slaves who were considering rebelling against the oppressive system.

26. We bear witness to this widespread attack on the slave community at Abena's public lynching where her fellow slaves, including her young daughter, Tituba, were forced to witness her execution.

27. Fanon's text additionally proves effective for my theorizing of patriarchy, since he examines power relations through male-normative, hetero-normative lens. Furthermore, the Fanonian text here becomes pivotal in analyzing the relationship between John Indian and Goodwife Sarah Porter as it supports Fanon's theory about the black man's desire to be with a white woman.

28. The witch-woman or the soucouyant, including other figures of female resistance, is given full attention in chapter 6.

Chapter 4. Mothering the Nation

An earlier version of this essay bearing the same title appeared in *African American Review* 43.3 (Fall 2011): 373-90.

1. Patricia J. Williams also says that AIDS was regarded as an affliction of minorities, including Haitians.

2. This quote is taken from *Mountains beyond Mountains: The Quest of Dr. Paul Farmer, a Man Who Would Cure the World*, Tracy Kidder's phenomenal biographical account of Farmer's selfless philanthropic efforts. Many of the quotes are direct quotes by Farmer; henceforth, Farmer will be cited intermittently as the original source; at other times, Kidder's indirect quotes will be referenced.

3. Under the Cuban Agreement Act, a U.S. federal law enacted in 1966, Cuban natives are granted permanent resident status after having resided in the United States for at least one year. Fellow Haitians have no such luck.

Addressing the U.S. discriminatory practices, in 2009 many Haitians, including Grammy-winning singer and ambassador Wyclef Jean, rallied in Florida at the Broward Transitional Center in Pompano Beach in an effort to reverse the U.S. plan to deport over 30,000 Haitians. About 600 were held in detention, while another 243 were detained under a form of house arrest and monitored with electronic ankle bracelets. In his appeal to the small crowd gathered, Jean said: "It's important that Haitians get the justice that our Cuban brothers and sisters get. This is not a Haitian cause, it's a human being cause." Since establishing Temporary Protected Status in 1990, Washington has "granted 260,000 Salvadorans, 82,000 Hondurans, and 5,000 Nicaraguans protection, which was extended on October 1, 2008. Haiti was not among the countries granted extension." For additional details, see the article appropriately titled "A Double Standard?" in CaribWorldNews.com, March 2, 2009, http://www.caribbeanworldnews.com/middle_top_news_detail.php?mid=2171.

4. After the 2010 earthquake, the U.S. government halted all deportations to Haiti.

Notwithstanding, TPS has a shelf life of only eighteen months. Responding to the brevity of this government grant, the Department of Homeland Security extended the initial 180-day registration period from January 21 to July 20, 2010, through January 18, 2011. It must be noted, however, that TPS was not granted to Haitians who entered the country after January 12, 2010.

5. Prior to the publication of her 2007 memoir, *Brother, I'm Dying*, in which she catalogs her father's and her uncle's experiences and deaths, Danticat, protesting the treatment of her uncle, "appeared" on several media outlets, including online interviews, internet blogs, and CBS's *60 Minutes*.

6. The difference in spelling of Danticat's and her uncle's last names is the result of a clerical error made on her father's birth certificate.

7. "Haitian Pastor Dies on U.S. Doorsteps," *St. Petersburg Times*, November 19, 2004.

8. *Washington Post*, May 11, 2008.

9. Edwidge Danticat, "A Very Haitian Story," *New York Times* Op-ed, November 24, 2004, http://www.nytimes.com/2004/11/24/opinion/24danticat.html.

10. Further exposing the U.S. government's bias in the treatment of Haitians, Danticat calls our attention to the relief aid—recently renewed for the fourth time—that Hondurans and Nicaraguans received after Hurricane Mitch in 1998. At the same time, Haitians have yet to receive protection, not only in regard to the political upheavals but also resulting from the flash floods caused by tropical storm Jeanne that killed 2,000 residents in 2004. In 2008, Haiti was ravaged yet again by tropical storm Fay, hurricane Gustav, and tropical storm Hanna in three weeks. Officials concluded that the death toll and damage were on par with tropical storm Jean.

11. Various claims have been made that U.S. officials have gone as far as arguing that Haitians represent a national security threat. See *St. Petersburg Times*, November 19, 2004.

12. Jean Dominique, who steadfastly articulated his discontent with successive dictatorships, was assassinated on April 3, 2000, as he reported to work at Radio Haiti. His murder remains unsolved. However, his relentless criticism of Dany Toussaint, a former police chief and Haitian senator, and subsequent attacks on the radio station by Toussaint's lawyers and supporters led many to perceive Toussaint as the prime suspect.

13. Laguerre draws attention to three peak periods of Haitian immigration to the United States: the Haitian revolutionary era and its aftermath (1791–1810), the period of the U.S. occupation of Haiti (1915–34), and the Duvalier and immediate post-Duvalier era (1957–94). See Laguerre's *Diasporic Citizenship: Haitian Americans in Transnational America*. I am concerned with the third wave, when thousands of Haitians were forced to choose between exile and death. Danticat herself, only twelve years of age, left Haiti during this period.

14. Before 9/11 and the restrictive revised immigration policies, many residents of Caribbean countries opted not to become passport holders as a symbolic gesture to maintaining ties and pledging allegiance to their respective home countries. As a post-9/11 compromise, many have settled for dual citizenship. Carole Boyce Davies chronicles her mother's journeys between the Caribbean and the United States as ones of constant remembering and reconnection. See *Black Women, Writing, and Identity: Migrations of the Subject*.

15. Ironically, the very repressive Duvalier regime has not only forced/forged the formation of various anti-Duvalierist women's groups, but it has also contributed to women's political consciousness. Carolle Charles addresses this paradox of women's increased politicization and raised consciousness in "Gender and Politics in Contemporary Haiti: The Duvalierist State, Transnationalism, and the Emergence of a New Feminism."

16. Some of these iconic representations used to denigrate black women include Mammy, Jezebel, Topsy Turvy, Aunt Jemima, and Sapphire.

17. The term *Tonton Macoute* is derived from the Creole term for a mythological bogeyman. These bogeymen, the rural militia, formally named the Volunteers for National Security, not only invaded the myths and legends of Haiti but also disrupted the daily lives of Haitian people, primarily women. Danticat's novel is set during what is commonly referred to as the Duvalier regime. The country was under the leadership of a father-son team, François and Jean-Claude Duvalier, from 1957 to 1986. The conflation of father and son under the banner of the Duvalier regime is no coincidence. The atrocities meted out by father and son were equally sadistic, as the young Jean-Claude inherited his father's violence and despotic rule.

It is worth mentioning that the United States backed the military dictatorship of François and Jean-Claude Duvalier.

18. Moira Ferguson captures this land/body conflation in the title of her book, *Jamaica Kincaid: Where the Land Meets the Body*. Ferguson's theory, however, is focused on the imperial presence and colonial domination that condition the mother-daughter relationship in the novel.

19. Paradoxically, the "neuterizing of nationalism" speaks to how nationalism is tangibly gendered as it reinforces male hegemony.

20. In 1957 François Duvalier took office, after which he declared himself President for Life in 1964. By 1967, he had executed some 2,000 political prisoners, while others were driven into exile.

Although Haiti gained its independence from France in 1804, the French colonial regime left its mark on the Haitian landscape. Almost a century later (1915), a shift occurred from French to U.S. hegemony when the United States occupied Haiti for almost twenty years. The United States continues to dabble in Haiti's political affairs.

21. The history of violence and discrimination in Uganda against women frighteningly mirrors that in Haiti, in that Ugandan women were also coerced to obey the decree by mobs of men or by soldiers who were empowered by the state to arrest and even enjoy sexual license over these women.

In 1972 Idi Amin consolidated his control over the nation by legislating that women had to wear dresses that covered their knees.

22. Other Caribbean women writers who employ the trope of daffodils in their work include Jamaica Kincaid and Lorna Goodison.

23. Despite her eventual migration to the United States, Martine's thirst for difference is not quenched. She travels not to France, the home of the French buds, but to the United States, where she substitutes one colonized space for another. As the dominant nation-state, the United States exercises power and control over other smaller (insignificant) states. As a result, its policies, in significant ways, mirror the policies of former imperial powers, Britain and France.

24. Several times at night Martine pulled the yellow sheets over both her and Sophie's bodies. She also insisted that she was giving Sophie the doll, which was like a friend to her, for safekeeping.

25. The term *colonization in reverse* is borrowed from the Jamaican dub poet Louise Bennett, whose poem bears the same title. In this poem, Bennett chronicles the migration cum reverse colonization of Caribbean people to Great Britain.

26. As documented in the *Encyclopedia Britannica*, Marc's last name, Chevalier, is a French title originally equivalent to the English knight and later denoting membership in any order of chivalry and used by men of noble birth. It attests to his noble status. His complete name is Marc Jolibois Francis Legrand Moravien Chevalier.

27. As a permanent resident alien (a non-citizen), Martine is entitled to enjoy the social and civil rights accorded a citizen. Notwithstanding, her noninvolvement, which is arguably by choice, in transnational activities, her lack of membership to any diasporic (Haitian) communities, is palpable.

28. For further detail, see *Flexible Citizenship: The Cultural Logics of Transnationality*, 3.

29. Within the citizenship or permanent resident alien status there exist specific membership categories and boundaries that classify immigrants further into citizens and non-citizens. However, Laguerre argues that citizenship as constructed in the American imaginary is limiting because it fails to recognize the transnational aspect of the practice. Instead, he opts for the term *diasporic citizenship*, which validates belonging to two or more nation-states.

30. It is worth mentioning that the word *amnesty* is not referenced in the Immigration Reform and Control Act of 1986. The term seems to evoke much ire among various groups as evidenced by the ongoing debates over granting amnesty to the estimated 12 million illegal immigrants currently in the United States.

31. Martine's desire for amnesia is countered by Sophie, whose face resembles the rapist's and serves as a constant reminder of the past that Martine desperately tries to suppress. One of the interesting points here is that although Martine claims never to have seen the face of her rapist, his presence is hauntingly etched in her imagination/memory. I contend that the widespread terror afflicted by the Tontons Macoutes upon Haitian citizens has become part of the Haitian imaginary. While Martine speaks of her discomfort about returning to Haiti, the only connection to Haiti that she remembers/acknowledges is her rape.

32. Carolle Charles speaks about the respectability accorded to marriage, but more importantly to married women.

33. In actuality, Martine does perceive Marc as her protector. In conversation with Sophie, she admits that he saves her every night when she experiences the recurring nightmare.

34. In the given situation, Martine's repudiation of amnesty is measured by her refusal to engage in the masculinist discourse.

35. Here I wish to illuminate Martine's status as victim not as a result of her taking her own life but because of her being deprived of realizing citizenship.

As I have argued, Martine's attempt to realize citizenship, on her own terms, becomes evident when she replaces the transplanted daffodils with her renewed attraction for the tropical, indigenous hibiscus.

36. Martine's fascination with the ideal body is not just its diametrical form but includes the body's appearance. To achieve desired or accepted results in appearance, modeled after European assumptions, she uses skin bleach.

37. Collins stresses that in order to avoid race suicide and maintain racial purity, which is critical to racial categorization in the United States, white women of varying social classes are encouraged to become mothers with white men.

38. While Neti employs menstrual blood as the theme of protest in her article, Danticat's narrative involves all forms of female body flows, where the flow of blood trumps other body excretions. However, the common language is of pain and torture and eventual freedom and redemption.

39. Furthermore, Martine's insistence that Sophie acquire an education is a common factor, reflective of the (unrealized) dreams and aspirations of the newly arrived (Caribbean) immigrant. I purposely limit this analysis to the Caribbean in keeping with the novel's focus. Chancy additionally underscores the freedom of will that Sophie can exercise and enjoy having migrated to the United States.

40. Neti additionally notes the birth potential of blood. Drawing on this theorization, I locate birth in relation to reproduction, but I also interpret birth as an allegorical process, namely, the birth of freedom, self-deliverance, self-renewal, or self-rejuvenation.

41. The story of the Marassas that Martine relates to Sophie to distract her from the "testing" is one of doubling and duplicity, of inseparable lovers, who were the same person but duplicates of each other.

42. Expanding the operatives of systemic violence, Sunita Peacock links the violence experienced by newly arrived immigrants, specifically women, to neocolonial concerns.

Chapter 5. Performing the Body

1. *The Fat Black Woman's Poems* has four sections. Nevertheless, this article focuses on the first section, which bears the same title as the book.

2. Mindful of the fact that some critics, among them Peter Stallybrass and Allon White, take issue with Bakhtin's gender-neutral grotesque/classical opposition, his theoretical musings still remain useful to this discussion. By the same token, Bakhtin's numerous references to birth, death, pregnancy, and other bodily transformations allude to a gendered body and bodily acts that Stukator ascertains have "an uncanny affinity with women" (202).

3. I use the terms *vulgar/ity* and *grotesque* interchangeably.

4. Beauty pageants like Miss World (Universe) are exclusive affairs. The sites or spaces within which these events are staged are undoubtedly homogeneous and racialized, reinforced by the fact that the contestants are predominantly white, not to mention noticeably thin. For a protracted period, black women were not featured contestants in beauty pageants; in other words they were "blacked out." Then again, in recent pageants, one can point out that efforts have been made to colorize the industry. However, the presence of

blacks is comparatively minimal in relation to white presence. For additional details on the history of beauty pageants, see Shaw's *The Embodiment of Disobedience*.

Sarah Banet-Weiser pontificates that black female presence in beauty pageants is in response to accusations of the pageants' exclusion of women of color. On another level, this acknowledged presence disguises and erases the racist histories for which beauty pageants are known (125). See Banet-Weiser's *The Most Beautiful Girl in the World*.

5. On July 3, 2010, Miss Jamaica Universe, Yendi Phillips, was crowned; coincidentally, I was conducting research for this chapter. Although the controversy this time around did not stem from the erasure of blackness—the crowned queen is of black and partial Indo-Jamaican descent—many local residents complained that the contest was rigged. Not only was Ms. Phillips allegedly paid to enter the competition, but she was also guaranteed that she would win.

6. This is a borrowed term from Susan Bordo's book *Unbearable Weight: Feminism, Western Culture, and the Body*.

7. In recent years the issue of body weight (deficiency) has escalated to unprecedented proportions and has consumed young females as early as the onset of puberty; hence the rise in cases of bulimia and anorexia. Cecilia Hartley refers to this obsession as the "tyranny of slenderness." For a full-length discussion of this body deficiency, see Hartley, "Letting Ourselves Go," 60.

8. In his brilliant assessment of Rabelais's work, Bakhtin remarks that wine is chosen over oil as the marker of revelry and celebration because oil is the "symbol of Lenten, pious seriousness."

9. This community of white female contestants is rendered "diasporic" because it stands apart (literally and bodily) from the general female population as the contestants are not a true representation of women's reality.

10. Apart from being a talented actress who worked in vaudeville theaters as a young woman, Mae West (born Mary Jane West) was an outspoken sex symbol; she decked her trademark hourglass figure in long, tight dresses. This quote was uttered in her 1933 movie *She Done Him Wrong*. West sardonically alludes to the ideal of purity and chastity in the movie *I'm No Angel* (1933) in the famous quote, "I used to be Snow White, but I drifted."

11. In analyzing how disabled women are marginalized in our culture, Garland-Thomson remarks that the Barbie doll, restricted within her "sequined gowns, crowns, and push-up bras" is revered. This analogy can be effectively applied to the beauty pageants discussed earlier in this chapter.

12. Black women's breasts during slavery were a prime object of commodification and consumption in great part because black women functioned as wet nurses for white women who safeguarded white femininity at all costs.

13. The coinage "stolen woman" is a reappropriation of the title of Gail Wyatt's book.

14. Patricia Hill Collins, Barbara Christian, Michelle Wallace, and Trudier Harris are among the black critics who have vigorously objected to the portrayal of black women as contented mammies.

15. Here I use *namesake* not in the conventional sense but rather to suggest that the Fat Black Woman is modeled after Saartjie Baartman as a way to pay her tribute and to

validate her. Furthermore, the unnamed Fat Black Woman is everywoman. This identitarian politics delivers another resounding denunciation of western/Victorian gender ideology and ideals.

16. This obsession is not unique to Britain. As I mentioned in chapter 1, Don Imus and others' likening the tennis champions Venus and Serena Williams to animals functions as a subtext for their dehumanization and marginalization, even as it underscores men's covert fixation on posteriors.

17. This analysis is limited to the first section of this poetry collection.

18. This poem, "The Body Reclining," is dedicated to Walt Whitman, most likely for his employment of free verse and the overt sexuality depicted in his poems. His poetry collection *Leaves of Grass* was notably controversial.

19. As Khoisan poet Diana Ferrus reminds us in her poetic tribute to Baartman, imperialism is the man-made monster.

Chapter 6. Bodies and DisEase

1. Beyond social and racial injustices, different diseases affect various communities differently. Additionally, some diseases are innate to geographic locations.

2. *Indigenous medicine* is used interchangeably with *homeopathic medicine*.

3. I interpret the role of medicine, the medical discourse, as a nationalistic undertaking due to the preponderance of maleness that commandeers the profession. This argument is poignantly articulated in chapter 2. In light of this fact, the terms *nation* and *medicine* or *medical discourse* are used interchangeably.

4. Essentially, Farmer's discourse on illness overlaps with Lorde's, especially in relation to women from poor immigrant communities.

5. "Haitian Pastor Dies on U.S. Doorsteps," *St. Petersburg Times*, November 19, 2004.

6. Morrison writes: "Black people are generally viewed as patients, victims, wards, and pathologies . . . not as participants" ("City Limits" 37).

7. Lorde does not identify the medical institution to which she refers. Rather, she discloses that she was an outpatient (referred by her own doctor) at a leading cancer hospital in New York City where a specialist in liver tumors saw her.

8. Notably, Annie's doctor, Dr. Stephens, hails from England.

9. One can safely argue that these powerful female characters are present in every one of Morrison's novels; a similar argument can be made about this pervasive presence in the work of many other black female writers. This study only examines a small sample of such works.

10. The following quote catalogs an interesting confluence of modern and local/folk medicine: "Take the milk of a woman suckling a male child. Also take a cat and cut off its ear or part of it. Let the blood flow into the milk. Get the patient to drink this mixture. Repeat three times a day" (Condé, *Tituba*, 1992: 112).

11. This rebirth process is given full attention in my earlier book, *Mother Imagery in the Novels of Afro-Caribbean Women*, 69–70.

12. See "Mothers-to-Be and HMOs Help Deliver Resurgence of Midwives," *Los Angeles Times*, May 4, 1997.

Additionally, the article details that more than 220,000 babies were expected to be delivered by midwives in the United States in 2007; while most would be born in hospitals, more than 10,000 would be delivered at home.

13. I merge the words *witch* and *woman* to emphasize female empowerment and potency. This conflation, the synonymous use of *witch* and *woman* intimates that powerful women were saddled with the label of *witch*.

14. See King-Aribisala's *The Hangman's Game*; Nalo Hopkinson's *Brown Girl in the Ring* and *Skin Folk*; Morrison's *The Bluest Eye* and *Song of Solomon*, and Danticat's *Breath, Eyes, Memory*.

15. A parallel variant of this story details Africans walking back home on water. In *Mother Imagery*, I argue that the trope of Africans walking on water parallels the biblical story of Jesus walking on water.

16. Whereas in some versions of this tale, the witch-woman's skin is peppered, in other versions her skin is salted. I would further like to link this process of "salting" with the "seasoning" process that enslaved Africans underwent as a way to "break" them. Like her forebears, the witch-woman was salted in an effort to break her spirit and to transform her transgressive body into a docile one.

17. Despite the fact that Anzaldúa specifically discusses alternative sexuality, "doubling" strongly resonates with this theme and is equally relevant to her analysis.

18. The practice of "testing" is discussed in detail in chapter 4.

19. "Shedding skin" is an act of self-deliberation; by refusing to shed skin or bleed, the bride rejects imposed conjugal obligation.

20. After consummating his marriage on his wedding night, the following morning the husband was expected to hang a blood spotted sheet in his courtyard to serve as evidence of his prized possession.

21. Grandmè Ifé is named for the native African people, the Ifé, who inhabit the southwestern region of Nigeria. According to Yorùbá legend, Ilé-Ifè is where the deities Odùduwà and Obàtàlà created the world.

22. After shedding her skin, the old higue transforms into a ball of fire before she ascends into the skies/heavens.

23. Sophie's resistance to "testing" is given full attention in chapter 4.

24. See chapter 4 for an in-depth analysis.

25. This theme is developed further in chapter 3.

26. Shango is the god of thunder and the ancestor of the Yoruba people of Nigeria.

27. Of noted interest, Sophie also resides in the United States where she has acquired resident alien status.

28. Perhaps the deuil that Grandmè Ifé wears has a double meaning: she is mourning the passing of her husband and the loss of her daughter. This assumption materializes as Martine eventually passes away.

29. Hope also notes that men are increasingly appropriating the practice of bleaching.

30. Many African cultures regard weight as a sign of wealth. Pauline Uwakweh finds that some cultures had a traditional "fattening room" where adolescent girls were groomed into "robust marriageable maidens." For additional detail, see Uwakweh's "Debunking Patriarchy."

31. In the given example, half of the women are migrants. Notwithstanding, the overriding concern here is to reveal their shared class and attendant disease.

32. The titular protagonist, Lucy, compares the charmed lives of her employer, Mariah, and her friend, Dinah, with those of the women of her impoverished community, particularly Sylvie, who had a scar on her right cheek, imprinted by a bite mark from another woman.

33. Avey receives her final rite of initiation from Rosalie Parvay, the daughter of the androgynous healer, Lebert Joseph. Marie-Noëlle receives spiritual guidance from the clairvoyant, Madame Esmondas.

Bibliography

Adams, David. "Haitian Pastor Dies on U.S. Doorstep." *St. Petersburg Times*, November 19, 2004.

Aldama, Arturo J., ed. *Violence and the Body: Race, Gender, and the State*. Bloomington: Indiana University Press, 2003.

Alexander, Elizabeth. "'Coming Out Blackened and Whole': Fragmentation and Reintegration in Audre Lorde's *Zami* and *The Cancer Journals*." In *Skin Deep, Spirit Strong: The Black Female Body in American Culture*, ed. Kimberly Wallace-Sanders. Ann Arbor: University of Michigan Press, 2002.

Alexander, M. Jacqui. "Not Just (Any) Body Can Be a Citizen: The Politics of Law, Sexuality, Postcoloniality in Trinidad and Tobago and the Bahamas." *Feminist Review* 48 (Autumn 1994): 5–23.

———. *Pedagogies of Crossing: Meditations on Feminism, Sexual Politics, Memory, and the Sacred*. Durham: Duke University Press, 2005.

Alexander, M. Jacqui, and Chandra Talpade Mohanty, eds. *Feminist Genealogies, Colonial Legacies, Democratic Futures*. New York: Routledge, 1997.

Alexander, Simone A. James. "Bearing Witness: De/Cultivating Violence in Edwidge Danticat's *The Farming of Bones*." Spec. issue: *Violence in Paradise: The Caribbean. Anglistica* 14.1 (2010): 57–70.

———. *Mother Imagery in the Novels of Afro-Caribbean Women*. Columbia: University of Missouri Press, 2001.

———. "M/Othering the Nation: Women's Bodies as Nationalist Trope in Edwidge Danticat's *Breath, Eyes, Memory*." *African American Review* 43.3 (fall 2011): 373-390.

———. "'Mouthing a New Beginning': Diaspora Identity and Consciousness in Grace Nichols' *The Fat Black Woman's Poems*." *New Mango Season* 2.1 (2008): 33–48.

———. "Racial and Cultural Categorizations of Language: The Evolution of Kamau Brathwaite's Nation Language in the Fiction of Paule Marshall." *Revista Review InteRamericana* 31.1–4 (2001).

Allsopp, Richard. *The Caribbean Multilingual Dictionary of Flora, Fauna, and Foods in English, French, French Creole, and Spanish*. Kingston, Jamaica: Arawak, 2003.

———. *Dictionary of Caribbean English Usage*. New York: Oxford University Press, 1996.

Amadiume, Ifi. *Male Daughters, Female Husbands: Gender and Sex in an African Society*. London: Zed Books, 1987.

———. *Reinventing Africa: Matriarchy, Religion, and Culture*. London: Zed Books, 1997.

Anatol, Giselle Liza. "A Feminist Reading of Soucouyants in Nalo Hopkinson's *Brown Girl in the Ring* and *Skin Folk.*" *Mosaic: A Journal for the Interdisciplinary Study of Literature* 37.3 (September 2004): 33–50.

Anderson, Benedict. *Imagined Communities: Reflection on the Origin and Spread of Nationalism.* London: Verso, 1983.

Anglin, Mary. "Whose Health? Whose Justice? Examining Quality Care and Forms of Advocacy for Women Diagnosed with Breast Cancer." In *Gender, Race, Class, and Health: Intersectional Approaches*, ed. Amy J. Schulz and Leith Mullings, 313–41. San Francisco: Jossey-Bass, 2006.

Anzaldúa, Gloria. *Borderlands: La Frontera. The New Mestiza.* San Francisco: Aunt Lute Books, 1999.

Arnold, A. James. "From the Problematic Maroon to a Woman-Centered Creole Project in the Literature of the French West Indies." In *Slavery in the Caribbean Francophone World: Distant Voices, Forgotten Acts, Forged Identities*, ed. Doris Y. Kadish, 164–75. Athens: University of Georgia Press, 2000.

Bakare-Yusuf, Bibi. "The Economy of Violence: Black Bodies and the Unspeakable Terror." In *Feminist Theory and the Body: A Reader*, ed. Janet Price and Margrit Shildrick, 311–23. New York: Routledge, 1999.

Bakhtin, Mikhail. *Rabelais and His World.* Trans. Helene Iswolsky. Bloomington: Indiana University Press, 1984.

Bambara, Toni Cade. *The Salt Eaters.* New York: Random House, 1980.

Bammer, Angelika, ed. *Displacements: Cultural Identities in Question.* Bloomington: Indiana University Press, 1994.

Banet-Weiser, Sarah. *The Most Beautiful Girl in the World: Beauty Pageants and National Identity.* Berkeley: University of California Press, 1999.

Barnet, Miguel. *Afro-Cuban Religions.* Trans. Christine Renata Ayorinde. Kingston, Jamaica: Ian Randle, 2001.

Baum, Robert. "Religious Views of Evil and Suffering." *Encyclopedia of Africa.* Ed. Henry Louis Gates and Kwame Anthony Appiah.

Beam, Dorri Rabung. "The Flower of Black Female Sexuality in Pauline Hopkins's *Winona.*" In *Recovering the Black Female Body: Self-Representations by African American Women*, ed. Michael Bennett and Vanessa Dickerson, 71–96. New Brunswick: Rutgers University Press, 2000.

Bell, Beverly. *Walking on Fire: Haitian Women's Stories of Survival and Resistance.* Ithaca: Cornell University Press, 2001.

Bennett, Louise. "Bennett on Bennett." By Dennis Scott. *Caribbean Quarterly* 14 (March–June 1968): 97–101.

———. "Colonisation in Reverse." In *Jamaica Labrish.* Kingston: Jamaica: Sangster's Bookstore, 1966, 179–80.

———. *Jamaica Labrish.* Kingston, Jamaica: Sangster's Book Store. 1966.

Bennett, Michael, and Vanessa Dickerson, eds. *Recovering the Black Female Body: Self-Representations by African American Women.* New Brunswick: Rutgers University Press, 2000.

Bennett, Michael, and Vanessa D. Dickerson, eds. *Recovering the Black Female Body: Self-Representation by African American Women*. New Brunswick: Rutgers University Press, 2001.

Benoit, Olga. "Assuming the Title 'Feminist.'" In *Walking on Fire: Haitian Women's Stories of Survival and Resistance*, ed. Beverly Bell, 184–86. Ithaca: Cornell University Press, 2001.

Bertone, Andrea Marie. "Sexual Trafficking in Women: International Political Economy and the Politics of Sex." *Gender Issues* 18 (December 1999): 4–22.

Biseswar, Indrawatie. "A New Discourse on 'Gender' in Ethiopia." *African Identities* 6.8 (November 2008): 405–29.

Bordo, Susan. "The Body and the Reproduction of Femininity." In *Writing on the Body: Female Embodiment and Feminist Theory*, ed. Katie Conboy, Nadia Medina, and Sarah Stanbury, 90–112. New York: Columbia University Press, 1997.

———. "Feminism, Foucault, and the Politics of the Body." In *Feminist Theory and the Body: A Reader*, ed. Janet Price and Margrit Shildrick, 246–57. New York: Routledge, 1999.

———. "Reading the Slender Body." In *Body/Politics: Women and the Discourses of Science*, ed. Mary Jacobus, Evelyn Fox Keller, and Sally Shuttleworth. New York: Routledge, 1990.

———. *Unbearable Weight: Feminism, Western Culture, and the Body*. Berkeley: University of California Press, 1993.

Bowles, Gloria, M. Giulia Fabi, and Arlene R. Keizer, eds. *New Black Feminist Criticism, 1985–2000*. Urbana: University of Illinois Press, 2007.

Brathwaite, Kamau. *Roots*. Ann Arbor: University of Michigan Press, 1993.

Braziel, Jana Evans, and Kathleen LeBesco, eds. *Bodies Out of Bounds: Fatness and Transgression*. Berkeley: University of California Press, 2001.

———. "Daffodils, Rhizomes, Migrations: Narrative of Coming of Age in the Diasporic Writings of Edwidge Danticat and Jamaica Kincaid." *Meridians* 3:2 (2003): 110–31.

Braziel, Jana Evans, and Anita Mannur, eds. *Theorizing Diaspora: A Reader*. Malden, MA: Blackwell, 2003.

Brooks, Daphne. *Bodies in Dissent: Spectacular Performances of Race and Freedom, 1850–1910*. Durham: Duke University Press, 2006.

———. "'The Deeds Done in My Body': Black Feminist Theory, Performance, and the Truth about Adah Isaacs Menken." In *Recovering the Black Female Body: Self-Representation by African American Women*, ed. Michael Bennett and Vanessa D. Dickerson, 41–70. New Brunswick: Rutgers University Press, 2001.

Brown-Glaude, Winnifred. "The Fact of Blackness? The Bleached Body in Contemporary Jamaica." *Small Axe* 11.3 (October 2007): 34–51.

Bunch, Charlotte. "Not for Lesbians Only." In *Materialist Feminism: A Reader in Class Difference and Women's Lives*, ed. Rosemary Hennessy and Chrys Ingraham, 54–58. New York: Routledge, 1997.

Bush, Barbara. *Slave Women in Caribbean Society, 1650–1838*. Bloomington: Indiana University Press, 1990.

Carter, Thatcher. "Body Count: Autobiographies by Women Living with Breast Cancer." *Journal of Popular Culture* 33.4 (Spring 2003): 653–68.

Caruth, Cathy. *Unclaimed Experience: Trauma, Narrative, and History*. Baltimore: Johns Hopkins University Press, 1996.

Chancy, Myriam J. A. *Framing Silence: Revolutionary Novels by Haitian Women*. New Brunswick: Rutgers University Press, 1997.

———. *Searching for Safe Spaces: Afro-Caribbean Women Writers in Exile*. Philadelphia: Temple University Press, 1997.

Charles, Carolle. "Gender and Politics in Contemporary Haiti: The Duvalerist State, Transnationalism, and the Emergence of a New Feminism." *Feminist Studies* 21.1 (Spring 1995): 135–64.

Christian, Barbara. *Black Feminist Criticism: Perspectives on Black Women Writers*. New York: Pergamon Press, 1985.

———. *Black Women Novelists: The Development of a Tradition, 1892–1976*. Westport, CT: Greenwood Press, 1980.

———. "The Contemporary Fables of Toni Morrison." In *Black Women Novelists: The Development of a Tradition, 1892–1976*, 137–79. Westport, CT: Greenwood P, 1980.

———. "The Race for Theory." In *New Black Feminist Criticism, 1985–2000*, ed. Gloria Bowles, M. Giulia Fabi, and Arlene R. Keizer, 40–50. Urbana: University of Illinois Press, 2007.

Christophe, Marc A. "Truth, Half-Truths, and Beautiful Lies: Edwidge Danticat and the Recuperation of Memory in *Breath, Eyes, Memory*." *Journal of Haitian Studies* 7:2 (Fall 2001): 96–107.

Clark, Vèvè A. "Diaspora Literacy." In *Encyclopedia of the African Diaspora: Origins, Experiences, and Cultures*, ed. Carole Boyce Davies, 382–83. Santa Barbara: ABC-CLIO, 2008.

———. "Developing Diaspora Literacy and Marassa Consciousness." In *Comparative American Identities: Race, Sex, and Nationality in the Modern Text*, ed. Hortense Spillers, 40–61. New York: Routledge, 1991.

Clarke, Austin. *The Polished Hoe*. Kingston, Jamaica: Ian Randle, 2003.

Cobb-Clark, Deborah A., and Sherrie A. Kossoudji. "Did Legalization Matter for Women? Amnesty and the Wages of Formerly Unauthorized Workers." *Gender Issues* 17.4 (Fall 1999): 5–15.

Cole, Johnnetta Betsch, and Beverly Guy-Sheftall. *Gender Talk: The Struggle for Women's Equality in African American Communities*. New York: Ballantine Books, 2003.

Colligan, Sumi. "Why the Intersexed Shouldn't Be Fixed: Insights from Queer Theory and Disability Studies." In *Gendering Disability*, ed. Bonnie G. Smith and Beth Hutchison, 45–60. New Brunswick: Rutgers University Press, 2004.

Collins, Patricia Hill. *Black Feminist Thought: Knowledge, Consciousness, and the Politics of Empowerment*. New York: Routledge, 2000.

———. *Black Sexual Politics: African Americans, Gender, and the New Racism*. New York: Routledge, 2004.

———. "Producing the Mothers of the Nation: Race, Class, and Contemporary U.S. Population Policies." In *Women, Citizenship, and Difference*, ed. Nira Yuval-Davis and Pnina Werbner, 118–29. New York: Zed Books, 1999.

Condé, Maryse. *Desirada*. New York: Soho Press, 2000.
———. *I, Tituba, Black Witch of Salem*. Trans. Richard Philcox. New York: Ballantine Books, 1992.
Cooper, Carolyn. *Noises in the Blood: Orality, Gender, and the 'Vulgar' Body of Jamaican Popular Culture*. Durham: Duke University Press, 1995.
———. *Sound Clash: Jamaican Dancehall Culture at Large*. New York: Palgrave Macmillan, 2004.
Cornell, Drucilla, ed. *Feminism and Pornography: Oxford Readings in Feminism*. London: Oxford University Press, 2000.
Couser, G. Thomas. *Recovering Bodies: Illness, Disability, and Life Writing*. Madison: University of Wisconsin Press, 1997.
Crais, Clifton, and Pamela Scully. *Sara Baartman and the Hottentot Venus: A Ghost Story and a Biography*. Princeton: Princeton University Press, 2009.
Creed, Barbara. "Lesbian Bodies: Tirades, Tomboys, and Tarts." In *Feminist Theory and the Body: A Reader*, ed. Janet Price and Margrit Shildrick, 111–24. New York: Routledge 1999.
Dangarembga, Tsitsi. *Nervous Conditions*. Seattle: Seal Press, 1988.
Danticat, Edwidge. "Belles Lettres Interview." By Renée H. Shea. *Belle Lettres* 10.3 (Summer 1995): 12–15.
———. *Breath, Eyes, Memory*. London: Abacus, 1994.
———. *Brother, I'm Dying*. New York: Knopf, 2007.
———. *The Butterfly's Way: Voices from the Haitian Dyaspora in the United States*. New York: Soho Press, 2001.
———. *Create Dangerously: The Immigrant Artist at Work*. New York: Vintage, 2011.
———. "An Interview with Edwidge Danticat." By Bonnie Lyons. *Contemporary Literature* 44.2 (Summer 2003): 183–98.
———. *Krik? Krak!* New York: Vintage Books, 1996.
———. "A Very Haitian Story." *New York Times*, November 24, 2004.
Davies, Carole Boyce. *Black Women, Writing, and Identity: Migrations of the Subject*. New York: Routledge, 1994.
———. "Carnivalized Caribbean Female Bodies: Taking Space/Making Space." *Thamyris* 5.2 (Autumn 1998): 333–46.
Davis, Angela Y. Foreword. *I, Tituba, Black Witch of Salem*. By Maryse Condé. Trans. Richard Philcox. New York: Ballantine Books, 1992.
———. "Reflections on the Black Woman's Role in the Community of Slaves." *Black Scholar* 3.4 (December 1971): 2–15.
———. "Sick and Tired of Being Sick and Tired: The Politics of Black Women's Health." In *The Black Women's Health Book: Speaking for Ourselves*, ed. Evelyn C. White, 18–26. Seattle: Seal Press, 1994.
———. *Women, Race, and Class*. New York: Vintage Books, 1983.
Dayan, Joan. "Erzulie: A Women's History of Haiti." *Research in African Literatures* 25.2 (Summer 1994): 5–31.
———. *Haiti, History, and the Gods*. Berkeley: University of California Press, 1995.
deCaires Narain, Denise. *Contemporary Caribbean Women's Poetry: Making Style*. New York: Routledge, 2002.

DeHernandez, Jennifer Browdy, ed. *Women Writing Resistance: Essays on Latin America and the Caribbean.* Cambridge, MA: South End Press, 2003.

DeShazer, Mary K. *Fractured Borders: Reading Women's Cancer Literature.* Ann Arbor: University of Michigan Press, 2005.

De Souza, Pascale. "Creolizing Anancy: Signifyin(g) Processes in New World Spider Tales." *Matatu* 27–28 (2003): 339–63.

De Veaux, Alexis. *Warrior Poet: A Biography of Audre Lorde.* New York: W. W. Norton, 2004.

Dickerson, Vanessa. "Summoning SomeBody: The Flesh Made Word in Toni Morrison's Fiction." In *Recovering the Black Female Body: Self-Representations by African American Women*, ed. Michael Bennett and Vanessa Dickerson, 195–216. New Brunswick: Rutgers University Press, 2000.

Diedrich, Maria, Henry Louis Gates Jr., and Carl Pedersen, eds. *Black Imagination and the Middle Passage.* New York: Oxford University Press, 1999.

Douglas, Mary. *Purity and Danger: An Analysis on the Concept of Pollution and Taboo.* New York: Routledge, 2002.

Duany, Jorge. *Blurred Borders: Transnational Migration between the Hispanic Caribbean and the United States.* Chapel Hill: University of North Carolina Press, 2011.

Dunbar, Paul Laurence. "We Wear the Mask." In *The Prentice Hall Anthology of African American Literature.* New York: Prentice Hall, 1999.

Dworkin, Andrea. "Against the Male Flood: Censorship, Pornography, and Equality." In *Feminism and Pornography: Oxford Readings in Feminism*, ed. Drucilla Cornell, 19–29. London: Oxford University Press, 2000.

———. "Pornography and Grief." In *Feminism and Pornography: Oxford Readings in Feminism*, ed. Drucilla Cornell, 39–44. London: Oxford University Press, 2000.

Edwards, Brent Hayes. *The Practice of Diaspora: Literature, Translation, and the Rise of Black Internationalism.* Cambridge: Harvard University Press, 2003.

Ehrenreich, Barbara, and Arlie Russell Hochschild, eds. *Global Woman: Nannies, Maids, and Sex Workers in the New Economy.* New York: Metropolitan Books, 2002.

Esteves, Carmen C., and Lizabeth Paravisini-Gebert, eds. *Green Cane and Juicy Flotsam: Short Stories by Caribbean Women.* New Brunswick: Rutgers University Press, 1991.

Fabi, M. Giulia. "Sexual Violence and the Black Atlantic: On Alice Walker's *Possessing the Secret of Joy*." In *Black Imagination and the Middle Passage*, ed. Maria Diedrich, Henry Louis Gates Jr., and Carl Pedersen. New York: Oxford University Press, 1999.

Fanon, Frantz. *Black Skin, White Masks.* Trans. Charles Lam Markmann. New York: Grove Press, 1967.

Fausto-Sterling, Anne. "Gender, Race, and Nation: The Comparative Anatomy of 'Hottentot' Women in Europe, 1815–17." In *Skin Deep, Spirit Strong: The Black Female Body in American Culture*, ed. Kimberly Wallace-Sanders. Ann Arbor: University of Michigan Press, 2002.

Ferguson, Moira. *Jamaica Kincaid: Where the Land Meets the Body.* Charlottesville: University of Virginia Press, 1994.

Ferrus, Diana. "I've Come to Take You Home." In *Venus 2010: They Called Her 'Hottentot,'* ed. Deborah Willis, 213–14. Philadelphia: Temple University Press, 2010.

Fleetwood, Nicole R. *Troubling Vision: Performance, Visibility, and Blackness*. Chicago: University of Chicago Press, 2011.

Flores-Ortiz, Yvette. "Re/membering the Body: *Latina Testimonies of Social and Family Violence*." In *Violence and the Body: Race, Gender, and the State*, ed. Arturo J. Aldama, 347–59. Bloomington: Indiana University Press, 2003.

Francis, Donette A. "'Silences Too Horrific to Disturb': Writing Sexual Histories in Edwidge Danticat's *Breath, Eyes, Memory*. *Research in African Literatures* 35.2 (Summer 2004): 75–90.

Friedman, May, and Silvia Schultermandl. *Growing Up Transnational: Identity and Kinship in a Global Era*. Toronto: University of Toronto Press, 2011.

Frith, Susan. "Searching for Sara Baartman." *Johns Hopkins Magazine* 61.3 (June 2009). http://www.jhu.edu/jhumag/0609web/sara.html.

Gadsby, Meredith M. *Sucking Salt: Caribbean Women Writers, Migration, and Survival*. Columbia: University of Missouri Press, 2006.

Gaitskell, Deborah, and Elaine Unterhalter. "Mothers of the Nation: A Comparative Analysis of Nation, Race, and Motherhood in Afrikaner Nationalism and the African National Congress." In *Woman-Nation-State*, ed. Nira Yuval-Davis and Floya Anthias, 58–78. New York: St. Martin's Press, 1989.

Garland-Thomson, Rosemarie. *Extraordinary Bodies: Figuring Physical Disability in American Culture and Literature*. New York: Columbia University Press, 1997.

———, ed. *Freakery: Cultural Spectacles of the Extraordinary Body*. New York: New York University Press, 1996.

———. "Integrating Disability, Transforming Feminist Theory." In *Gendering Disability*, ed. Bonnie G. Smith and Beth Hutchison, 73–103. New Brunswick: Rutgers University Press, 2004.

Gatens, Moira. "Corporeal Representation in/and the Body Politic." In *Writing on the Body: Female Embodiment and Feminist Theory*, ed. Katie Conboy, Nadia Medina, and Sarah Stanbury, 80–89. New York: Columbia University Press, 1997.

Gates, Henry Louis, Jr. *The Signifying Monkey: A Theory of African American Literary Criticism*. New York: Oxford University Press, 1988.

Gauthier, Xavière. "Why Witches?" In *New French Feminism: An Anthology*, ed. Elaine Marks and Isabelle de Courtivron, 199–203. Amherst: University of Massachusetts Press, 1980.

Gerber, Nancy F. "Binding the Narrative Thread: Storytelling and the Mother-Daughter Relationship in Edwidge Danticat's *Breath, Eyes, Memory*." *Journal of the Association for Research on Mothering* 2:2 (Fall–Winter 2000): 188–99.

Gilbert, Sandra, and Susan Gubar. *Madwoman in the Attic: The Woman Writer and the Nineteenth-Century Literary Imagination*. New Haven: Yale University Press, 1979.

Gilman, Sander L. "Black Bodies, White Bodies: Toward an Iconography of Female Sexuality in Late Nineteenth-Century Art, Medicine, and Literature" in *"Race," Writing, and Difference*, ed. Henry Louis Gates. Chicago: University of Chicago Press, 1986.

———. *Difference and Pathology: Stereotypes of Sexuality, Race, and Madness*. Ithaca: Cornell University Press, 1985.

Gilroy, Paul. *The Black Atlantic: Modernity and Double Consciousness*. Cambridge: Harvard University Press, 1995.

Glissant, Edouard. *Caribbean Discourse: Selected Essays*. Charlottesville: University Press of Virginia, 1999.

———. *Poetics of Relation*. Trans. Betsy Wing. Ann Arbor: University of Michigan Press, 1997.

Goodison, Lorna. *I Am Becoming My Mother*. London: New Beacon Books, 1986.

Gottlieb, Karla. *"The Mother of Us All": A History of Queen Nanny Leader of the Windward Jamaican Maroons*. Trenton, NJ: Africa World Press, 2000.

Gould, Stephen J. *The Flamingo's Smile: Reflections in Natural History*. New York: W. W. Norton, 1985.

Grewal, Inderpal, and Caren Kaplan, eds. *Scattered Hegemonies: Postmodern and Transnational Feminist Practices*. Minneapolis: University of Minnesota Press, 2002.

Grosz, Elizabeth. *Volatile Bodies: Toward a Corporeal Feminism*. Bloomington: Indiana University Press, 1994.

Halberstam, Judith. "F2M: The Making of Female Masculinity." In *Feminist Theory and the Body: A Reader*, ed. Janet Price and Margrit Shildrick, 125–33. New York: Routledge, 1999.

Hall, Stuart. "Cultural Identity and Diaspora." In *Theorizing Diaspora: A Reader*, ed. Jana Evans Braziel and Anita Mannur, 233–46. Malden, MA: Blackwell, 2003.

Hamilton, Virginia. *The People Could Fly: American Black Folktales*. New York: Scholastic, 1985.

Hammonds, Evelynn M. "Toward a Genealogy of Black Female Sexuality: The Problematic of Silence." In *Feminist Genealogies, Colonial Legacies, Democratic Futures*, ed. M. Jacqui Alexander and Chandra Talpade Mohanty, 170–82. New York: Routledge, 1997.

Hartley, Cecilia. "Letting Ourselves Go: Making Room for the Fat Body in Feminist Scholarship." In *Bodies out of Bounds: Fatness and Transgression*, ed. Jana Evans Braziel and Kathleen LeBesco, 60–73. Berkeley: University of California Press, 2001.

Hartman, Saidiya. *Lose Your Mother: A Journey along the Atlantic Slave Route*. New York: Farrar, Straus and Giroux, 2008.

———. *Scenes of Subjection: Terror, Slavery, and Self-Making in Nineteenth-Century America*. New York: Oxford University Press, 1997.

Hasecic, Dzenita Hrelja. "Transnationalism and Transformative Knowledge: Travelling Practices by Women in Bosnia and Herzegovina." http://www.inter-disciplinary.net/at-the-interface/wp-content/uploads/2012/08/hreljamulpaper.pdf.

Henderson, Carol E. *Scarring the Black Body: Race and Representation in African American Literature*. Columbia: University of Missouri Press, 2002.

Hobson, Janell. *Venus in the Dark: Blackness and Beauty in Popular Culture*. New York: Routledge, 2005.

Holloway, Karla F. C. *Codes of Conduct: Race, Ethics, and the Color of Our Character*. New Brunswick: Rutgers University Press, 1995.

———. *Passed On: African American Mourning Stories*. Durham: Duke University Press, 2002.

———. *Private Bodies, Public Texts: Race, Gender, and a Cultural Bioethics*. Durham: Duke University Press, 2011.

Holmes, Helen Bequaert, and Laura M. Purdy, eds. *Feminist Perspectives in Medical Ethics*. Bloomington: Indiana University Press, 1992.

Holmes, Rachel. *African Queen: The Real Life of the Hottentot Venus*. New York: Random House, 2007.

hooks, bell. *Black Looks: Race and Representation*. Boston: South End Press, 1992.

———. *Feminist Theory: From the Margin to the Center*. Cambridge, MA: South End Press, 2000.

Hope, Donna P. *Man Vibes: Masculinities in the Jamaican Dancehall*. Kingston, Jamaica: Ian Randle, 2010.

Hopkinson, Nalo. *Brown Girl in the Ring*. New York: Warner Books, 1998.

———. *Skin Folk*. New York: Warner Books, 2001.

Hudson, Nicholas. "The 'Hottentot Venus,' Sexuality, and the Changing Aesthetics of Race, 1650–1850." *Mosaic* 41.1 (March 2008): 19–41.

Hughes, Langston. "The Negro Artist and the Racial Mountain." In *Prentice Hall Anthology of African American Literature*, ed. Rochelle Smith and Sharon L. Jones, 955–58. Upper Saddle River, NJ: Prentice Hall, 1999.

Hurley, E. Anthony, Renée Larrier, and Joseph McLaren, eds. *Migrating Words and Worlds: Pan-Africanism Updated*. Trenton, NJ: Africa World Press, 1999.

Hurston, Zora Neale. *Mules and Men*. New York: Harper Perennial, 1990.

"Imus Called Women's Basketball Team 'Nappy-Headed Hos.'" *MediaMatters for America*, April 4, 2007.

Jaggi, Maya. "Island Memories." *Guardian*, November 20, 2004.

John, Catherine A. *Clear Word and Third Sight: Folk Groundings and Diasporic Consciousness in African Caribbean Writing*. Durham: Duke University Press, 2003.

Kadish, Doris Y., ed. *Slavery in the Caribbean Francophone World: Distant Voices, Forgotten Acts, Forged Identities*. Athens: University of Georgia Press, 2000.

Kandiyoti, Deniz. "Identity and Its Discontent: Women and Nation." In *Colonial Discourse and Post-Colonial Theory: A Reader*, ed. Patrick Williams and Laura Chrisman, 376–91. New York: Columbia University Press, 1994.

Kaplan, Caren, Norma Alarcón, and Minoo Moallem, eds. *Between Woman and Nation: Nationalisms, Transnational Feminisms, and the State*. Durham: Duke University Press, 1999.

Kidder, Tracy. *Mountains beyond Mountains: The Quest of Dr. Paul Farmer, a Man Who Could Cure the World*. New York: Random House, 2003.

Kincaid, Jamaica. *Annie John*. New York: Penguin Books, 1986.

———. *The Autobiography of My Mother*. New York: Penguin Books, 1997.

———. *Lucy*. New York: Penguin Books, 1991.

———. *A Small Place*. New York: Penguin Books, 1988.

King, Debra Walker. *African Americans and the Culture of Pain*. Charlottesville: University of Virginia Press, 2008.

King-Aribisala, Karen. *The Hangman's Game*. London: Peepal Tree Press, 2007.

Kiple, Kenneth F. *Another Dimension to the Black Diaspora: Diet, Disease, and Racism*. New York: Cambridge University Press, 1981.

Laguerre, Michel S. *Diasporic Citizenship: Haitian Americans in Transnational America*. New York: St. Martin's Press, 1998.

The Life and Times of Sara Baartman. Dir. Zola Maseko. Perf. Phillip Tobias, Francois-Xavier Fauvelle, Yvette Abrahams, Steve Martin, and Brian Daubney. First Run Icarus Films, 1998. Film.

Lindsley, Syd. "The Gendered Assault on Immigrants." In *Policing the National Body: Sex, Race, and Criminalization*, ed. Jael Silliman and Anannya Bhattacharjee, 175–96. Cambridge, MA: South End Press, 2002.

A Litany for Survival: The Life and Work of Audre Lorde. Dir. Michelle Parkerson. Perf. Ada Gay Griffin. Third World Newsreel, 1998. Film.

Loichot, Valèrie. "Edwidge Danticat's Kitchen History." *Meridians* 5.1 (2004): 92–116.

Lorde, Audre. "Age, Race, Class, and Sex: Women Redefining Difference." In *the Cancer Journal*, 114–23. San Francisco: Aunt Lute Books, 1980.

———. *A Burst of Light: Essays by Audre Lorde.* Ithaca, NY: Firebrand Books, 1988.

———. *The Cancer Journals.* San Francisco: Aunt Lute Books, 1980.

———. *A Litany for Survival: The Life and Work of Audre Lorde.* Screenplay by Ada Gay Griffin. Dir. Michelle Parkerson. Third World Newsreel, 1998.

———. "The Master's Tools Will Never Dismantle the Master's House." In *Sister Outsider: Essays and Speeches*, 110–13. Berkeley: Crossing Press, 1984.

———. "Uses of the Erotic: The Erotic as Power." In *Sister Outsider: Essays and Speeches*, 53–59. Berkeley: Crossing Press, 1984.

———. *Zami: A New Spelling of My Name.* Berkeley: Crossing Press, 1982.

Louis, Yvette. "Body Language: The Black Female Body and the Word in Suzan-Lori Parks's *The Death of the Last Black Man in the Whole World*." In *Recovering the Black Female Body: Self-Representations by African American Women*, ed. Michael Bennett and Vanessa Dickerson, 141–64. New Brunswick: Rutgers University Press, 2000.

Lovelace, Earl. *Salt.* New York: Persea Books, 1998.

Mabura, Lily G. N. "Black Women Walking Zimbabwe: Refuge and Prospect in the Landscapes of Yvonne Vera's *The Stone Virgins* and Tsiti Dangarembga's *Nervous Conditions* and Its Sequel, *The Book of Not*." *Research in African Literatures* 41.3 (2010): 88–111.

Magubane, Zine. "Which Bodies Matter? Feminism, Poststructuralism, Race, and the Curious Theoretical Odyssey of the 'Hottentot Venus.'" *Gender and Society* 15.6 (2001): 816–34.

Manby, Bronwen. *Struggles for Citizenship in Africa.* London: Zed Books, 2009. http://www.afrimap.org/english/images/report/Struggles-for-Citizenship-Ch1-print.pdf.

Marcheim, E. A., ed. *Hinterland: Caribbean Poetry from the West Indies and Britain.* Newcastle upon Tyne: Bloodaxe Books, 1989.

Marshall, Paule. *Praisesong for the Widow.* New York: Penguin Books, 1983.

———. *Reena and Other Stories.* New York: Feminist Press, 1983.

Mathurin, Lucille. *The Rebel Woman in the British West Indies during Slavery.* Kingston: Institute of Jamaica for the African-Caribbean Institute of Jamaica, 1975.

Mayer, Tamara. *Gender Ironies of Nationalism: Sexing the Nation.* New York: Routledge, 1999.

McCormick, Robert H. "Return Passages: Maryse Condé Brings Tituba Back to

Barbados." In *Black Imagination and the Middle Passage*, ed. Maria Diedrich, Henry Louis Gates Jr., and Carl Pedersen. New York: Oxford University Press, 1999.

McDowell, Deborah E. "Recovery Missions: Imaging the Body Ideals." In *Recovering the Black Female Body: Self-Representation by African American Women*, ed. Michael Bennett and Vanessa D. Dickerson, 296–317. New Brunswick: Rutgers University Press, 2001.

Mendoza, Martha. "Mothers-to-be and HMOs Help Deliver Resurgence of Midwives." *Los Angeles Times*, May 4, 1997.

Mhando, Lindah. "Under Ivory-Tower Eyes: Influence of Womanist Warriors as Public Intellectuals." *Feminist Wire*, October 29, 2012. http://thefeministwire.com/2012/10/under-ivory-tower-eyes-influence-of-womanist-warriors-as-public-intellectuals/.

Morgan, Jennifer L. *Laboring Women: Reproduction and Gender in New World Slavery*. Philadelphia: University of Pennsylvania Press, 2004.

Morris, Margaret Kissam. "Audre Lorde: Textual Authority and the Embodied Self." *Frontiers: A Journal of Women Studies* 35.2 (June 2002): 168–89.

Morrison, Andrew R., and Rachel A. May. "Escape from Terror: Violence and Migration in Post-Revolutionary Guatemala." *Latin America Research Review* 29.2 (1994): 111–32.

Morrison, Toni. *Beloved*. New York: Penguin, 1988.

———. *The Bluest Eye*. New York: Plume, 1994.

———. "City Limits, Village Values: Concepts of the Neighborhood in Black Fiction." In *Literature and the Urban Experience: Essays on the City and Literature*, ed. Michael C. Taye and Ann Chalmers Watts, 35–43. New Brunswick: Rutgers University Press, 1981.

———. *Playing in the Dark: Whiteness and the Literary Imagination*. New York: Vintage Books, 1992.

———. "Rootedness: The Ancestor as Foundation." In *Black Women Writers, 1950–1980*, ed. Mari Evans, 339–45. Garden City, NY: Doubleday, Anchor Press, 1984.

———. *Song of Solomon*. New York: Penguin, 1987.

———. *Sula*. New York: Penguin, 1973.

Mosher, Howard Frank. "Staying Alive." *New York Times*, October 25, 1992.

Moudelino, Lydie. "Returning Remains: Saartjie Baartman or the 'Hottentot Venus' as Transnational Postcolonial Icon." *Forum for Modern Language Studies* 45.2 (2009): 200–212.

Mugabane, Khanyi. "Celebrating the Power of Women." August 14, 2008. http://www.mediaclubsouthafrica.com/culture/629-celebrating-power-of-women.

Mwaria, Cheryl. "Biomedical Ethics, Gender, and Ethnicity: Implications for Black Feminist Anthropology." In *Black Feminist Anthropology: Theory, Politics, Praxis, and Poetics*, ed. Irma McClaurin, 187–210. New Brunswick: Rutgers University Press, 2001.

Natarajan, Nalini. "Woman, Nation, and Narration in Midnight's Children." In *Feminist Theory and the Body: A Reader*, ed. Janet Price and Margrit Shildrick, 399–409. New York: Routledge, 1999.

Ndinda, Catherine, and Korwa Adar. "The Interaction of Nationalist and Feminist Goals with Reference to the South African Liberation Movement." *JENDA: A Journal of Culture and African Women Studies* 7 (2005).

Neti, Leila. "Blood and Dirt: Politics of Women's Protest in Armagh Prison, Northern Ireland." In *Violence and the Body: Race, Gender, and the State*, ed. Arturo J. Aldama, 77–93. Bloomington: Indiana University Press, 2003.

Ngcobo, Lauretta, ed. *Essays by Black Woman in Britain*. London: Pluto, 1987.

Nichols, Grace. "The Battle with Language." In *Caribbean Women Writers: Essays from the First International Conference*, ed. Selwyn Cudjoe, 283–89. Wellesley: Calaloux, 1990.

———. *The Fat Black Woman's Poems*. London: Virago Press, 1984.

———. *I Is a Long Memoried Woman*. London: Karnak House, 1983.

———. *Lazy Thoughts of a Lazy Woman*. London: Virago Press, 1989.

N'Zengou-Tayo, Marie-Jose. "Rewriting Folklore: Traditional Beliefs and Popular Culture in Edwidge Danticat's *Breath, Eyes, Memory* and *Krik? Krak!*" *MaComere* 3 (2000): 123–40.

Obbo, Christine. "Sexuality and Economic Domination in Uganda." In *Woman-Nation-State*, ed. Nira Yuval-Davis and Floya Anthias, 79–91. New York: St. Martin's Press, 1989.

O'Callaghan, Evelyn. *Woman Version: Theoretical Approaches to West Indian Fiction by Women*. New York: St. Martin's Press, 1993.

Oleksy, Elzbieta H., Jeff Hearn, and Dorota Golanska, eds. *The Limits of Gendered Citizenship: Contexts and Complexities*. New York: Routledge, 2011.

Olmos, Margarite Fernández, and Lizabeth Paravisini-Gebert, eds. *Sacred Possessions: Vodou, Santería, Obeah, and the Caribbean*. New Brunswick: Rutgers University Press, 1997.

Ong, Aihwa. *Flexible Citizenship: The Cultural Logics of Transnationality*. Durham: Duke University Press, 1999.

Oyěwùmí, Oyèrónkẹ́. "Abiyamo: Theorizing African Motherhood." *JENDA: A Journal of Culture and African Women* 4.1 (2003).

———, ed. *African Women and Feminism: Reflecting on the Politics of Sisterhood*. Trenton, NJ: Africa World Press, 2003.

———. *The Invention of Women: Making an African Sense of Western Gender Discourses*. Minneapolis: University of Minnesota Press, 1997.

Peacock, Sunita. "Sita's War and the Body Politic: Violence and Abuse in the Lives of South Asian Women." In *Violence and the Body: Race, Gender, and the State*, ed. Arturo J. Aldama, 360–74. Bloomington: Indiana University Press, 2003.

Pfaff, Françoise. *Conversations with Maryse Condé*. Lincoln: University of Nebraska Press, 1996.

Philip, Marlene Nourbese, ed. *A Genealogy of Resistance and Other Essays*. Toronto: Mercury Press, 1997.

———. *She Tries Her Tongue: Her Silence Softly Breaks*. Charlottetown, Canada: Ragweed Press, 1993.

Potts, Laura K, ed. *Ideologies of Breast Cancer: Feminist Perspectives*. New York: St. Martin's Press, 2000.

Poussaint, Alvin F., and Amy Alexander. *Lay My Burden Down: Suicide and the Mental Health Crisis among African Americans*. New York: Beacon Press, 2001.

Price, Janet, and Margrit Shildrick, eds. *Feminist Theory and the Body: A Reader*. New York: Routledge, 1999.

———. "Openings on the Body: A Critical Introduction." In *Feminist Theory and the Body: A Reader*, ed. Janet Price and Margrit Shildrick, 1–14. New York: Routledge, 1999.

Remmler, Karen. "Sheltering Battered Bodies in Language: Imprisonment Once More?" In *Cultural Identities in Question: Displacements*, ed. Angelika Bammer, 216–32. Bloomington: Indiana University Press, 1994.

The Return of Sarah Bartman. Dir. Zola Maseko. Perf. Gail Smith. First Run/Icarus Films, 2003. Film.

Roberts, Diane. *The Myth of Aunt Jemima: Representations of Race and Region*. New York: Routledge, 1994.

Roberts, Dorothy. *Fatal Invention: How Science, Politics, and Big Business Re-create Race in the Twenty-First Century*. New York: New Press, 2011.

———. *Killing the Black Body: Race, Reproduction, and the Meaning of Liberty*. New York: Vintage Books, 1997.

Saigol, Rubina. "Militarisation, Nation, and Gender: Women's Bodies as Arenas of Violent Conflict." In *Making Enemies, Creating Conflicts: Pakistan's Crises of State and Society*, ed. Zia Mian and Iftikhar Ahmad. Lahore, Pakistan: Mashal Books, 1997.

Saywell, Cherise, with Lesley Henderson and Liza Beattie. "Sexualized Illness: The Newsworthy Body in Media Representations of Breast Cancer." In *Ideologies of Breast Cancer: Feminist Perspectives*, ed. Laura K. Potts, 37–62. New York: St. Martin's Press, 2000.

Scanlon, Mara. "The Divine Body in Grace Nichols's *The Fat Black Woman's Poems*." *World Literature Today*. 72.1 (Winter 1998): 59–67.

Scarry, Elaine. *The Body in Pain: The Making and Unmaking of the World*. New York: Oxford University Press, 1985.

Schiebinger, Londa. *Plants and Empire: Colonial Bioprospecting in the Atlantic World*. Cambridge: Harvard University Press, 2004.

Schulz, Amy J., and Leith Mullings, eds. *Gender, Race, Class, and Health: Intersectional Approaches*. San Francisco: Jossey-Bass, 2006.

Schwarz-Bart, Simone. *The Bridge of Beyond*. Trans. Barbara Bray. Portsmouth, NH: Heinemann, 1982.

Scully, Pamela, and Clifton Crais. "Race and Erasure: Sara Baartman and Hendrik Cesars in Capetown and London." *Journal of British Studies* 47.2 (April 2008): 301–23.

Shaw, Andrea Elizabeth. *The Embodiment of Disobedience: Fat Black Women's Unruly Political Bodies*. New York: Lexington Books, 2006.

Sherwin, Susan. "Feminist and Medical Ethics: Two Different Approaches to Contextual Ethics." In *Feminist Perspectives in Medical Ethics*, ed. Helen Bequaert Holmes and Laura M. Purdy, 17–31. Bloomington: Indiana University Press, 1992.

Shildrick, Margrit, and Janet Price. "Breaking the Boundaries of the Broken Body." In *Feminist Theory and the Body: A Reader*, ed. Janet Price and Margrit Shildrick, 432–44. New York: Routledge, 1999.

Silliman, Jael, and Anannya Bhattacharjee, eds. *Policing the National Body: Sex, Race, and Criminalization.* Cambridge, MA: South End Press, 2002.

Singer, Debra S. "Reclaiming Venus: The Presence of Sarah Bartmann in Contemporary Art." In *Venus 2010: They Called Her 'Hottentot,'* ed. Deborah Willis, 87–95. Philadelphia: Temple University Press, 2010.

Smith, Barbara. *Toward a Black Feminist Criticism.* Trumansburg, NY: Out & Out Books, 1982.

Smith, Bonnie G., and Beth Hutchison, ed. *Gendering Disability.* New Brunswick: Rutgers University Press, 2004.

Smith, Faith, ed. *Sex and the Citizen: Interrogating the Caribbean.* Charlottesville: University of Virginia Press, 2011.

Spillers, Hortense J. *Black, White, and in Color: Essays on American Literature and Culture.* Chicago: University of Chicago Press, 2003.

———. "Mama's Baby, Papa's Maybe: An American Grammar Book. *Diacritics* 17.2 (Summer 1987): 65–80.

Stallybrass, Peter, and Allon White. *The Politics and Poetics of Transgression.* Ithaca: Cornell University Press, 1986.

Stanford, Ann Folwell. *Bodies in a Broken World: Women Novelists of Color and the Politics of Medicine.* Chapel Hill: University of North Carolina Press, 2003.

———. "Mechanisms of Disease: African-American Women Writers, Social Pathologies, and the Limits of Medicine." *NWSA Journal* 6.1 (Spring 1994): 28–47.

Stukator, Angela. "'It's Not Over until the Fat Lady Sings'": Comedy, the Carnivalesque, and Body Politics." In *Bodies out of Bounds: Fatness and Transgression,* ed. Jana Evans Braziel and Kathleen LeBesco, 197–213. Berkeley: University of California Press, 2001.

Tate, Claudia. *Black Women Writers at Work.* New York: Continuum, 1983.

Terry, Jennifer. "Anxious Slippages between 'Us' and 'Them': A Brief History of the Scientific Search for Homosexual Bodies." In *Deviant Bodies: Critical Perspectives on Difference in Science and Popular Culture,* ed. Jennifer Terry and Jacqueline Urla, 129–69. Bloomington: Indiana University Press, 1995.

Terry, Jennifer, and Jacqueline Urla, eds. *Deviant Bodies: Critical Perspectives on Difference in Science and Popular Culture.* Bloomington: Indiana University Press, 1995.

Thomas, Deborah, A. *Exceptional Violence: Embodied Citizenship in Transnational Jamaica.* Durham: Duke University Press, 2011.

Tiffin, Helen. "'Flowers of Evil,' Flowers of Empire: Roses and Daffodils in the Work of Jamaica Kincaid, Olive Senior, and Lorna Goodison." *Span* 46 (April 1998): 58–71.

Uwakweh, Pauline Ada. "Debunking Patriarchy: The Liberational Quality of Voicing in Tsitsi Dangarembga's *Nervous Conditions. Research in African Literatures* 26.1 (Spring 1995): 75–84.

Van Hear, Nicholas. *New Diasporas: The Mass Exodus, Dispersal, and Regrouping of Migrant Communities.* Seattle: University of Washington Press, 1998.

Van Thompson, Carlyle. *Eating the Black Body: Miscegenation as Sexual Consumption in African American Literature and Culture.* New York: Peter Lang, 2006.

Varadarajan, Latha. *The Domestic Abroad: Diasporas in International Relations*. London: Oxford University Press, 2010.

Wallace, Michelle. *Black Macho and the Myth of the Superwoman*. New York: Verso, 1990.

Wallace-Sanders, Kimberly, ed. *Skin Deep, Spirit Strong: The Black Female Body in American Culture*. Ann Arbor: University of Michigan Press, 2002.

Warren, Virginia L. "Feminist Directions in Medical Ethics." In *Feminist Perspectives in Medical Ethics*, ed. Helen Bequaert Holmes and Laura M. Purdy, 32–45. Bloomington: Indiana University Press, 1992.

Washington, Harriet A. *Medical Apartheid: The Dark History of Medical Experimentation on Black Americans from Colonial Times to the Present*. New York: Doubleday, 2006.

Washington, Mary Helen. *Black-Eyed Susans: Classic Stories by and about Black Women*. New York: Anchor Books, 1975.

Wendell, Susan. "Feminism, Disability, and the Transcendence of the Body." *Feminist Perspectives in Medical Ethics*, ed. Helen Bequaert Holmes and Laura M. Purdy, 325–33. Bloomington: Indiana University Press, 1992.

———. "Toward a Feminist Theory of Disability." In *Feminist Perspectives in Medical Ethics*, ed. Helen Bequaert Holmes and Laura M. Purdy, 63–81. Bloomington: Indiana University Press, 1992.

White, Deborah Gray. *Ar'n't I a Woman? Female Slaves in the Plantation South*. New York: W. W. Norton, 1999.

White, Evelyn C. *The Black Women's Health Book: Speaking for Ourselves*. Seattle: Seal Press, 1994.

Williams, Patricia J. *Alchemy of Race and Rights: Diary of a Law Professor*. Cambridge: Harvard University Press, 1991.

Williams, Patrick, and Laura Chrisman, eds. *Colonial Discourse and Post-Colonial Theory: A Reader*. New York: Columbia University Press, 1994.

Willis, Deborah, ed. *Venus 2010: They Called Her 'Hottentot.'* Philadelphia: Temple University Press, 2010.

Wilson, Elizabeth. "'Le Voyage et l'espace clos'—Island and Journey as Metaphor: Aspects of Woman's Experience in the Works of Francophone Caribbean Women Novelists." In *Out of the Kumbla*, ed. Carole Boyce Davies and Elaine Savory Fido. Trenton, NJ: Africa World Press, 1990.

Wu, Cynthia. "Marked Bodies, Marking Time: Reclaiming the Warrior in Audre Lorde's *The Cancer Journal*." *Auto/Biography Studies* 17.2 (Winter 2002): 245–61.

Wyatt, Gail Elizabeth. *Stolen Women: Reclaiming Our Sexuality, Taking Back Our Lives*. New York: John Wiley & Sons, 1997.

Yancy, George. *Black Bodies, White Gazes: The Continuing Significance of Race*. New York: Rowman and Littlefield, 2008.

Young, Harvey. *Embodying Black Experience: Stillness, Critical Memory, and the Black Body*. Ann Arbor: University of Michigan Press, 2010.

Young, Iris Marion. *Throwing Like a Girl and Other Essays in Feminist Philosophy and Social Theory*. Bloomington: Indiana University Press, 1990.

Yuval-Davis, Nira. *Gender & Nation*. New York: Sage, 1997.

Yuval-Davis, Nira, and Floya Anthias, eds. *Woman-Nation-State*. New York: St. Martin's Press, 1989.
Yuval-Davis, Nira, and Marcel Stoetzler. "Imagined Boundaries and Borders: A Gendered Gaze." *European Journal of Women's Studies* 9.3 (2002): 329-44.
Yuval-Davis, Nira, and Pnina Werbner, eds. *Women, Citizenship, and Difference*. New York: Zed Books, 1999.

Index

Able-bodiedness, 17, 42, 57, 161
Abortions, 70, 72, 85, 118
Adar, Korwa, 32, 33, 34, 35, 196nn17,18
Africa(n), 6, 8, 9, 20, 21, 22, 25, 28, 30, 31, 33, 34, 35, 36, 39, 44, 47, 68, 69, 70, 93, 94, 97, 129, 130, 132, 145, 157, 164, 165, 171, 173, 183, 186, 187, 193n6, 195n14, 196nn17,18,23, 197n6, 200n20, 208nn15,16,21,30
African National Congress (ANC), 34, 196n23; Women's League, 30
Africanness, 30
Afrikaner, 34, 105, 116
Afro-America, 9
AIDS, 96, 97, 98, 159, 161, 163, 198n11, 201n1
Alarcón, Norma, 104
Alexander, M. Jacqui, 14, 40, 41, 43, 52, 53, 54, 56, 60, 63, 64, 65, 66, 106, 111, 159, 197n1
Alternative cures, 160, 166, 191
Alternative discourse, 14, 43, 50, 72
Alternative subjectivity, 16
Amadiume, Ifi, 6, 8, 128, 129
Amazonian (women), 51, 58, 198n10
Amazon women, 51
America, 16, 21, 42, 46, 63, 66, 75, 97, 101, 105, 111, 133, 164, 165, 167, 179, 198n15, 199n20
American Cancer Society, 42, 43, 52
Americanization, 184
Amnesia, 113, 204n31
Amnesty, 37, 111, 112, 113, 118, 204n30
Amputation, 54, 60, 64, 199n20

Anatol, Giselle, 173, 174
Anderson, Benedict, 8, 10
Androcentric, 25
Anglophone, 12
Anorexia, 182, 183, 185, 186, 206n7
Anthias, Floya, 115, 125
Antifeminist, 70
Antigua, 19
Antiwoman, 70
Anzaldúa, Gloria, 175, 176, 177, 189, 208n17
Apartheid, 13, 22, 30, 31, 32, 33, 34, 35, 42, 45, 46, 47, 196nn21,22, 197n23; politics of, 13
Asexualization, 143
Assimilation, 114, 182
Asylum, 98, 113
Atlantic slave trade, 22
Aunt Jemima, 144, 203n16

Baartman, Saartjie, 12, 13, 17, 20–26, 28–30, 32–38, 42, 47, 48, 56, 63, 64, 67, 70, 130, 140, 146–50, 155, 194n1, 195nn10,12,13,14,15, 196nn15,21, 197nn24,25,26,27, 206n15, 207n19
Bad Mother Syndrome, 119
Bakhtin, Mikhail, 16, 130, 131, 135, 138, 139, 142, 146, 152, 156, 205n2, 206n8; Bakhtinian, 155
Baldwin, James, 9, 194n12
Bambara, Toni Cade, 178, 179, 197n4; *The Salt Eaters*, 178
Banet-Weiser, Sarah, 150, 206n4
Bantu's Women League, 30

Barbados, 14, 69, 71, 77, 95
Barnet, Miguel, 188
Beauty pageants, 134, 148, 154, 205n4, 206n11
Benoit, Olga, 80
Bermuda Triangle, 157
Bertone, Andrea Marie, 23, 26
Bestiality, 24, 65, 75
Biological disorder, 186
Biomedical science, 11
Birmingham, Alabama, 45
Biseswar, Indrawatie, 33, 196n16
Black immigrant woman, 119, 190
Black lesbian, 14, 53, 55, 59, 60, 61, 65, 66
Black mothers, 104
Black Nationalist movement, 34
Bleaching, 18, 179, 180, 181, 183, 185, 208n29; of skin, 18, 179, 180
Bodily extravagance, 142
Bodily restrictions, 154, 190
Bodily ruptures, 191
Bodily silence, 115
Bodily violation, 22
Body, 1, 8, 11, 12, 15, 18, 19, 20, 21, 24, 30, 36, 37, 43, 45, 49, 54, 55, 59, 62, 65, 66, 71, 73, 74, 75, 76, 78, 81, 86, 89, 96, 98, 102, 105, 106, 108, 110, 113, 115, 117, 118, 121, 122, 124, 127, 131, 132, 133, 134, 135, 137, 141, 144, 147, 152, 153, 154, 155, 156, 159, 160, 161, 163, 164, 166, 168, 170, 171, 172, 173, 174, 175, 176, 178, 181, 182, 184, 185, 186, 187, 188, 191, 195nn8,11, 197n2, 198n16, 203n18, 205n38, 206n7, 207n18, 208n16; anomalous, 22, 63; black female, 13, 17, 23, 25, 26, 29, 39, 44, 56, 60, 67, 72, 107, 123, 143, 148, 149, 150; as text, 4, 72, 140; disfigurement, 64; disorder, 183; erasure, 29; estrangement, 180, 183; expulsion, 109; management, 138, 139; politic, 130, 136, 140, 146, 158; posturing, 61; violation, 69, 72, 90; deviant, 5, 41, 52, 67; diseased, 13, 41; expendability of black bodies, 57; freakish, 142, 146; ideal, 16, 44, 53, 58, 119, 129, 140, 142, 143, 205n36; Idealized feminine, 51; Normative, 42, 53, 194n2; nonnormative, 52; queer, 14; theft of the, 22, 40, 44; Visceral, 142; vulgar, 130
Border crossing(s), 3, 70, 200n18
Borderlands, 41, 161
Border politics, 23
Borders, 2, 14, 17, 18, 19, 23, 30, 32, 40, 42, 44, 45, 59, 70, 71, 84, 105, 112, 113, 125, 130, 133, 149, 155, 156, 160, 165, 170, 171, 175, 188, 194n19, 200n18; impermeable, 32
Bordo, Susan, 53, 54, 58, 133, 134, 135, 139, 140, 151, 153, 182, 184, 186, 187, 193n1, 206n6
Botha, P. W., 34, 42, 45, 49
Boundaries, 10, 17, 19, 23, 30, 42, 44, 49, 51, 54, 58, 59, 66, 67, 70, 71, 81, 85, 107, 114, 115, 126, 130, 133, 138, 140, 142, 149, 155, 156, 160, 165, 168, 171, 188, 193n2, 194n19, 204n29; elastic, 10
Boyd, Monica, 10, 194n14
Breast cancer, 3, 3, 18, 42, 43, 44, 48, 49, 50, 51, 52, 60, 61, 165, 181, 193n7, 197n3, 198n7, 199n17
British, 22, 34, 127, 128, 147, 156
Brooks, Daphne, 133, 136, 137, 143
Brown-Glaude, Winnifred, 180
Bulimia, 18, 182, 183, 184, 185, 186, 206n7
Bunch, Charlotte, 67, 193n1
Bush, Barbara, 88, 89
Byrd, James, Jr., 57, 198n14

Camus, Albert, 3, 193n4
Cannibalization, 17, 25
Cape Town, 36
Captive, 12, 13, 22, 36, 38, 44, 46, 49, 68, 69, 121, 123, 144, 173
Caribbean, 9, 12, 25, 68, 93, 97, 103, 109, 118, 127, 131, 171, 173, 187, 202n14, 203n22, 204n25, 205n39
Carnivalesque, 137, 152
Carnivalization, 25
Carriacou, 181, 182

Caruth, Cathy, 71, 199n4
Castration, 157
Censorship, 110, 153, 173, 177, 190; self-, 57
Chancy, Myriam, 35, 102, 103, 105, 107, 108, 111, 119, 120, 122, 205n39
Charles, Carolle, 35, 103, 104, 105, 107, 114, 118, 203n15, 204n32
Chastity, 84, 107, 108, 117, 133, 136, 139, 175, 176, 206n10
Christian, Barbara, 4, 5, 6, 108, 122, 144, 145, 145, 193nn1,7, 194n10, 206n14
Citizen(s), 9, 14, 18, 24, 30, 31, 32, 33, 36, 39, 40, 41, 43, 44, 45, 46, 47, 48, 49, 50, 52, 53, 55, 65, 70, 77, 94, 95, 96, 99, 100, 105, 114, 115, 118, 119, 123, 129, 137, 140, 146, 147, 149, 153, 155, 160, 166, 170, 176, 181, 194nn16,22, 199n1, 204nn27,29,31; desirable, 52, 60, 95, 138, 169, 171, 191; ideal, 16, 44, 51, 52, 56, 64, 67, 74, 130, 149, 153, 155; second-class, 15, 102, 135; undesirable, 161, 172, 177
Citizenship, 9, 10, 12, 15, 18, 19, 30, 31, 33, 37, 40, 46, 50, 54, 58, 60, 61, 67, 69, 77, 79, 80, 81, 83, 89, 90, 93, 94, 97, 101, 113, 114, 115, 120, 127, 135, 137–38, 140, 147, 149, 153, 157, 159, 166, 171, 174, 204nn29,35; attainment of, 13, 20, 22, 23, 96, 99, 102, 156; black, 28; conditional, 32, 133, 154, 172, 182; denial of, 11, 17, 20, 21, 24, 47, 130; dual, 202n14; exceptional, 132, 167; exclusionary, 16, 70, 129; exemplary, 169; flexible, 99, 100, 112, 136, 156, 170, 175, 194n22, 200n13; ideal, 16, 129, 130, 139, 160; second-class, 48; transnational, 14, 41, 47, 70, 71, 100, 130, 156, 165, 194n22; unconditional, 51, 59, 104; unworthy of, 57, 119, 141, 160
Clark, Vèvè, 9, 33
Class consciousness, 50
Classed difference, 190
Clitoridectomy, 188
Cobb-Clark, Deborah, 112
Cole, Johnnetta Betsch, 80

Collective consciousness, 10
Colligan, Sumi, 24, 62, 64, 138, 198
Collins, Patricia Hill, 102, 115, 119, 120, 144, 193n1, 205n37, 206n14
Colonialism, 22, 26, 28, 32, 34–37, 48, 87, 93, 94, 109, 110, 111, 115, 125, 127, 131, 155, 157, 185, 186, 203n18
Colonialist, 151, 155
Colonial occupation, 131, 157
Colonial paternalism, 132
Commercialization, 48, 55, 62, 134
Commodification, 28, 36, 43, 51, 62, 123, 144, 157, 176, 206n12
Commodity, 31, 49, 57, 62, 64, 75, 76, 148, 150, 178; profitable, 76
Compulsory normalcy, 51
Condé, Maryse, 3, 5, 12, 17, 68–73, 75, 76, 79–83, 86, 88, 90, 92, 95, 160, 164, 165, 169, 183, 190, 200nn16,18,24, 207n10; *Desirada*, 183; *I, Tituba, Black Witch of Salem*, 14, 68, 169
Connor, Bull, 42, 45
Consumer culture, 133, 184
Consumerism, 182
Consumerist, 54, 62; culture, 54
Consumption, 25–26, 29, 53, 57, 63–64, 73, 135–36, 138–39, 143, 148, 150, 177–78, 181–82, 184–85, 206n12; European, 25, 64; male, 26, 57, 65, 75, 135, 148; object of western, 63; public, 25, 29, 42, 66
Contamination, 84, 152, 185
Cooper, Carolyn, 16, 130, 140–41, 152, 155, 158
Coronation, 138
Counter discourse, 11, 16–17, 77, 102, 160
Counter narrative, 30, 149, 190
Crais, Clifton, 21, 22, 23, 32, 33, 35, 155, 195n13, 196n21, 197n30
Creed, Barbara, 58, 65–66, 193n1, 198n16
Creole, 100, 127, 203n17
Criminality, 21, 65
Criminalization, 14, 33, 40, 98
Criminalized, 14, 98
Crisscrossing, 17, 19, 42, 133, 156, 170

Critical race theory, 11
Cubans, 97, 99
Cult of True Womanhood, 84, 107
Cultural imperialism, 6, 70
Cultural moorings, 93
Cuvier, Baron Georges, 26, 64, 195n8

Dahomey, 51
Dangarembga, Tsitsi, 185–86; *Nervous Conditions*, 185
Dantica, Joseph, 63, 98–99, 167
Danticat, Edwidge, 1–3, 5, 10–12, 15–18, 85, 96, 98–111, 113–17, 119–25, 160, 163–64, 173–77, 179, 183–85, 187–88, 190, 193n4, 197n4, 200n20, 202nn5,6,9,10,13, 203n17, 205n38, 208n14; *Create Dangerously*, 1–3, 99, 193n4
Davies, Carole Boyce, 11, 25–26, 150–51, 157, 176, 195n7, 202n14
Davis, Angela, 18, 39–40, 42, 44, 71, 118, 193n1, 199nn1,5
Dayan, Joan, 177
deCaires Narain, Denise, 158
Decolonizing, 131
Decontaminant, 185
De-familiarization, 185
Defeminization, 51, 66
Defiance, 41, 43, 85, 88, 108, 117, 125, 141, 147, 154
Degeneracy, 25
Dehumanization, 30, 47, 74, 90, 104, 135, 153, 160, 166, 207n16
Delegitimization, 98, 104, 140
Demonization, 17–18, 36, 56, 70, 82, 107, 118, 148, 163, 172, 173
Denationalization, 17, 161
Dependence, 76–77, 184
Depersonalization, 54–55, 62
Depoliticization, 33, 62
Deracialization, 51
De Veaux, Alexis, 5, 43, 46–47, 50, 59, 62, 65, 193n8, 197n6
Deviance, 13–14, 16–17, 41–43, 51, 58, 60, 130, 142, 149, 160, 180, 194n17; axis of, 13, 24; blanketed, 43; embodied, 52; sexual, 11
Deviant(s), 5, 11, 14–15, 22, 40–43, 52, 58–60, 64, 67, 104, 108, 138, 161, 176–77, 180, 190–91
Diagnosis, 1, 5, 170, 187, 189, 198n7
Diaspora, 8–9, 10–12, 18, 31–33, 39, 42, 50, 69, 72, 77, 99, 109, 111, 156, 170, 187; African, 22, 33, 47, 68, 132; Black, 14, 17, 40, 161; female, 41–43, 46, 70, 77, 85, 172, 199n5; female-centered, 19, 169
"Diaspora literacy," 9, 33
Diasporic connections, 42
Diasporic kinship, 10, 178
Dickerson, Vanessa, 107, 121, 123
Disarmament, 60
Discursive, 2, 5, 13, 16, 29, 33, 37, 45, 92, 124, 129, 140–41, 151, 154, 170, 175, 186, 200n18
Disease(s), 2, 3, 4, 17, 40, 42, 43, 44, 45, 48–50, 97, 152, 159–62, 164–67, 169, 171, 179–91, 193n3, 198nn7,11, 207n1, 209n31; biological, 186; social, 179, 186
Disembodiment, 54, 60, 137, 161, 179, 180–81
Disfiguration, 26, 185
Disfigurement, 64, 138
Displaced bodies, 190
Displacement(s), 8, 12, 68, 79, 90, 100, 138, 171, 182
Disrobing, 26, 134–35
Dominique, Jean, 99, 202n12
Doubling, 86–87, 120, 168, 174–75, 186–87, 205n41, 208n17
Duany, Jorge, 8, 17, 18, 130, 169
Dunbar, Paul Laurence, 93
Dunlop, Alexander, 22, 195n6
Duvalier, François, 105, 203nn15,17,20
Duvalier regime, 99, 103, 105, 203n15
Dworkin, Andrea, 150

Eastern Cape, 22, 36
Emasculation, 78, 91
Embodiment, 48, 52, 93, 122–23, 137, 142

Enslavement, 14, 46, 70–71, 76, 89, 157, 160, 173
Epidemic, 97, 163, 164, 198n11
Erotic(ism)/eroticization, 56, 65, 124, 150, 151, 152, 155
Erzulie, 119, 120, 177, 188
Estrangement, 18, 55, 170, 179, 180, 181, 183
Ethiopia/Ethiopian, 33, 188, 196n16
Ethnicity, 1, 7, 9, 24, 28, 50 57, 114, 115, 116, 179
Ethnic mobilization, 15, 102, 116
Eurocentrism, 14, 25, 42, 63, 64; ideology, 58
European(s), 6, 22, 25, 26, 29, 39, 47, 59, 63, 64, 108, 109, 118, 119, 129, 135, 137, 148, 155, 167, 173, 181, 185, 205n36; audiences, 24–25
Europeanization, 182
Exceptionalism, 51, 133
Exoticization, 23
Exploitation, 17, 23, 24, 24, 26, 28, 29, 32, 35, 47, 48, 73, 75, 108, 130, 144, 148, 149, 155

Fabi, Guilia M., 68, 90
Family-centered religion, 188
Fanon, Frantz, 92, 93, 94, 201n27; *Black Skin, White Masks*, 92
Farmer, Paul, 17, 18, 96, 161
Federation of South African Women, 31
Female agency, 88, 94, 148, 151, 191
Female disempowerment, 26
Female eroticism, 151
Female healers, 18, 19, 170, 171
Female marginalization, 132, 169
Female propriety, 154, 176
Female reproduction, 87
Female sexuality, 51, 59, 60, 73, 75, 76, 77, 108, 114, 140, 141, 142, 148, 150, 152, 157, 170, 175
Female subjugation, 71, 75, 76, 175
Female subordination, 26, 137
Feminine values, 51, 118
Femininity, 16, 50, 51, 53, 58, 59, 101, 130, 135, 138, 142, 149, 153; homogeneous, 153; normative, 137; paragons of, 135; tenets of, 58; white, 50, 58, 59, 67, 84, 137, 140, 143, 149, 152, 154
Feminist(s), feminism, 1–8, 14, 19, 32, 33, 34, 40, 43, 48, 50, 53, 55, 58, 61, 63, 67, 70, 71, 77, 80–83, 94, 102, 103, 114, 129, 133, 144, 145, 172, 193n2, 194n10, 196n18, 203n15, 206n6
Feminist coalition, 32
Feminization, 10, 50, 141, 194n13
First-wave feminism, 71, 82, 83
Flesh, 13, 24, 32, 36–37, 39, 44, 46, 54, 69, 73, 81, 84, 121–24, 130, 148, 149, 174, 177, 186; captive, 12, 13, 36, 38, 46, 68–69; excess, 17, 24, 26, 63, 130, 143, 146, 149, 195n9; severed, 191; wounded, 25
Flores-Ortiz, Yvette, 186
Fluidity, 5
Francis, Donette, 113
Francophone, 12, 100
Frankenstein, 17, 154–55
Freakishness, 143
Freak of nature, 24, 146
Friedman, May, 3, 82
Frontier, 4

Gadsby, Meredith, 10–11
Gaitskell, Deborah, 35, 102, 105, 107, 115–16, 123
Garland-Thomson, Rosemarie, 30, 64, 132, 136, 142, 148, 155, 164, 190, 193n1, 206n11
Gatens, Moira, 140
Gauthier, Xavière, 172, 174, 176, 178
Gender-biased discourse, 4
Gender conformity, 54
Gender discrimination, 114
Gender disparity, 33, 38
Gender inequality, 7
Gender-neutral, 114, 205n2
Genitalia, 25, 63, 153, 157, 195n8
Geographic borders, 23
Geographic boundaries, 160

Geographic flexibility, 112
Gilbert, Sandra, 108
Gilman, Sander, 29, 30, 64, 195n14
Gilroy, Paul, 69, 71, 157
Ginwala, Frene, 34, 196n20
Glamorization, 51, 62–63
Global apartheid, 31
Goldstein, Laurence, 56–57
Gottlieb, Karla, 80, 94
Gould, Stephen, 29, 195n13
Grandmè Ifé, 108, 117, 178–81, 183, 186–88, 208n21
Grieco, Elizabeth, 10, 194n14
Grewal, Inderpal, 6, 7, 8, 13, 32, 45, 94
Grotesque, 16, 60, 63, 64, 130, 138, 139, 141, 146, 152, 156, 157, 205nn2,3
Grotesque realism, 138, 157
Guadeloupe/Guadeloupian, 94, 184
Gubar, Susan, 108
Guyanese, 127
Guy-Sheftall, Beverly, 80
Gynecological revolt, 78

Haiti/Haitians, 3, 10, 11, 18, 94, 96–101, 103–7, 109, 110, 111, 113, 114, 115, 117, 120–23, 161, 162, 163, 179–85, 190, 194n16, 201nn1,3,4, 202nn7,9,10,11,12,13, 203nn15,17,20,21, 204nn27,31, 207n5
Haitian Americans, 97
Haitianization, 101
Halberstam, Judith, 59, 61, 193n1
Hall, Stuart, 9, 11, 68
Hammonds, Evelynn M., 53, 54–55, 59, 60, 83, 84, 193n1, 198n11
Hartley, Cecilia, 135, 139, 141, 144, 206n7
Hartman, Saidiya, 21, 28, 160, 161
Hasecic, Dzenita Hrelja, 42
Hegemony, 12, 17, 33, 103, 158, 172, 186, 190, 203n19; cultural, 5, 6; and language, 190
Heteronormative, 12, 43
Heteronormativity, 17, 51, 130
Heterosexism, 40, 43; and society, 40
Heterosexual culture, 58, 66, 67
Heterosexuality, 51, 53, 58, 60, 65, 67, 114; compulsory, 13, 53, 59, 60, 81; patriarchal, 8
Heterosexual order, 43, 60, 66, 67
Hierarchy inversion, 142
Highbrow, 16, 130, 142, 155
High culture, 16, 156
Holistic, 166, 167
Holmes, Rachel, 26, 32, 33, 37, 38, 63, 147, 148, 195n15
Homeland(s), 22, 69, 97, 98, 99, 100, 111, 113, 157, 181
Homeland Security, U.S. Department of, 98, 99, 162, 202n4
Homeopathic, 19, 162, 163, 164–65, 166–69, 207n2
Homogenization, 52, 53, 107
Homophobic, 80
Homosexual(ity), 59, 65, 197n1; homosexuals, 96, 97
hooks, bell, 7, 54, 77, 79, 82, 83, 147, 148, 178; *Black Looks*, 54, 77, 79, 147, 148, 149, 178
Hope, Donna, 180, 208n29
Hopkinson, Nalo, 172, 208n14
"Hottentot Venus," 21, 35, 148, 149, 194n1
Hudson, Nicholas, 148, 149
Hurricane Katrina, 11
Hybridity, 8
Hypersexual(ity), 11, 17, 24, 28, 56, 63, 64–65, 89, 130, 144, 200n22
Hypersexualized, 11, 73
Hypertrophy, 63
Hypervisibility, 17, 24, 42, 130, 146, 195n9
Hyposexual(ity,) 25, 63, 64, 89, 202n22
Hypovisibility, 42, 195n9

Identity, 5, 9, 10, 13–14, 15, 17, 21, 24, 26, 28, 29, 35, 36, 37, 40, 41, 43, 51, 54, 59, 65, 67, 70, 72, 77, 92, 94, 95, 97, 99, 100, 101, 103, 110, 111, 116, 118, 119, 120, 127, 129, 130, 133, 136, 138, 139, 146, 155, 175, 182, 183, 198n13; alternative, 16, 17, 66, 129, 141, 159, 160, 174–75; flexible, 10, 59, 165; fluid, 16; politics of, 31, 47, 82, 90
Ilé-Ifè, 208n21

Illegitimacy, 44, 98, 121
Illegitimate, 56, 85, 98, 112, 114, 117, 163
Imagined community, 8
Immigration, 97–99, 111, 112, 202nn13,14, 204n30
Immigration Reform and Control Act, 111
Immobility, 171; female, 171
Imperial/ism, 6, 8, 70, 129, 207n19
Imperialistic expansion, 157
Impurity, 84, 121, 147, 176
Inaccessibility, 140, 143
Independence, 22, 72, 117, 158, 184, 193n5, 203n20
Indeterminacy, 187
Indigeneity, 9, 18, 160, 163, 165
Indigenization, 170
Indigenous, 9, 110, 160, 165, 167, 186, 205n35, 207n2
Indigenous cultures, 163
Inequality, 7, 18, 115, 161
Infanticide, 70, 72, 81, 84–88, 166, 179, 199n7, 200n20
Infantilization, 178
Infantilized, 48, 177
International Organization for Migration (IOM), 23
Intersectionality, 5, 7
Inversion, 92, 142, 156
Invisibility, 10, 20, 50, 71, 113, 121, 129, 161, 165, 181

Jamaican, 130, 134, 141, 200n17, 204n25, 206n5
Jamaican dancehall, 141
Jezebel, 56, 73, 74, 78, 120, 144, 200n22, 203n16
Johnson, Charles, 56

Kandiyoti, Deniz, 107, 112, 114, 115
Kaplan, Caren, 6, 7, 8, 13, 32, 45, 94, 104
Khoisan, 13, 24, 207n19
Kidder, Tracy, 96, 97, 161, 162, 163, 164, 189, 201n2
Kincaid, Jamaica, 17, 160, 164, 197n4, 203n18, 203n22; *Annie John*, 168, 170;

The Autobiography of My Mother, 200n20
King, Debra Walker, 36, 147
King-Aribisala, Karen, 172
Kossoudji, Sherrie, 112
Krome Detention Center, 97, 98

Laguerre, Michel, 100
Language of difference, 190
Language of female empowerment, 190
Lawlessness, 17, 161
Laziness, 16, 129, 151, 152–58
Lesbianism, 64, 65, 66, 81
Lesbians, 3, 6, 13, 14, 40–41, 43, 53, 55, 58, 59, 60, 61, 64, 65–67, 81, 193n2, 198n16
Liberation, 34, 37, 48, 54, 82, 178, 179, 196n18, 197n6
Linguistic silencing, 114
Loichot, Valérie, 182
Lorde, Audre, 1, 12, 21, 29, 40, 41, 42, 43–67, 124, 125, 150, 151, 164, 165–67, 190, 193nn1,2,6,7,9, 194nn18,19, 195n9, 197n2, 198nn10,12,17, 199nn20,3, 207nn4,7; *A Burst of Light: Essays*, 18, 45, 165, 166, 167, 194n19, 197n3; *The Cancer Journals*, 43, 49, 50, 52–55, 57–63, 193n8, 194n19; *Zami: A New Spelling of My Name*, 65, 66, 190, 194n21
Lord of the Rings, The, 98
Lovelace, Earl, 173; *Salt*, 173
Lowbrow, 16, 130
Low culture, 17
Lukas Klinik, 166, 167

Mabura, Lily, 185
Male dominance, 102, 135
Male-dominated, 5, 48, 157
Male hegemony, 12, 103, 186, 190, 203n19
Male inheritance, 168
Mammy, 16, 56, 73, 129, 143, 144, 145, 200n22, 203n16
Manby, Bronwen, 21
Mandela, Nelson, 33, 34, 35, 37, 196nn19,21,22,23
Manhood, 101, 114, 195n11

"Marassas," 124, 205n41
Marginalization, 18, 33, 41, 57, 61, 94, 121, 132, 134, 142, 146, 169, 170, 172, 189, 207n16
Maroon(s), 71, 72, 79, 80, 93, 94
Marshall, Paule, 17, 153, 160, 164, 181, 190, 197n4
Masculine desire(s), 15, 76, 105
Masculinism, 7, 11, 13, 14, 15, 32, 33, 34, 43, 47, 52, 70, 92, 96, 101, 124, 125, 126, 132, 153, 171, 172, 190, 204n34
Masculinity, 101; hegemonic, 15, 102; white, 135, 137
Masking, 57, 61, 93, 144, 174
Mastectomy, 13, 42, 51, 52, 53, 64, 198n13
Mathurin, Lucille, 80
Mbeki, Thabo, 26, 33, 35, 196nn20,23
McCormick, Robert H., Jr., 80, 81, 82, 85
McDowell, Deborah, 135, 136
Medical Apartheid, 22, 46
Medical authority, 18, 19, 171
Medical industry, 41, 48, 49, 50
Medical malfeasance, 47
Medical profiling, 43, 47
Medicine, 19, 39, 43, 46, 47, 55, 88, 89, 98, 159, 160, 162, 163, 165, 166–72, 187, 188, 189, 207nn3,10; alternative, 167; commercialization of, 55; and highly charged masculinist discourse, 190; homeopathic, 207n2; Indigenous, 160, 207n2; institutionalized, 188; nontraditional medicine, 162, 170; nonwestern, 98, 163, 164, 169; western patriarchal, 170
Memory, 143, 163, 204n31
Mercantile, 29
Mhando, Lindah, 159
Middle Passage, 69, 157
Midwife/midwives, 18, 19, 89, 72, 88, 168, 169, 171, 172, 187, 207n12
Migrant(s), 9, 10, 12, 16, 17, 23, 29, 31, 101, 112, 189, 209n31; commercialized, 29; economic, 22
Migrant status, 9, 16
Migration, 4, 8, 10–14, 16, 19, 20, 22, 23, 29, 36, 38, 51, 200n13, 203n23, 204n25; coercive, 23; feminization of, 10, 194n13; labor-determined, 101; labor, 194n13; noncoercive, 78
Migratory experiences, 11, 12, 18, 190
Migratory flow, 10
Migratory movements, 10, 101
Militancy, 46, 49
Militaristic engagement, 51
Militaristic language, 49
Militaristic scrutiny, 15, 103
Militarization, 15, 45, 46, 103, 199n3
Military, 49, 50, 94, 103, 104, 203n17
Minstrelsy, 93
Misdiagnosis, 188
Moallem, Minoo, 104
Mobility, 14, 119, 122, 142; female, 10, 18, 77, 173; loss of, 184
Mobilization, 15, 46, 102, 116
Monolithic, 4, 5, 8, 11, 16, 56, 101, 129
Monstrosity, 140, 155
Monstrous, 21, 26, 29, 139, 155
Morgan, Jennifer, 26, 78
Morris, Margaret Kissam, 3
Morrison, Toni, 2, 9, 13, 17, 21, 26, 30, 36, 37, 70, 79, 160, 166, 168, 169, 194nn11,12, 199n5, 207nn6,9, 208n14; *Beloved*, 26, 27, 36, 169; *The Bluest Eye*, 168, 208n14; *Song of Solomon*, 169, 208n14
Mother Africa, 37, 38
Motherhood, 15, 16, 86–87, 89, 102–4, 106, 116–20, 145, 197n26; obligatory, 70, 72, 75, 76, 78, 79
Mothering, 15, 70, 72, 76, 87, 89, 106, 116, 119, 197n26
Motherland, 35, 95, 175, 180
Mother Poets, 153
"Mother(s) of the nation," 15, 116, 119
Moudelino, Lydie, 35, 36
Mugabane, Zine, 30, 31
Mullings, Leith, 7, 29
Multifaceted, 109; community, 159, 160
Mummification, 23
Musée de l'Homme, 47, 195n8
Mwaria, Cheryl, 63

Nanny of the Maroons, 72, 93, 94
Natarajan, Nalini, 106, 115, 116, 120
Nation(s), 8, 10, 11, 13, 15, 17, 19, 28, 32, 35, 37, 40, 41, 49, 51, 53, 54, 56, 59, 63, 65, 66, 70, 71, 76, 78, 101–5, 107, 113, 115, 116, 118, 120, 130, 146, 147, 148, 156, 160, 161, 169, 172, 179, 189, 194n20, 196n21, 199n2, 203n21, 207n3
Nationalism, 196n17
Nationalist(ic), 15, 16, 32–35, 96, 101, 102, 103, 107, 114–18, 126, 196n18, 207n3; language, 15, 101, 102; regime, 15, 103
Nation-building, 13, 34, 37, 66
Nationhood, 82, 101
Ndinda, Catherine, 32, 33, 34, 35, 196nn17,18
New World Africans, 173
New World religion, 168
Nichols, Grace, 3, 5, 12, 16, 17, 127–32, 134, 136, 137, 139, 140, 142–47, 151–58
Nomadism, 8
Non-beings, 62
Non-citizen(s), 48, 54, 56, 91, 129, 131, 132, 157, 163, 189, 204nn27,29
Non-person(s), 46, 69, 78, 90, 129
Normalcy, 13, 44, 51, 52, 54, 66, 130, 136, 154
Normality, 51, 52, 61; abnormality, 65, 161, 198n17
Normalization, 17, 50, 54, 56, 61, 62, 66, 101, 139, 140, 147, 153; de-normalization, 199n20

Obbo, Christine, 108, 114
Obeah, 170
Objectification, 22, 25, 68, 77, 78, 84, 134, 135
Old World culture, 167
Old World values, 168
Ol'Higue/old higue, 18 94, 171, 178, 179, 208n22
Olmos, Margarite Fernández, 173, 174
Ong, Aihwa, 100, 112
Oppression(s), 14, 28, 31, 32, 40, 42, 47, 48, 53, 71, 74, 78, 79, 82, 83, 88, 90, 92, 94, 95, 105, 132, 134, 143, 145, 161, 163, 164, 165, 174, 175, 185, 186, 193n2; female, 7, 41, 46, 77, 82, 140, 165, 173, 176, 188; global female, 188
Othering, 11, 23, 96, 103
Overdiagnosis, 188
Overmedicalized, 188
Oyěwùmí, Oyèrónkẹ́, 7, 25, 26

Paravisini-Gebert, Lizabeth, 173, 174
Passbook(s), 30, 31, 32, 45, 47, 196n15
Pathological, 26, 64, 70, 104, 128, 172, 190
Pathology, 29, 43, 52, 84, 89
Patriarchy, 6, 66, 70, 74, 76, 77, 80, 82, 89, 90, 91, 92, 121, 125, 132, 146, 150, 155, 157, 165, 176, 179, 190, 201n27, 208n30; conventions of, 136; dictates of, 70, 171, 172, 173, 176; dominance of, 177, 178; gaze of, 13; ideology of, 141; and interference, 132; limits of, 158; tool of, 190; white male, 190; white, 74, 91, 92, 165
Performative, 57, 133, 136, 148
Personhood, 22, 28, 30, 32, 69, 153, 159
Peterson, Laci, 57, 198n13
Peterson, Scott, 57, 198n13
Phallic, 73, 110, 124, 125
Piccadilly, 47, 155
Pigeonholed, 16, 102, 144
Point de Ralliement (Rallying Force), 114
Policing, regimental, 24, 122
Political inequities, 164, 166
Politicization, 44, 203n15
Politics: of exclusion, 46, 58; of inclusion, 61, 94, 160, 163; of liberation, 48; of normalization, 139; of satiety, 142
Pollutant, 121
Polluted, 121, 152, 178
Pollution, 122, 152
Pornographic display, 25
Pornographic exposure, 25, 64
Pornography, 25, 26, 149, 150, 151
Postcolonial(ity), 11, 40, 179
Postcolonialism, 145
Postmodern(ism), 11, 59
Post-recovery, 53

Post-traumatic, 161
Poussaint, Alvin, 160, 161
Pretoria, 30
Price, Janetk, 65, 66, 125, 136
Priestess, 187
Primitivism, 24
Procreation, 145
Profit-making, 27, 29, 48
Propertied possession, 27, 29, 74, 79, 90, 133
Prophylaxis, 164
Propriety, 13, 17, 130, 133, 139, 141, 154, 176
Prosthesis, 13, 14, 43, 48, 51–58, 60–63, 134, 181
Puppeteering, 93
Purging, 182, 184, 185
Puritans, 75, 76, 77, 80, 84, 85, 86, 89, 90–93
Purity, 107, 108, 133, 152, 175, 176, 205n37, 206n10

Queen Mother, 94
"Queering the nation," 14, 41
Queerness, 52

Race, 2–9, 11, 12, 13, 16, 20, 21, 22, 29, 30, 35, 43, 45, 46, 48, 50, 51, 55, 60, 61, 75, 82, 83, 90, 111, 115, 129, 141, 147, 148, 159, 160, 161, 165, 180, 182, 190, 193n1, 196n15, 198n7, 205n37
Race politics, 4, 45, 165
Racial abuse, 68
Racialized, 11, 45, 80, 90, 104, 118, 133, 135, 179, 189, 205n4
Racial profiling, 43, 47
Racism, 2, 6, 7, 8, 18, 26, 28, 29, 32, 42, 43, 45, 50, 54, 72, 83, 90, 129, 133, 134, 160, 164, 165, 183, 185
Racist ideology, 20, 190
Rape, 69, 72, 73, 74, 90, 91, 92, 103, 105, 106, 107, 109, 174, 183, 196n18, 199nn2,6
Reach for Recovery, 52, 53, 58, 61
Recuperative, 14, 68, 122
Redemption, 14, 68, 69, 205n38

Reductionism, 29, 104, 157
Regimental policing, 24, 122
Renegade, 18
Repatriation, 14, 35, 69, 70, 71, 95, 196n21
Reproduction, 65, 87, 107, 115, 118, 120, 205n40
Reproductive control, 47
Resilience, 3, 32, 52, 58, 71, 94, 174, 190
Resistance, 1, 3, 5, 8, 11–14, 30, 31, 32, 42–44, 47, 52, 54, 58, 59, 67–70, 73–74, 77, 79, 80, 82, 84–89, 91, 93, 94, 102, 117, 122, 125, 127, 132, 133, 138, 140, 147, 157, 158, 160, 166, 173, 174, 175, 179, 185, 186, 193n5, 199n7, 200n20, 201n28, 208n23; political, 12, 47; politics of, 11, 77, 185
Respectability, 58, 63, 73, 131, 133, 138, 149, 176, 177, 204n32; female, 58; white, 84
Rich, Adrienne, 7
Roberts, Diane, 143
Roberts, Dorothy, 47, 85, 86, 87, 88, 104, 119, 120, 159, 160, 166

Salem Witch trials, 71
Same-sex desire, 65, 66
Same-sex relationships, 81
Santería, 187, 188
Saywell, Cherise, 51, 53, 120
Scarry, Elaine, 121, 125
Schiebinger, Londa, 109
Schultermandl, Silvia, 3, 82
Schulz, Amy, 7, 29
Scientific racism, 26
Scully, Pamela, 21, 22, 23, 32, 33, 35, 155, 195n13, 196n21, 197n30
Self-distortion, 57
Self-reflexivity, 6
Sexism, 4, 28, 45, 46, 62, 72, 79, 105, 125, 133, 164, 165, 189; ideology, 190
Sex tourists/sex tourism, 97
Sexual autonomy, 77, 119, 123
Sexual availability, 28
Sexual bondage, 26
Sexual desire(s), 75, 120
Sexual exploitation, 17, 23, 73, 75, 108, 148

Sexual independence, 158
Shaw, Andrea, 132, 133, 134, 139, 142, 151, 185, 206n4
Shelley, Mary, 155
Sherwin, Susan, 63
Shildrick, Margrit, 65, 66, 125, 136
Silencing, 21, 44, 52, 68, 69, 107, 115, 147, 150, 166, 178, 181
Singer, Debra S., 148, 150
Sisulu, Walter, 37
Slackness, 140, 141
Slavery, 12, 14, 21, 26, 32, 36, 38, 68–72, 74, 78, 84, 87–90, 104, 125, 143, 151, 157, 160, 198n15, 200n20, 206n12
Smith, Barbara, 5, 7, 194n10
Smith, Faith, 13, 76
Social disorder, 186
Socioeconomic, 17, 18, 22, 83, 164, 183, 186
Sociosomatic, 17, 164, 168, 189
Soucouyant, 18, 94, 171, 173, 201n28
South Africa/South African(s), 13, 14, 20, 21, 26, 28, 30–37, 41, 42, 45–48, 105, 196nn15,17,18,20,21,22, 197nn23,29,6
Spectatorship, 137
Spillers, Hortense, 2, 4, 20, 22, 23, 29, 32, 39, 44, 46, 48, 49, 121, 122; "Mama's Baby, Papa's Maybe," 20, 22, 39, 44, 123
Stallybrass, Peter, 146, 152, 155, 156, 205n2
Stanford, Ann Folwell, 159, 160, 187, 188, 189
Steatopygia, 24, 147
Stigmatization, 162
Stoetzler, Marcel, 23
Stukator, Angela, 142, 148, 149, 205n2
Subhuman, 13, 24, 27, 48
Subversive, 11, 60, 65, 121, 136, 140, 142, 143, 149
Suffering mother, 35, 115, 116
Suicide, 81, 115, 205n37
Supernatural, 79, 168, 175, 177
Surgical erasure, 64
Survival, 11, 20, 45, 46, 49, 54, 65, 71, 77, 127, 143, 160, 166, 174

Tambo, Oliver, 37
Temporary Protected Status (TPS), 97, 201n3
Terry, Jennifer, 24, 52
Testing, 18, 107, 115, 117, 124, 125, 175, 176, 178, 202n5, 205n41, 208nn18,23
Third World, 6, 11, 41, 58, 103, 129, 163, 189
Tontons Macoutes, 105, 203n17
Trafficking, 23, 26
Transgression(s), 15, 18, 43, 66, 77, 172, 176
Transmigratory subject, 77
Transnationalism, 3, 8, 14, 70, 78, 90, 99, 165, 175, 203n15; alliances, 10, 14, 19, 32, 46, 69; coalitions, 32, 58, 85; exchanges, 8, 12; feminism, 5, 14, 32, 44, 82, 94; partnership, 33; sensibility, 9, 41; solidarity, 46
Truth, Sojourner, 143
Tuberculosis, 18, 161, 162, 183, 184
Tuskegee Syphilis Study, 47

Unbelonging, 9, 18, 22, 112
United States, 3, 4, 11, 14, 21, 30, 31, 46, 47, 97–100, 105, 109–13, 115, 119, 121, 122, 133, 159, 162, 179, 180, 181, 184, 190, 194n16, 197n5, 201n3, 202nn13,14, 203nn17,20,23, 204n30, 205nn37,39, 208nn12,27
Unterhalter, Elaine, 35, 102, 105, 107, 115–16, 123
Urla, Jacqueline, 52

Victimhood, 127, 200n18
Victimization, 69, 108, 116, 119, 128, 149, 175
Victorian, 77, 107, 119, 207n15; aesthetics, 139; ideals, 16, 130, 139, 149
Vilification, 56, 107, 124, 163
Violence: colonial, 36; domestic, 31; gendered, 14; patriarchal, 87
Virchow, Rudolf, 163, 164, 166
Virginity cult, 125, 176
Vodou, 163
Voyeurism/Voyeurs, 26, 47, 149, 201n24

Voyeuristic, 22, 25, 26, 29, 42; desires, 148; fascination, 200n24; gaze, 26, 64;
Vulgarity, 11, 16, 17, 21, 130, 131, 152, 205n3; vulgarization, 155

Wallace-Sanders, Kimberly, 56
Washington, Harriet A., 22, 46, 195n13
Washington, Mary Helen, 4
Wendell, Susan, 187
Werbner, Pnina, 118
West, Mae, 140, 141, 206n10
Western: cultural imperialism, 70, 132, 163, 173, 190; feminism, 103, 128, 129; gaze, 24, 25, 30, 63, 135; ideals of beauty/womanhood, 51, 119, 132, 139, 141, 182, 207n15; ideology, 9, 11, , 26, 124, 141, 148, 163, 165, 173, 179, 185, 186; literature, 6, 8; medicine, 18, 19, 160, 162–72, 179, 187–90; thought, 5, 6, 11
"We Wear the Mask," 93
White, Allon, 146, 152, 155, 156, 205n2
White feminists, 2, 50, 129, 193n2
White gaze, 43, 181
White imagination, 21, 148
White racist ideology, 20, 190
White supremacy, 26, 33, 46, 47, 92, 195n11

White, Deborah Gray, 73, 74, 75, 86, 87, 88, 89, 143, 144, 145, 166, 198n15, 199n9, 200nn10,14
White, Evelyn C., 39
Wholeness, 115, 120, 171, 182
Williams, Patricia J., 31, 105, 201n1
Williams, Serena, 199n19, 207n16
Williams, Venus, 199n19, 207n16
Witch, 70, 72, 77, 86, 169, 173, 174, 177, 200n16
Witchcraft, 76, 77, 84, 87, 90, 91, 174
Witch-wife, witch-woman, 93, 171–73, 174, 175, 176, 179, 201n28, 208nn13,16
Womanhood, 58, 73, 76, 80, 101, 102, 108, 117, 119, 152, 171; black, 129, 158; ideal, 51, 119; proper, 15, 81, 101; white, 77
Women migrants, 10
Women warriors, 51
Wu, Cynthia, 50, 51, 136
Wyatt, Gail, 144, 206n13

Yancy, George, 17, 20, 21, 29, 31, 43, 161, 194n2, 197n2
Yuval-Davis, Nira, 23, 101, 102, 115, 118, 122, 125; *Gender & Nation*, 101

Zamani Soweto Sisters, 47

Simone A. James Alexander is professor of English and Africana Studies at Seton Hall University and the author of *Mother Imagery in the Novels of Afro-Caribbean Women*. She is the co-editor of *Feminist and Critical Perspectives on Caribbean Mothering*.

The University Press of Florida is the scholarly publishing agency for the State University System of Florida, comprising Florida A&M University, Florida Atlantic University, Florida Gulf Coast University, Florida International University, Florida State University, New College of Florida, University of Central Florida, University of Florida, University of North Florida, University of South Florida, and University of West Florida.

www.ingramcontent.com/pod-product-compliance
Lightning Source LLC
Chambersburg PA
CBHW031434160426
43195CB00010BB/725